DISCARD

THEODORE ROOSEVELT

Theodore Roosevelt

A PROFILE

EDITED BY

MORTON KELLER

AMERICAN PROFILES

General Editor: Aïda DiPace Donald

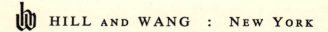

HILL AND WANG : NEW YORK

Contents

Introduction   vii

Brief Biography of Theodore Roosevelt   xvii

Theodore Roosevelt: The Years of Decision   I
   JOHN M. BLUM

Theodore Roosevelt   17
   WILLIAM ALLEN WHITE

Roosevelt and the National Psychology   33
   STUART P. SHERMAN

Roosevelt I   52
   H. L. MENCKEN

The Progressive Mind in Action   66
   JOHN R. CHAMBERLAIN

T.R.   80
   LOUIS FILLER

Rough Rider   93
        DIXON WECTER

Theodore Roosevelt: The American as Progressive   107
        HAMILTON BASSO

Theodore Roosevelt: The Conservative as Progressive   122
        RICHARD HOFSTADTER

Theodore Roosevelt and the Rise of America to World
    Power   155
        HOWARD K. BEALE

The Republican Roosevelt   169
        JOHN M. BLUM

Bibliography   191

Contributors   193

Introduction

We cling to the memory of our Presidents for two reasons. One has to do with the idea that the chief executive is the sum of the national character, is in some way the embodiment of his people and his time. Then, too, there is the aura of power that surrounds the office. The man who is President of the United States has a unique and awesome access to the instruments of national sovereignty, of political power, of public opinion. A President who responds to these potentialities, or at least appears to do so, cannot help but pique the imagination.

Presidents, in short, are both symbols and leaders. Theodore Roosevelt was the first chief executive after Lincoln to lay claim to attention as a major figure in the mythos of the office and as an important shaper of national policy. The selections that follow probe these central themes of Roosevelt and his Presidency.

I

A certain degree of personal drama and historical significance accrues to every President; it is inherent in the office. But Theodore Roosevelt's impact as an evocative figure in American life had little to do with his title. He made the American Presidency into something new and arresting, not the reverse. Presidents since Andrew Jackson's time had come of humble or middling origins;

not since John Quincy Adams could they lay claim to distinguished birth or high culture. Roosevelt broke the established pattern. He was as much the aristocrat and intellectual as American society would permit one of its leaders to be. To old-family New York and Harvard he added the unique ingredients of gentlemanly adventuring in the West and in the Spanish-American War. He united a passion for blood sports with respectable attainments as a historian and naturalist. His flamboyant personality was worlds away from those of his comfortable, phlegmatic predecessors.

Even more dramatic was the abrupt transition of generations that occurred when Roosevelt entered the Presidency on William McKinley's death in 1901. The average age of incoming Presidents to this time was about sixty; T.R., the youngest chief executive in our history, was not yet forty-three when he took office. (Some idea of what this age difference meant in experience—and could mean in outlook—comes when we recall that McKinley had been a major and a hero in the Civil War; T.R. as a boy of seven had watched Abraham Lincoln's New York City funeral procession in 1865.)

The style of Roosevelt's Presidency reinforced this sense of sharp and sudden change. He behaved in a manner quite unlike anything Americans had come to expect of their chief executives. Not since Jefferson, and not again until Kennedy, was the White House so open to men of diverse accomplishments. T.R., most of all, infused a vitality, almost an electric intensity, in everything he did—politics, science, scholarship, sports. Henry Adams, who did not like Roosevelt, summed him up in a classic observation: "[He] showed the singular primitive quality that belongs to ultimate matter—the quality that medieval theology assigned to God—he was pure act."

Roosevelt's hypertension was real enough. He died worn out at sixty, a victim of "malignant endocarditis, and an embolism in the coronary arteries." But his instinctive flair for the full, dramatic life was made to serve the hard, grubby purposes of politics and policy. What might otherwise have been a colorful but frivolous personality became, in the office of the Presidency, a subject of profound concern for contemporaries and later commentators. It was for this reason that the critical Stuart Sherman found Roosevelt to be "the most interesting man of our times."

That unabashed admirer William Allen White saw a single theme in Roosevelt's personal style and Presidential role: the uplifting of American life. Others, less kind, have decided that T.R.'s baroque public performance served as a façade for essentially empty or regressive policies. But all observers of Roosevelt have been struck by a peculiar, pervasive paradox. The man who had one of the most remarkable careers in American history had also, it would seem, an extraordinary ability to represent, to address himself to the American average: to be, in Richard Hofstadter's words, "the master therapist of the middle classes." White looked on Roosevelt not only as a revered leader but as a kindred spirit; as a man who was at one with the disturbed petite bourgeoisie. H. L. Mencken found T.R., for all the fact that he was a consummate showman, to be "a perfectly typical politician." Dixon Wecter, treating Roosevelt as one of America's mythic heroes, nevertheless was struck by his essential ordinariness. John Dewey noted at the time of Roosevelt's death that as the Man of Action he was the "typical representative," indeed the "living embodiment," of the generation that came to its maturity around 1900.[1]

For all the color and sophistication of his life, Roosevelt remains best remembered for an underlying, an almost eccentric simplicity. The Rough Rider, the tamer of the Dakota badlands and the Dakota badmen, Hemingway's great American boy-child romping in the White House: this is the Roosevelt that has persisted in the memory of Americans.

And yet, as John M. Blum and Howard K. Beale among others have noted, there are sufficient grounds for arguing that Roosevelt went about his policy-making with considerable subtlety of style and purpose. The interesting question, of course, is why Roosevelt for so long, and on so many different levels of apprehension, has been regarded as a classic American innocent. The answer lies in the nature and function of his Presidential performance.

[1] John Dewey, "Theodore Roosevelt," *Characters and Events* (New York, 1929), I, 87. Unless otherwise noted, quotations are from the commentaries collected in this volume.

II

For all the fascination of Roosevelt's personality, it is his career as a politician and a shaper of public policy that is the primary measure of his historical significance. And again we find an elusive relationship between form and substance—between promise and performance—commanding the attention of commentators.

For contemporary—and later—idolators he is the great figure of the Progressive movement of reform that swept over American life in the early twentieth century. White, for one, has no doubts as to the significance and substance of Roosevelt's Presidential achievement. He sees T.R. as the wise and effective overseer of the transition—"critical, dangerous, and but for him terrible"—from rural individuality to the highly industrialized, urbanized social order of the twentieth century. But even for White there are difficulties when one examines this performance in detail. "For some strange reason," he muses, "the labor movement never followed in his train." Nor did the administration that succeeded T.R.'s triumphal election in 1904 seem, in retrospect, to hold very much of substance, and White is forced to resort to rhetoric: "The actual list of achievements of Roosevelt in his second term, viewed as a legislative or administrative program, is not imposing; viewed as a crusade for justice it is a revolution." Another admirer, the literary critic Harry Thurston Peck, said much the same thing of T.R. in October, 1908: "He will be remembered as the President who stirred the conscience of the people to a righteous indignation. He has accomplished little except this; and yet there was nothing else so absolutely needed at the time."[2]

Others have found it far more difficult to see him as a significant figure in the tradition of American political reform. The First World War, and Roosevelt's important public role in it as a spokesman of preparedness, intervention, and militant American-ism, colored many early evaluations of his career. Because of Roosevelt's role in the conflict, Stuart Sherman declared, "he can

[2] Harry T. Peck, "Mr. Roosevelt and His Future," *Forum* (October 1908), p. 375.

never again greatly inspire the popular liberal movement in America." Indeed, in retrospect T.R.'s major political contribution was the regressive one of transforming "the unimaginative plutocratic psychology . . . into the psychology of efficient, militant, imperialistic nationalism."

Mencken took T.R. less seriously. He concerned himself with Roosevelt's style as a political demagogue rather than with his substance as a national leader—which, of course, was in itself a comment on that leadership. "He didn't believe in democracy; he believed simply in government," declared the great iconoclast. T.R.'s policies existed only to serve his demagoguery: "The issues that won him most votes were issues that, at bottom, he didn't believe in."

Consideration of Roosevelt flagged during the 1920's. He had, it seemed, equally little to offer those who followed George W. Norris and Robert La Follette and those who followed Harding and Coolidge. He was remembered chiefly as the exemplification of sterling American virtues—Hermann Hagedorn and the Roosevelt Memorial Association fostered the cult of the Rough Rider— or as a figure of fun. Henry F. Pringle's often caustic Pulitzer Prize biography in 1931 portrayed an amusing but hardly a major figure in American history.

The Great Depression of the 1930's, and the appearance of the New Deal stimulated a renewed interest in F.D.R.'s cousin and the Progressive movement of which he was so prominent a part. But he remained an unattractive figure to angry critics of American life. John Chamberlain, comparing Roosevelt and La Follette in a Marxist interpretation of Progressivism, found T.R. distinctly less significant than the Wisconsin Senator. Roosevelt's conception of himself as the spokesman of a core middle class preyed upon by capital and labor had little viability, said Chamberlain. The true American reality, rather, was that of oppressed labor confronting avaricious corporations; and to this Roosevelt did not address himself. The radical Chamberlain of the early 1930's found T.R.'s romanticism not exhilarating but unscientific and hence destructive: Roosevelt, he complained, "never understood the spirit of the laboratory—which was the one hope of the Progressive, or

Liberal, movement." Matthew Josephson, in *The President Makers,* was more inclusive and concrete in rejecting Roosevelt as a reformer. He drew a picture of T.R. as the close associate—and in many respects the spokesman—of the great finance capitalists and corporation lawyers of the time.[3]

Louis Filler, too, in 1939 had little patience with Roosevelt's evident insufficiency in the face of the problems of an industrial society. "Each year," he observed, "Roosevelt becomes less impressive in retrospect, and it is unlikely that he will ever resume the stature he enjoyed in his days of triumph." The coming of F.D.R. and the New Deal gave T.R. legitimacy as a reformer, but little more: "Roosevelt was a promise rather than a fulfillment. The excitement that attended him was mainly the excitement of anticipation." Richard Hofstadter, writing in the wake of World War II, added to the well-established theme of Roosevelt's inadequacy as a shaper of public policy in an industrial age the element that had concerned Stuart Sherman and H. L. Mencken in 1919: T.R.'s authoritarianism and militarism.

In recent years interpretations of Theodore Roosevelt have taken an interesting turn. The Second World War, and the mix of welfare and warfare that has characterized American government since then, gives new significance to the Roosevelt policies. American society—in which social order, administrative efficiency, and an intermixed devotion to international *Realpolitik* and domestic reform are highly prized—inevitably finds in Roosevelt's career something more than therapy and entertainment.

One can see the change at work in Hamilton Basso's World War II assessment of T.R. The ironic amusement of Pringle and the angry disapproval of Chamberlain are gone. In their place is a respectful consideration of Roosevelt as the first American President to propose using the state to discipline and democratize the economy and to bring order into international power politics.

John M. Blum develops the ramifications of this new appreciation of Roosevelt. Nelson Aldrich's estimate of T.R. as "the greatest politician of his time" was a gauge of derision in the

[3] Matthew Josephson, *The President Makers* (New York, 1940).

1920's and contempt in the 1930's; by the 1950's it had become a measure of his significance. The political art took on increasing importance as an instrument of social betterment—and of social control. Blum's Roosevelt emerges as the archetypal enlightened conservative: "an institutionalist, a gradualist, a moralist" whose prime achievement lay in the fact that he created a viable governmental response to the tremendous economic, intellectual, and demographic forces that were transforming American life. Roosevelt's goals—and now they have come to seem important and desirable ones—were consolidation, conservation, stability: "He broadened power precisely for the purpose of establishing order." His great lack, says Blum, was an equivalent commitment to the pursuit of happiness: to a dynamic rather than a static vision of the Good Society. Carleton Putnam, Roosevelt's most recent biographer, echoes Blum's conclusions: "three traits . . . were the pillars of Roosevelt's personality—a belief in the leadership principle, a stern respect for duly constituted authority and a devotion to the ideal of freedom and self-dependence for the individual."[4]

Another recent appraisal of Roosevelt as a sophisticated conservative dwells on these traits with less satisfaction than those of Blum and Putnam. Gabriel Kolko, elaborating upon the earlier insights of Matthew Josephson and John Chamberlain, sees Roosevelt as the spokesman of a large-scale financial and industrial capitalism seeking a more rationalized and controllable economic order. In his view, Roosevelt's relationships to men such as George W. Perkins of J. P. Morgan and Company, and his readiness to support forms of government regulation that major corporate interests—railroad, insurance, banking, and the like—themselves wanted constitute the central theme of his Presidency.[5]

Closely analogous in spirit is Howard K. Beale's examination of T.R.'s foreign policy. Here, too, *Machtpolitik* and *Realpolitik* coincide. Beale concedes that Roosevelt's conduct of American international relations was restrained by a strong sense of social responsibility and by an underlying commitment to persuasion and

[4] Carleton Putnam, *Theodore Roosevelt: The Formative Years* (New York, 1958) pp. 605–606.
[5] Gabriel Kolko, *The Triumph of Conservatism* (New York, 1963).

the democratic process. But he is disturbed by Roosevelt's desire "for sufficient power to be able to do as he pleases without restraint."

III

What can be said in sum of a man who for half a century has been the subject of such diverse opinion? Surely—especially since the publication of the magnificent edition of *The Letters of Theodore Roosevelt* in the 1950's—the important facts about T.R. the man and the President are available to us. And presumably we are sufficiently removed from his generation to evaluate his place in history without the strong sense of personal involvement that he engendered in so many of his contemporaries.

What first commands recognition is the extraordinary vividness of Roosevelt's life. Poseur or genius, T.R. remains one of the commanding personalities in American history. Judgments may vary as to the nature and worth of the use to which he put his great personal talents. But there can be no question of his impact as a dramatic human being upon his contemporaries. For the first time since Lincoln, the Presidency became a meaningful institution for Americans who were accustomed to regard national politics as beneath—or above—their concern. Men of education and social conscience generally found T.R. a sympathetic figure. Those who had cause to account themselves among the dispossessed of American life could not help but respond to a President who lunched with Booker T. Washington, appointed a Jew to his cabinet, and publicly sided with a labor union during a strike. As the first chief executive explicitly to recognize the fact that the United States was becoming a nation of cities, of workers, of great ethnic diversity, Roosevelt's place in American history is secure.

The precise weight and direction of his policy-making is more difficult to determine. Certainly no legislation of great significance to twentieth-century American life came about under his aegis. The proposals for business regulation and conservation that were such important parts of his Presidency hardly compare with the institutional changes of the New Deal and after. Nor do his adventures in the field of foreign policy, for all the clamor that attended them, rank in significance with the activities of Woodrow Wilson or of Franklin D. Roosevelt and his successors. T.R. cannot even be accounted, for all his incontestable political skill, a seminal figure in the history of party politics. His effort to bring the Republican party to a sophisticated apprehension of the realities of twentieth-century American life hardly achieved success. Finally, for all the token recognition that he accorded Negroes, Jews, Catholics, organized labor—and reformers—the fact remains that he presided over an America where racist assumptions (among them his own) remained strong, where unions remained weak, where the conditions of life of the industrial and agrarian poor improved little.

The quality that makes Roosevelt a significant President despite this litany of insufficiencies is precisely the one that has been the subject of fiercest criticism: his ideological and political fluidity. He seems to lend himself with equal facility to each of a bewildering lot of interpretations: as the representative of a middle class that is fearful of change—or is demanding it; as the front man of sophisticated finance capitalism; as the first spokesman of the new America or the last great defender of the old.

If in his career Roosevelt seemed to speak with so many voices, to represent so many divergent yet contemporaneous interests, this may be a measure not of his duplicity but of his skill. Perhaps this is what sets him apart from other great figures of his time, who represented narrower, more parochial points of view: La Follette, Debs, Bryan. But he belongs in their company insofar as the central theme of his political career was to respond to the conditions imposed on American life by massive industrialization, urbanization, and immigration.

Ultimately he was no better able than these others, or his successor Woodrow Wilson, to ride out the political storms of early twentieth-century American life. After his last great effort of 1912 ended in defeat he became a frivolous, restless, and unsettled figure, vainly trying to reassert his place in the political order. The hysterical, chauvinistic Roosevelt of the wartime years has much in common with the shrilly fundamentalist Bryan of the 1920's, or the shattered, vindictive Wilson after Versailles.

Even before he was borne under, Roosevelt's response to the social changes of his time was less concrete and specific, less materially creative, than those of his distinguished contemporaries. In consequence his role in that story of political adaptation to the conditions of modern America is especially difficult to fix, to categorize. It is obscured, too, by the highly-colored huckster's manner with which he went about the business of national leadership. But it is well to bear in mind how overwhelming was the need to adapt old and deeply entrenched social values to spectacularly new social conditions, and how great was the potential for social chaos. In this context Roosevelt's flamboyance and adaptability become not impediments but instruments: the instruments of the great political teacher-broker of the Progressive era.

MORTON KELLER

Cambridge, Mass.
May 1, 1967

Theodore Roosevelt, 1858-1919

Theodore Roosevelt was born in New York City on October 27, 1858, into a comfortable and socially prominent family. He graduated from Harvard in 1880, and in that year married Alice H. Lee. Roosevelt first sought a career in the law, but quickly was drawn into political life. (His father had combined banking with a prominent role in genteel reform politics.) He served from 1882 to 1884 as a Republican member of the New York State Assembly. In 1884 his wife died, and Roosevelt devoted much of his time during the next two years to ranching in the Dakota Territory. (He had one daughter, Alice, from his first marriage; he would have four sons—Theodore, Kermit, Archibald, and Quentin—and a daughter, Ethel, from his second.)

In 1886 he married Edith Kermit Carow. Soon after he returned to public life, running as the Republican candidate for Mayor of New York against Henry George and Abram S. Hewitt. Although he finished last, his prominent place in this notable election added to his reputation as a respectable, reform-minded, loyal Republican. President Benjamin Harrison recognized these qualities by appointing him to the United States Civil Service Commission in 1889, where he served until 1895. T.R. then returned to New York affairs as president of the New York City Board of Police Commissioners from 1895 to 1897, under reform Mayor William L. Strong. In 1897 and 1898 he was McKinley's Assistant Secretary of the Navy. He won intellectual as well as political stature during these years by writing books on history, current affairs, and Western ranching and hunting life.

Until 1898 Roosevelt's public career was marked more by appointive than by electoral success. But in that year the Spanish-American War gave him the opportunity to make himself a nationally popular figure. He served spectacularly as the head of the Rough Riders, the First Regiment of U.S. Cavalry Volunteers. The *réclame* attending that venture and his strong place in Republican party politics won him the New York gubernatorial nomination—and election—in 1898. By the standards of the day Roosevelt was a reform Governor, tilting with organization stalwarts and with corporate interests. His prominence made him a natural Vice-Presidential running mate for William McKinley in 1900. In September, 1901, when McKinley died from gunshot wounds inflicted by an anarchist, Roosevelt assumed the Presidency.

It is not difficult to find a pattern of verbal boldness and cautious action characterizing Roosevelt's foreign and domestic Presidential leadership. He effectively used the weight of his office, and of his personality, to set under way the construction of the Panama Canal. He actively intervened to settle disputes in Latin America, the Far East, and Europe. Yet the United States as a world power was less overtly expansionist during his Presidency than it was during the McKinley years.

Roosevelt's domestic policies focused primarily on the problem of the large corporation. The Elkins (1903) and Hepburn (1906) acts extended the powers of the Interstate Commerce Commission over railroad rate-making. A government suit against the Northern Securities Company (1902) revived the dormant Sherman Anti-Trust Act. Roosevelt sponsored the Pure Food and Drugs and Meat Inspection acts of 1906. Other issues engaged him, too. The Newlands Act (1902)—as much the cause of Mark Hanna as of Theodore Roosevelt—made funds available for reclamation projects in the arid regions of the West. In 1902 he intervened judiciously to mediate a major coal strike. If his public visage was that of a great popular champion, his Presidential performance for the most part stressed the arts of the mediator.

Roosevelt while President was a strong and active party leader. He took the GOP to a major electoral triumph in 1904, and avoided an intraparty conflict over the issue of a tariff revision.

T.R. left the Presidency in 1909 at the age of fifty-one, still a remarkably vigorous man. He hunted in Africa and toured Europe, returning to the United States in 1910. He became editor of *The Outlook* (a post he held until 1914), and quickly re-entered active political life—this time more venturesomely than before. He broke publicly with his chosen successor William Howard Taft, and in 1912 ran for President as the candidate of the new Progressive party. In lieu of organizational support he relied upon his great personal popularity, and on the theme of the New Nationalism— an attempt to catch up the reformist fervor of the Progressive movement. During the campaign he called on government to use its power to regulate rather than dissolve the large corporations, and pledged himself to a wide range of social, labor, and industrial reforms. He was defeated by Woodrow Wilson, but drew substantially more votes than did the Republican candidate Taft.

One final time T.R. sought relief in travel: during 1913 and 1914 he explored the Brazilian interior. From 1915 to 1917 Roosevelt was a leading spokesman for military preparedness and intervention on the side of the Allies. After the United States declaration of war in April, 1917, he attempted to raise and serve at the head of a volunteer division of American troops. He died on January 6, 1919, in the midst of preparations for an assault on the 1920 Republican nomination.

M.K.

THEODORE ROOSEVELT

Theodore Roosevelt:
The Years of Decision

Age, for the biographer, poses a formidable obstacle to under-standing. The familiar image of the mature man has a timeless quality that obscures the adjustments of youth, the resolution of contradictory emotional and intellectual forces. This timelessness occurs especially in the case of Theodore Roosevelt because, as he realized, he "rose like a rocket," reaching his pinnacle of power in four decades. In terms of public responsibility he had little oppor-tunity to be young. The young man in the state legislature, the still young man in the Navy Department assume, in the mind's eye, the characteristics of the statesman in the White House or the orator at Osawatomie. This inversion, however, is no less misleading because of the velocity of Roosevelt's career. To read Armaged-don back into 1890 or 1900 is to overlook a period of develop-ment without which there would have been no Armageddon.

In his first forty productive years Roosevelt knew the awful perplexity of a man of convictions who felt compelled to realize them in action. He matured in an exciting time—the age, in America, of rapid industrialization, Darwinism, the beginnings of

Reprinted by permission of the publishers from Elting E. Morison, editor, *The Letters of Theodore Roosevelt* (Cambridge, Mass.: Harvard University Press). Copyright, 1951, 1952, 1954, by the President and Fellows of Harvard College.

2

JOHN M. BLUMJOHN M. BLUM

scientific scholarship and critical realism. Omniverously curious, the young Roosevelt zealously studied these separate but often related phenomena. Gradually he formed basic conclusions on nature, society, literature, and government. But in this period he also became committed to a career which imposed continuing tests both on the practicability and durability of his convictions.

The measures of political success are the abilities to attain and administer office. In both cases the nature of political institutions, of parties and of government, makes compromise the essence of procedure. While indiscriminate willingness to compromise produces sterile opportunism, unfaltering adherence to theories—no matter how true they may be—limits the sphere for constructive action. Avoiding these extremes, Roosevelt brought the findings of his actual political experience into adjustment with the products of his intellectual experience. This continuing adjustment was painful. But the result was a body of doctrine which Roosevelt maintained with integrity.

Roosevelt's early public life gave him a vigorous indoctrination in the problems of making and administering law. In the New York Assembly he chafed at delay and incompetence. As civil service commissioner, police commissioner, and Assistant Secretary of the Navy he learned the frustrations of government service. Often ignored or actively opposed by legislators, the agencies he served were constantly wanting the personnel, funds, and authority to implement their programs. Woodrow Wilson, in the seclusion of his study, decided that parliamentary government, as Bagehot had described it, should become the American system. Roosevelt, increasingly distrustful of the capacity of legislative bodies to set policy, sharply conscious of their capacity to impede, concluded that the executive should be separate and dominate.

Roosevelt was even more impressed by the lessons of partisan politics. His reputation as an assemblyman rested on his outspoken allegiance to the movement for clean government, a reform favored by conservative men of property who otherwise abjured politics. The approval of many of these men, Roosevelt's friends and original sponsors, as well as his own reputation, turned on his role in the election of 1884. Roosevelt had fought the nomination of Blaine. He decided, however, after much hesitation to support Blaine's campaign. Personal ambition, the prejudices of birth and inheritance, the character of the Democracy in New York, the postwar tradition equating the Republican party with Union prompted this decision. As soon as it was announced Roosevelt became the target of the majority of civil service reformers whose vituperation he returned in kind. From 1884 on he insisted that a "healthy party spirit" was "prerequisite to the performance of effective work in American political life." Later experience sustained this observation. The repeated failures of independent tickets in New York, some of which Roosevelt endorsed, helped Tammany control the city by splitting the Republican vote. The opposition of single-minded reformers in Albany and Washington prevented or delayed compromise legislation which would have accomplished a part of their purpose. Distrusting Democrats no less than Independents, particularly after the Democracy absorbed Populism, Roosevelt settled on a restless but regular Republicanism. He cooperated with leaders of whom he disapproved, and voted the party ticket even when assailed by doubts. Within the party, however, or in office on party sufferance, he attempted to further his own ideas for political and social improvement. These were rooted in large part in his nonpolitical experience.

While the lessons of public life were molding Roosevelt, less-examined facets of his youth also affected his thinking. As student, author, and critic, he expended his enormous energy in pursuing simultaneously each of his many interests. The conclusions he reached, recorded in his letters and essays, in spite of their superficial disorganization suggest the controlling principles of his public career.

The earliest consuming interest of Roosevelt's boyhood was nature. Encouraged by his father, a director of the Museum of Natural History, he found favored playmates among mice, guinea pigs, chipmunks, and squirrels. Spectacles, a shotgun, and lessons in taxidermy introduced him to the world of birds. While hunting them and studying their habits, he read precociously what books he could find. Roosevelt's careful inspection of the coloring of Old World chats, made in his teens with the aid of an ornithological treatise, supplied evidence which he used years later to challenge a too-generalized theory of protective coloring. At college and in the Dakotas he continued to examine and record the life of birds and animals in their natural habitats. His intimate familiarity with the wapiti, cougar, and other creatures of the Western plains and Long Island swamps, his sound inductive conclusions on the nature of species and subspecies, proved valuable to professional scientists.

Roosevelt's investigation of nature stopped short of the laboratory. Audubon and Waterton were his preceptors; the researches of young Agassiz at Harvard held no appeal for him. Disliking confinement, he gloried in life in the wilds rather than in the science of the microscope and dissecting table. If Roosevelt would not be a biologist, he nevertheless followed scientific thought with eager understanding. He studied Marsh and Leidy on paleontology with "a devotion . . . usually attended by a dreary lack of reward." At Harvard, working under William James and Nathaniel Shaler, reading Dana on geology, Buchan on meteorology, Gray on botany, he won "honorable mention" in natural sciences. And especially in Darwin and Huxley he found both delight and reward.

The influence of Darwinian thought on Roosevelt's generation was profound. Historians, sociologists, and economists transposed Darwin's theses on evolution to their disciplines, sometimes with caution and salutary effect, more often indiscriminately and with regrettable results. Following Herbert Spencer, they identified the conception of the survival of the fittest with divine purpose. Evolution, animal or social, was a progressive movement toward a better life. Its course was not to be altered or interrupted. Roosevelt, approaching Darwin with a nice appreciation of the subject, accepted evolution through struggle as an axiom in all his thinking. Life, for him, was strife. Individuals and societies progressed or retrogressed depending on their ability to fight and to adjust. But Roosevelt, a competent naturalist, comprehended the limitations of Darwin's hypotheses. He realized that Darwin's postulates, especially when transposed to human experience, needed documentation and refinement. Furthermore, he had no sense of divine purpose. For him the evolutionary process was secular and scientific. Roosevelt, therefore, tempered his Darwinism with inductive conclusions and nonbiological premises and prejudices.

"The progress of mankind in past ages," Roosevelt observed in 1895, "can only have been made under, and in accordance with, certain biological laws and . . . these laws continue to work in human society at the present day. . . . [They] govern the reproduction of mankind from generation to generation, precisely as they govern the reproduction of the lower animals, and . . . therefore, largely govern his progress." But, taking issue with Benjamin Kidd, Roosevelt gave natural selection no monopoly in the determination of human progress. Eugenics, especially social eugenics, Roosevelt had learned from his pets and from Francis Bowen, was a complicated process. To a degree selection was most rigid, Roosevelt pointed out, where fecundity was greatest, but the species which had the greatest fecundity made the least progress. Consider the fate of the guinea pig. As Kidd had overgeneralized biological laws, so had he overlooked certain "curious features" in human society. Where the struggle for life was too intense, energy was dissipated in seeking bare existence, and national progress was inhibited. The English and German peoples had fared better than the Italians, Poles, and Irish. On the other hand, loss of fecundity was fatal. A declining population, witness the French, endangered a nation. Insofar as the biological analogy applied, progress in human society depended on the steady rise of the lower class to the level of the upper as the latter tended to vanish. This improvement, Roosevelt had earlier declared, was "due mainly to the transmission of acquired characters, a process which in every civilized State operates so strongly as to counterbalance the operation of that baleful law of natural selection which tells against the survival of some of the most desirable classes."

Agreeing with Kidd that many of the plans proposed in the interest of oppressed individuals were destructive of social growth, Roosevelt would not reject all such plans. He denied Kidd's contention that scientific development showed the interests of the group and the individual to be antagonistic. On the contrary, Roosevelt argued, the individual had a rational interest in conduct subordinate to the welfare of society, for in the process of social

evolution men had reached the stage where they felt "more shame
and misery from neglect of duty, from cowardice or dishonesty"
than could be offset by the gratification of individual desires.
Character had kept pace with animal evolution, making the growth
of rationalism, when accompanied by the growth of ethics and
morality, the key to human progress. Intellect and morality,
progressing together, Roosevelt declared, "will persistently war
against the individuals in whom the spirit of selfishness . . .
shows itself strongly." The development of intellect, while necessary, was less important than the development of character, for the
"prime factor" in social evolution was the "power to attain a high
degree of social efficiency." "Social efficiency," in turn, derived
from "love of order, ability to fight well and breed well, capacity to
subordinate the interests of the individual to the interests of the
community, . . . and similar rather hum-drum qualities." Progress, Roosevelt had maintained in another context, might be
assured "if we but live wise, brave, and upright lives," if each plays
"his part, manfully, as a man among men."

These interpretations permitted Roosevelt at once to reject
Henry George or Collis P. Huntington and to embrace Lyman
Abbott or Richard C. Ely. George could be categorized with the
reformers Kidd chastised; Huntington's crassness could not be
excused. As for the doctrines of Abbott or Ely, Roosevelt concluded that "the true function of the State, as it interferes in social
life, should be to make the chances of competition more even, not
to abolish them." Earlier Roosevelt had stated his belief that
raising the standard of living for the mass of people did not
necessarily mean lowering the standard of "the fortunate few."
Contemplating communities of the future without extremes of
poverty and wealth, he suggested that for such a development "the
sphere of the State's action may be vastly increased without in any
way diminishing the happiness of either the many or the few."
State socialism was neither necessary nor probable, but Sumnerian
laissez faire was patently inadequate for the "greatest victories
. . . yet to be won."

Roosevelt had no hesitation in maintaining that not all groups
were equally endowed with the qualities prerequisite for social

efficiency. The black and yellow peoples, he believed, were igno-
rant and unprogressive. While not excluding the possibility that
they might improve their lot, he clearly relegated them to an
inferior evolutionary status. He more often classified societies by
nation than by color. Here the inferior "races" were the southern
and eastern Europeans. Depressed conditions in those areas, he
implied, evidenced a lack of potential in the national struggle for
existence. Of the northern Europeans, the favored people, Roosevelt championed the Anglo-Americans. His *Winning of the West*
suggests that the Anglo-Americans enjoyed a biological as well as
a cultural supremacy. Within the United States he considered the
"native American" communities most progressive. With these
classifications in mind, Roosevelt declared that "what Le Bon says
of race is very fine and true." This strain of thought took political
expression in Lodge's arguments for a literacy test, which Roosevelt endorsed.

Nevertheless, Roosevelt opposed the intolerant nativism of the
A.P.A. His faith in Anglo-American institutions sustained his faith
in the efficacy of the "melting pot." The immigrants of the slums
he blamed in part for corrupt government, but he confidently
expected that second and third generation Americans would overcome the weaknesses of their forebears as they learned from the
American environment. Roosevelt, therefore, did not fear "the
mass." Le Bon, he concluded, fell "into fundamental errors." The
proletariat could be assisted by the state. And like the vulgar rich,
they could improve themselves by following the example set by
men "of good blood . . . meaning blood that had flowed through
the veins of generations of self-restraint and courage and hard
work, and careful training in mind and in the manly virtues." So
long as the "melting pot" was not overcrowded, Americans of all
origins, given time, would develop the character necessary for their
own progress.

The attitudes with which Roosevelt qualified Kidd, Sumner, and
Le Bon were rooted in his childhood. From his father and his
father's friends Roosevelt received his introduction to the social
gospel. Familiar from youth with the ethics of the Bible, he was
even more familiar with their application in philanthropy and

social work. The inequalities evidenced in the lives of the very
poor impressed Roosevelt long before he read Jacob Riis. Only
with time did he modify the patrician noblesse of his father's
ministrations to impecunious newsboys, but as Sunday-school
teacher, legislator, and police commissioner he daily observed that
the race was not necessarily to the swift, for the swift too often
were kept from the post. Like Francis Bowen, a potent intellectual
force at Harvard in his day, Roosevelt rejected the attitude toward
poverty of the Malthusians and social Darwinists. He was not,
ordinarily, a compassionate man. Perhaps, however much he may
have understood, he did not love mankind. But he was gregarious.
In politics, at roundups, in battle, he worked and fought with all
types of men and won their admiration. Very rarely, and then only
reluctantly, did he appoint impoverished or unlettered men to
responsible office. But he felt that they deserved better housing,
shorter hours of labor, increased opportunities to reach a higher
level of existence. In dealing with the poor, Roosevelt was never
intimate, but neither was he satisfied with hymns and handouts as
antidotes for destitution.

From his childhood Roosevelt also carried over the American
bourgeois morality. In his world a heart of gold beat gently in each
fair feminine breast, a leg was a limb, and sex a description of
gender. Others, while concurring in those virtuous views of physical
conduct, were peculiarly indifferent to social morality. But not Roosevelt. He believed in the gospel of work. He also believed that the
eighth and ninth commandments should restrain the pursuit of
success. In part because, unlike Collis P. Huntington, he had no
need to defend a newly acquired fortune, and, unlike Blaine, to
excuse a suspicious political past, Roosevelt established for himself a stern moral code by which he rejected the amorality of Jay
Gould as quickly as that of Maxim Gorki. Too much a political
realist to refuse to cooperate with the Huntingtons and the Blaines,
he was, nevertheless, neither personally dishonest nor given to
compromise where opinion was unfettered by political considerations. When expounding theory, he aggressively asserted that the
struggle for existence in human society was subject to rules of
behavior inapplicable to other species.

Roosevelt approached literature with these moral criteria. Like most men, he enjoyed a good story, and like most of his contemporaries, he favored romanticism in belles-lettres. But his primary requirements were that a novel demonstrate the validity of his rules of behavior and do so in genteel language. Roosevelt made no allowance for the spirit or the vocabulary of other times. Chaucer, he felt, was "altogether needlessly filthy." Plot was even more important than vocabulary. If a heroine were to be shot, she should be wounded, not killed. It was not proper to kill women, even fictional women. It was equally improper to seduce them or to be seduced by them. Flora A. Steel's *On the Face of the Waters* was "tedious" and "morbid in its everlasting insistence on the unhealthy sides of sex-relationship." In Tolstoi's *Anna Karenina* the history of Levin and Kitty was "not only very powerfully and naturally told," but also "perfectly healthy." Roosevelt thought that Tolstoi was too detached in dealing with Anna's adultery, but he was gratified that, in the end, she committed suicide. Whereas Roosevelt had only grudging admiration for *Anna Karenina,* he had unstinted praise for Robert Grant's *Unleavened Bread,* the "strongest study of American life that has been written for many years." Grant's heroine, neglecting the duties of motherhood, descended from the proud security of her home with the inevitability of one of Milton's fallen angels. Judged by similar standards, Edgar Fawcett won Roosevelt's plaudits for his properly vindictive attitude toward the sinful rich. Hamlin Garland, on the other hand, was too "inclined to let certain crude theories warp his mind out of all proper proportion." Clearly Roosevelt believed in the Decalogue and judged in its terms. When the time came, it was natural for him to stand at Armageddon—he had never stood elsewhere.

Roosevelt shared the virulent patriotism of the Civil War generation. His maternal forebears were from the South and the war was in his household. Convinced while a boy of the justice of the Union cause, he welcomed the triumph. After the Union was saved, while the rest of the continent was being conquered, while the products of Mesabi and the open hearth attested to America's growing might, he gloried in the power of his country. National concern over military and physical preparedness, born with the war, soon languished. But Roosevelt, with a few others, kept it alive. His own boyhood fragility, conquered painfully and slowly, and, perhaps, resentment that his father's war service fell to a hired substitute, intensified this legitimate concern. A first venture into history, his study of the War of 1812, supplied further evidence of the national peril in unpreparedness. Darwinian biology substantiated the need for personal physical strength. Taken together, the memories, emotions, and neuroses of childhood, and the historical and biological investigations of youth formed the basis for the cult of strenuosity with which Roosevelt's name is irrevocably linked and for the martial chauvinism which set him apart from most of his more moderately nationalistic class. He neither understood nor tolerated the effete in any sphere of activity.

Roosevelt did not consider himself militaristic, but he clearly intended the nation to be both prepared and willing to fight. Benton's truculence on Oregon, Cleveland's message on Venezuela won his praise; Jefferson's embargo, Otis' Hartford Convention, and Schurz's views on the Spanish War evoked his ire. Enthusiastically embracing the doctrines of Alfred Thayer Mahan, Roosevelt admonished his countrymen to build up the navy. Elsewhere he urged the individual to improve himself. Through outdoor life and exercise, personal preparedness could be made the handmaiden of national rearmament. With adequate military equipment and a healthy citizenry, the United States could enforce its just demands, could participate as an equal in international affairs.

The combination of white supremacy, national glory, and moral obligation spelled imperialism. Mahan's naval strategy dictated the acquisition of bases in Hawaii, Guam, Cuba, Panama, and Porto Rico. Duty involved the liberation of the Cubans and the enforced improvement of the Filipinos. For these people Roosevelt felt genuine responsibility, insisting that tariff benefits accompany American occupation. While urging the United States to become a colonial power, he also urged the country to cast away the vestiges of colonialism in American diplomacy. Roosevelt respected the British and admired their contributions to American civilization, but he took an uncompromising position against them when, as in

Venezuela, Alaska, and the isthmus, their demands conflicted with his understanding of proper American policies or claims.

Roosevelt's views on foreign affairs, like his moral attitudes, were reflected in his judgment of literature. Literature was to be strenuous and patriotic. He thrilled to Sienkiewicz' epic of fighting men. Most of all he enjoyed accounts of American feats at arms, for "the man who has in him real fighting blood is sure to be more deeply stirred by the deeds of his own people than by those of any other folk." Consequently he took indiscriminate pleasure in the work of Parkman, Cooper, Churchill, John Fox, and Owen Wister. To protect American writers he joined Brander Matthews in the campaign for copyright legislation. Like Matthews, he resented criticism of American manners and American letters. Miss Wilkins made Roosevelt feel "uncomfortable," for he hated "to think that her types are really typical of our life." Frank Norris' "overstatement" was "so preposterous as to deprive his work of all value." Henry Adams' *Democracy* was "mean and foolish." The very worst in literature, Roosevelt held, were the products of the expatriates, of whom the worst was Henry James, "thank Heaven . . . now an avowedly British novelist." Roosevelt excoriated James, a "man in whom intense love of country is wanting . . . a very despicable creature, no matter how well equipped with all the minor virtues and graces, literary, artistic, and social." James was a "miserable little snob" whose "polished, pointless, uninteresting stories about the upper social classes of England" made "one blush to think he was once an American." Neither in diplomacy, in international yachting, nor in belles-lettres would Roosevelt tolerate any "strained humility toward foreigners, . . . especially toward Englishmen."

Roosevelt had built an eclectic intellectual home, its parts connected, but the whole more comfortable than integrated. It was designed to provide security for a man whose personality compelled him to act, whose profession required him to compromise, and whose moral beliefs forced him to justify everything he did. There was room for Roosevelt's Darwinism, his social gospel, his chauvinism and his strenuosity, and these were not tightly compartmented, but related each to the other. Still this complex man was not entirely secure. He had the assurance that comes with great physical courage, but he needed clear and continued evidence of approval. During every campaign he expected defeat. After each victory he was almost pathologically exuberant. His constant motion both released and revealed his constant tension. The violence with which he attacked his critics attested to his doubts. Yet he was sure enough to respond, when challenged, with argument as well as condemnation, and sure enough to act with purpose.

If Roosevelt had any supreme belief it was in character, individual character and national character. Feeling as he did, he was deeply impressed by Brooks Adams' *Law of Civilization and Decay*. He considered the book "brilliant," "very strong." Adams and Roosevelt, with many others of their class, resented the power of the new masters of American industry and finance. These men and their political agents, in the ruthlessness of their struggle for success, had abandoned ethical considerations in business and politics. Their manner of life, private as well as public, offended the sensibilities of more civilized men. To an alarming degree their methods and their taste permeated much of American society on every level. Reacting against this vulgarization, the Adamses foresaw doom; Henry James found etiquette in exile; Hay, Lodge, Roosevelt, and Spring Rice reminded each other of the gross cunning of international bankers who, as they often pointed out, were, conveniently for the Anglo-American reputation, usually Semitic.

Roosevelt, unlike Henry Adams and Henry James, did not retreat. He met the corrupt as well as the illiterate in political battle. But he shared with the Adamses and James a disdain for the vulgar rich. Their standards, he felt, were the historic ruination of social efficiency. A decade before Brooks Adams published his book, Roosevelt damned the propertied class of revolutionary France, the "despicable beings, the traders and merchants who have forgotten how to fight, the rich who are too timid to guard their wealth, the men of property, large or small, who need peace, and yet have not the sense and courage to be always prepared to conquer it." New York society, both the *nouveau riche* and "the people of good family" who had been corrupted, Roosevelt declared in 1891, were of this despicable stamp. The fashionable "took little interest in literature or politics; . . . did not care to explore and hunt and travel in their own country." Instead, "they put wealth above everything else, and therefore hopelessly vulgarized their lives."

Roosevelt, therefore, sympathized strongly with Adams' classifications of the imaginative and the economic man, but he was profoundly disturbed by Adams' prophetic conclusions. He simply could not admit that the United States was declining nor could he vote for silver at sixteen to one. He declared that Brooks Adams was "a little unhinged." But this was not enough. For his own peace of mind Roosevelt had to demonstrate that Adams' book was "from a false standpoint." Adams had made mistakes. Roosevelt found them. He pointed out that Adams had warped the facts in applying his thesis to Rome. Change from an imaginative to an economic society had occurred during expansion as well as during contraction of the currency. In the decline of Rome the currency factor was less important than the competition of Asiatic and African slaves and cheap Egyptian labor. These doomed the Italian husbandman. In the United States, Roosevelt maintained, emancipation of the slaves, convict labor laws, restriction of Chinese immigration, and the protective tariff prevented competition which might threaten "the free workingman." As for currency, wage earners and farmers in the United States and other "gold" countries stood "waist high above their brothers in Mexico and other communities that use[d] only silver."

Adams' thesis, Roosevelt continued, did not apply at all times or in all places. The Spaniards and Russians of the late nineteenth century, although not economic men, were inferior in martial prowess to the economic men of Germany, England, or the United States. National development need not correlate with economic life. Adams had overlooked more significant factors. Healthy children, the "virile" qualities, national honor—these were the vital determinants.

Like Brooks Adams, Roosevelt worried about the economic man. Unlike Adams, he was optimistic. He did not expect wealth to continue to corrupt American life because he had faith that men of character would understand the responsibility of power. Where such character was lacking, where the power of wealth was misdirected, Roosevelt was prepared to have the government intercede. Roosevelt was never radical. He attacked Altgeld, Bryan, Debs, Bellamy, and George with frenzied harshness. But, while resisting what seemed to him to be revolution, he welcomed change. From his rudimentary beginnings in the movements for civil service and for slum clearance, enlightened alike by the reformers he fought and the reformers he helped, he developed increasing concern over the abuses of great wealth, increasing inclination to listen, at least, to the demands of organized labor, and increasing determination to invest the state with authority to control the powerful and assist the weak.

The accidents of war and politics, making Roosevelt a national hero at the time Platt needed a hero in New York, gave Roosevelt the opportunity to test and administer his ideas as Governor of New York State. The times were conducive to change. But Roosevelt played a vital part in the development of the spirit of the times. A large body of the legislation he sponsored or approved pertained to political and social conditions which had attracted his attention years earlier. He supported measures reorganizing the civil service, improving the primary system and the machinery for the enforcement of election laws, keeping the police out of politics, and regulating the granting of municipal contracts and the use of campaign funds. He encouraged investigations of tenements and sweatshops and the expansion of the authority of the state's factory inspector.

Roosevelt turned also to other fields. The achievements of his administration in protecting and assisting New York's farmers and consumers, while not spectacular, were substantial. The state subsidized the cultivation of beet sugar and prevented the sale of artificially colored oleomargarine. The use of any poisonous food coloring and the adulteration of dairy products or fruit juices were forbidden. Union labor found Roosevelt a cautious friend, cool to most of the labor leaders who approached him, opposed to the major strikes of his term. But Roosevelt was not deaf to labor's demands. He sought the advice of Gompers, foremost labor spokesman of the time, of Henry White, a New York union leader, of Jacob Riis, and of George Gunton who, although discredited in labor circles, was a consistent advocate of shorter hours and higher pay. The widespread hostility to the measures passed in labor's behalf demonstrated the extent to which they departed from tradition. New York had earlier begun to restrict the working hours and regulate the conditions of employment of women and children. Continuing this precedent, Roosevelt helped prepare the way for more comprehensive legislation.

Of more immediate significance was Roosevelt's corporation program. Darwinian economists had expounded an evolutionary sanction for the growing concentration of money and power. Roosevelt, familiar with their arguments, appreciated the efficiency of size and the economic waste of unrestricted competition in many industries and services. With this appreciation and influenced by George W. Perkins, Roosevelt prevented limitations on the size of insurance companies. Where large size produced monopoly, however, he asserted the state's right to interfere. He sponsored many pieces of legislation which limited corporation privileges and practices. He signed a law prohibiting combinations in restraint of trade in the manufacture or sale of commodities in general use. Advised by essentially conservative economists and lawyers, particularly Jenks, Hadley, Ely, Root, Dill, and Griggs, he antagonized officials of public utility companies and street railways by supporting legislation restricting the tenure and terms of their franchises. His forceful action assured the passage of the Ford Bill, the most controversial measure of his administration. This law, reestablishing a practice previously abandoned in New York, but still untried in most states, provided for the taxation of franchises as real property. Roosevelt tried without success to secure legislation regulating corporations by stricter licensing and compulsory publicity. These remedies, the favored devices of moderate opinion in 1899, were the bases for Roosevelt's first national trust program. Their defeat in New York was partially offset by statutes Roosevelt signed which regulated the investment policies of savings banks, opened the books of membership corporations to inspection by public officials, and provided that the stock books of all corporations be open for inspection by all stockholders and creditors.

New York under Roosevelt assumed some of the characteristics of a protective state. Government, moving away from the principles of *laissez faire,* was still not paternalistic. It interceded more to prevent abuse than to impose a conceptualized social scheme. Roosevelt gave this process adroit and intelligent encouragement. Neither the labor vote, nor machine support, nor campaign contributions sufficiently explain his position. Just as, in the case of the Philippines or the Hay-Pauncefote Treaty, his political views were consistent with his dicta on race and nationalism, so in New York were they consistent with his other nonpolitical attitudes. His program for labor and corporations, permitting economic development "in accordance with certain biological laws," permitted also an increase in the sphere of the state's action, subordinating the interests of the individual to those of the community. By 1900 Roosevelt had effected a synthesis of experience which allowed him to act and to believe. By 1900 Roosevelt had begun to apply in politics standards of national character and social efficiency which contained the fundamental principles of the Big Stick, the Square Deal, and the New Nationalism. The first forty years, perplexing but fruitful, had produced an influential agent of responsible conservatism.

✪

Theodore Roosevelt[1]

Theodore Roosevelt was a giant, an overgrown personality. He was one of those sports that, appearing once or twice in a century or in an age, work tremendous havoc or harmony, and disappear apparently without spiritual progeny. Greatness, generally speaking, is an unusual quantity of a usual quality grafted upon a common man. The thing which the gods gave Roosevelt in excess was energy. He was Gargantuan in his capacity for work. It was one of those utterly unthinkable coincidences, coincidences so rare, so unbelievable that they almost force one to believe in the minute divine direction of human affairs, that a man of Roosevelt's enormous energy should come to the Presidency of exactly that country which at exactly that time was going through a transitional period—critical, dangerous, and but for him terrible—between an old rural, individual order and a new highly socialized industrial order. Of course the transition did not come abruptly. The transition period began in the 1850's, before the Civil War. It has not

[1] The reader should be warned that Theodore Roosevelt was my friend and probably I cannot be fair in estimating his weaknesses. This article was edited and somewhat rewritten more than nine years after his death. Yet he seems as vital now as he ever was in my life. Still his own justifications of incidents in his life—as, say, his cruise in Panama, or his quarrel with Wilson—seem to me reasonable and on the whole inevitable, being what he was, and on the whole tolerable. So what I tried to make an honest estimate is scarcely better than a eulogy.

Reprinted from William Allen White, "Theodore Roosevelt," *Masks in a Pageant* (New York: Macmillan, 1928), pp. 283–326.

17

closed as these lines are written in 1928, but the peak of crisis was passed somewhere between 1905 and 1916, a time during which Theodore Roosevelt was either in the White House or was a political leader of the first magnitude. In that period he went through his late forties into his early sixties, the ripest time of his life. He stood in 1912, when he was in the midst of his most important activity, a stocky man of five feet ten or eleven, long-legged, short-bodied, never pursy, though at times too heavy. He kept himself well trained physically; and electric energy seemed to exude from his body and emphasize his personality. His walk was a shoulder-shaking, assertive, heel-clicking, straightaway gait, rather consciously rapid as one who is habitually about his master's business. He shook hands vigorously with a powerful downward pull like a pumper, with a firm but never rough handclasp. His shoulders sloped a little off the square line, and his head often, perhaps generally, was thrust forward from the neck, a firm short pedestal for his face; indeed, his neck was a sort of muscular part of his face, which jammed his head forward without ever requiring a stoop of the shoulders. His countenance was dominated by a big, pugnacious nose, a mustache dropped to cover a sensitive mouth in which a heavy underlip sometimes protruded, indicating passion. Occasionally he used the loose lip as a shutter, purposely to uncover a double row of glittering teeth that were his pride. He knew that his display of teeth was effective as a gesture of humor or of rage. His slightly cleft chin could shoot out from a broad jaw, and when he was excited he worked his jaw muscles with an animal ferocity. They swelled and undulated in his moment of excitement, furnishing a physical outlet for his inner stress. Even in his thirties, when youth was still strong upon him, he had a wide, high brow, and to the end kept his hair intact. Probably his hair did not retreat a fraction of an inch in all his life. It was always stiff hair, inclined to curl, fairly close cropped, always trimmed, and gave his countenance an aspect of virility so real that, looking at Roosevelt's hair, one could understand how Delilah thought she would sap Samson's strength by shearing him. Roosevelt's eyes always peered through glasses, generally nose glasses when he was indoors or in civilized environment, and the glasses often gave a glint to his face which was absent when he took them off; for his grayish blue eyes were the least ferocious features in his face. Out of his countenance two men were wont to gaze at the world: One was a primitive—impetuous, imperious, splashing in a reservoir of vigor; the other was sophisticated, not ever quite furtive, but often feline. There, sometimes, glanced obliquely from his face the shadow of some inner femininity deeply suppressed, some exquisitely well-bred but devious female ancestress who sometimes flicked catwise out of his subconsciousness into the light and back again, as he clicked his glittering ivory teeth while purpose was surging from impulse into measured words. He rarely spoke hastily, but never acted tardily. Yet in his moments of inner debate one could see that old catlike great-grandmother hiding behind the shadow of his smile, or beneath the umbrage of a glare. She was always a minority report, but never entirely absent. Mostly Roosevelt was canine, and spiritually kicked dirt behind him and barked; perhaps in certain hours he gave tongue loudest to convince himself—barking at the treed cat of his own ancestry. But he surely was big, overwhelming, towering, monumental, a very Goliath of a personality inflated out of a common man by surplus energy. Every faculty, every purpose, every impulse, every physical and spiritual inch of him was overengined. Yet his qualities were coordinated. He made, with all his Cyclopean features, a well-balanced man and mind. If he was a freak, God and the times needed one. . . .

. . . if Theodore Roosevelt had died before September, 1901, his name in the tables of Vice-Presidents of the United States would probably mean no more a hundred years hence than the names of Daniel D. Tompkins, Richard M. Johnson, George M. Dallas, and other obscure Vice-Presidents. In dictionaries of American literature, two inches of brevier type would record that he had written ten or a dozen books, and give a list of the positions he had filled. An infinitesimally small number of Americans of the next century—historians, and advanced students of the period of American development from 1870 to 1899—would have a look at Roosevelt's *Winning of the West, American Ideals, With the Rough Riders in Cuba;* and insomuch as the style of these writings reveals the man, scholars would know him as a frank-spoken, sturdy fellow, a hater of shams, and a friend of everyone who gets things done and over with. No doubt American biography in the next century will tell stories of similar characters—fine enough, of course, but almost unknown and of limited influence. Roosevelt rose somewhat upon the ordinary rounds of political promotion: from a state legislator to a city office, Police Commissioner of New York City; from that to federal office, Civil Service Commissioner; and later to a higher federal office, Assistant Secretary of the Navy; and from that to Governor of New York. So he was trained in politics. But that does not explain his rise. Whence his strength? How did he win? To answer these questions, it is first necessary to find the keynote of Roosevelt's character. That was his ambition. And his ambition—the one great, ever-active purpose that, lying nearest to his heart, was the mainspring of his life—was to set an example before Americans, and especially youth. Always he saw himself in every public performance mirrored in the heart of youth. This reflection kept him always young. He was forever imagining himself as a man of the highest ideals, derived from good birth and liberal advantages, demonstrating to the youth of his country what such a man can do in politics in all honesty, without soiling his hands, for the betterment of American life and the progress of the world. In his early career he failed to realize his ambition. The country for the most part misread his motives. Men roughly regarded him as a pugnacious, impetuous, honest, but eccentric young man, or at best, perhaps, a harum-scarum, "bronco-busting" lover of notoriety, a poseur who liked a fight for its own sake and had no regard for the amenities of political relationship. Few of his partisans and fewer of his opponents saw, until he was well into his career, that they had a rare species of politician on their hands, one whose training had been moral rather than political. The American creed is that most politicians of all parties are bad, the worst ones generally being in the other party, and the good ones all dead or out of office. Americans believe that to get an office and enjoy it forever is the chief end of a politician's existence. Roosevelt had held office more than half his life, between his majority and the day he came to the White House. These offices entailed more labor and brought Roosevelt more enemies than glory or material reward. Only as Governor of New York and as Vice-President was his official salary as much as he could make writing for magazines and publishing books. But he never felt the need of money. . . .

The average man, sitting by the average grate fire in the average club living room in the United States in 1901, would have proclaimed the same opinion about civic morality and public honor that Roosevelt proclaimed. If Roosevelt had dropped in, there would have been amiable discussion, but few differences between the clubmen in spinning theories. But when the average man left his club for the caucus or convention, the legislature or Congress, he would accept things as they were and thank God he was not as other men. Roosevelt balked. He fought for things as they should be and can be. He spent his life trying to do much that the common man had dreamed should be done.

Moreover, Roosevelt started out to do many things that were left undone. And so, while Roosevelt had worked for a time as legislator, leaving that work unfinished; for a time as ranchman; as civil service commissioner; as Governor, leaving work to be done by others; even as President with rough ends showing; as agitator for liberalism—in the midst of his task he quit his career with certain definite achievements. His life as a whole was efficient, chiefly as a definite, consistent inspiration to like-minded Americans. In that much his ambition was fully realized. . . .

Early in his Presidential career Roosevelt had tremendously disturbed the reactionary wing of conservatism by his patronage fights with the Senate, by his demand for Cuban reciprocity over the opposition of the sugar interests, by the appointment of Oliver Wendell Holmes, Jr., to the Supreme Court. Holmes was regarded in Massachusetts as rather an unsafe and unsettling liberal, a book lawyer and a Puritan Brahmin. Finally, Roosevelt disturbed the right wing of conservatism by instituting a suit under the Sherman Anti-Trust Law against the Northern Pacific and the Great Northern railroads, charging them with establishing a merger in restraint of competitive trade. During his first year he made no important declaration of liberalism, but it was obvious to the more intelligent liberals of the country that Roosevelt was rather definitely committed to their cause, and also that he was using the thin edge of the wedge to drive his principles home.

Even at the end of his second year in the White House Roosevelt had not declared formal war upon the defenders of the citadel of special privilege. That citadel stood upon the firm foundation of Republican tradition. But Roosevelt was mining it. There sprang up out of the grass a group of young liberals, men at whom he had been unconsciously aiming all his life, who were coming into politics, and particularly into Republican party politics, not for the spoils, not to strengthen the machine, but for the fun of the game and the glory of God. They were mostly young men of means and some leisure, young business and professional men. For some strange reason, though Roosevelt all his life was the friend of labor, the labor movement never followed in his train. When he was a Bull Moose candidate ten years later, labor remained aloof from him. But this young liberal group, probably sons of mugwumps of the eighties—and Roosevelt was friendly with the mugwumps in the eighties—formed the nucleus of a faction inside the Republican party. It was evident in the second year of his administration that this faction might form. It was the first faction that had formed since the Silverites bolted in 1896.

For an impulsive man, Roosevelt was conspicuously cautious in those first years of his Presidency. Yet certainly he was noisier than McKinley. He filled the White House with all sorts and conditions of men: Western bull-whackers, city prizefighters, explorers, rich men, poor men, an occasional black man, editors, writers; and around his festal board gathered three times a day, from early morn until night, men whose faces never had been seen in the White House before. Party managers, to whom the White House table was an altar before which they bowed, were disturbed at the motley crew which Roosevelt called in. That assembly also was a sign of the times, a sign that Roosevelt had turned his back upon the citadel of privilege and all that it shielded and was looking into a new day to begin another struggle.

He was a book protectionist, not a political protectionist. He fried fat gingerly, holding his nose; whereas the party under the leadership of Hanna for twenty years inhaled the fumes of protective fat frying, as high priests love the blood of the altar. Roosevelt preached the simple life and became a book agent for a Swiss pastor's sermons on simplicity, advertising *The Simple Life* in a speech in which he attacked the trusts. And when he preached simplicity, it was a part of his cult to live his creed. In the White House his life as a father, as a husband, as a citizen, as a politician was most interesting, but almost primitive in its simplicity. Few forms were observed. He cut red tape. He talked state secrets in a loud voice to statesmen in the Presidential workroom, so that reporters could hear. He went on long walks through the parks in the environs of Washington, taking fat military officers with him, who panted along a step or two behind him. He tolerated no sacred cows. The generals of the army and the admirals of the navy, as generals and admirals, did not overcome him. Yet as an individual any man in the army or the navy or the State or Interior Department might command Roosevelt's esteem, even affection. But the officer's gold braid and rooster feather clearly got no homage from the President. He wore for the most part the black slouch hat of the type he had bought when he was police commissioner, fashionable in the early nineties. It became him. He liked the style. He stuck to it. And except upon extremely formal occasions, as when reviewing a fleet or when at a state function, Roosevelt wore his slouch hat and his business suit. The white-vested, black string-tied, gray-trousered McKinley in his Prince Albert coat had set a fashion for politicians. Roosevelt ruthlessly abolished the fashion. And, curiously enough, in abolishing the fashion of ceremonial garb—as in a score of other unconventional and revolutionary innovations—Roosevelt was dropping powder in the mine to blow up the citadel of privilege. So much of the cult of politics depends upon interior ceremonies, empty forms, tin cornice, and false fronts. His rejection of the pasteboard shams of life—social life, business life, political life—in and around the White House, as much as his antitrust suit against the Northern railways, and more than the appointment of Holmes to the Supreme Court, influenced the thought of the times, took away the magic of the cult of high priests, and turned America's heart from a solemn plutocracy to a rather noisy and aspiring democracy.

The death of Hanna, in 1903, removed the last possible aspirant for the Republican Presidential nomination, excepting Roosevelt, in the election of 1904. It was evident even before Hanna died that Roosevelt had overcome him. The President had the patronage of the White House, and in the Southern states showed his determination to use it. He had a growing acclaim in the Middle West. Academic, highly protected New England had small use for Roosevelt in those days; but that mattered little. He had settled a menacing coal strike. He had strengthened the trust laws. Before Hanna died Roosevelt had even contested Hanna's rule in Ohio—and won. He had cleaned out the thieves in the Postal Department. He had put new energy into the diplomatic wheels that were to build the Panama Canal, wheels that had been slowing down under McKinley. Roosevelt had wrestled publicly and successfully with the machine element in every state in the Union, where the machine had tried to impose upon him for federal appointment candidates whom Roosevelt regarded as unworthy men. And these tussles with the machine had always been advertised. His few defeats and inevitable compromises were forgotten. The spotlight of publicity followed Roosevelt all his life with curious devotion—by no means without Roosevelt's encouragement. Certainly McKinley had stood for clean men in high places. Many of McKinley's appointees had been men of the highest type. It is only fair to say that McKinley, on the whole, found better men for high places than Roosevelt chose. It was in choosing high-grade men for the minor appointments and fighting for these men that Roosevelt made his mark.

McKinley had a fine intuition for character in men. But if he fought the organization, he suppressed the news of the combat. He remained regular, a part of the established order. Roosevelt, in his battles with the Republican organization for men in minor places, called out the brass band, rang for the fire department, put on a military parade, and the nation saw the show. But in three years he had won.

He was unopposed for the Republican Presidential nomination in 1904, because he was right in the sense that he was following the deep and probably righteous tendency of his times. He had strength to review both sides of many proposals, and physical weakness did not tempt him ever to take the easy way. It was his habit to seek and follow the lines of greatest resistance, which habit made him seem deeply courageous where he was only mentally and morally acute. In these three years he had revealed to Congress and to the nation a man of abnormal energy. He often arose at six o'clock, took half an hour of violent exercise, breakfasted at seven, and was in his office at seven thirty, grinding away upon the day's work which a less energetic man might have postponed until mid-forenoon. At luncheon his table was crowded with visitors and he talked incessantly, yet never lingered over the table; ate heartily but not too heartily; enjoyed with a zest good food, and knew about it; drank one glass of sherry and no more; came back from lunch bursting into his office, where he saw Senators, cabinet members, bureau assistants, and chiefs, Congressmen and citizens in a long procession, and with the valves of his dynamic force pumped them through the White House in a steady stream. He decided minor questions quickly and with seemingly almost brutal casualness, even nonchalance, but really drawing from deep wells of past experience in each decision. Of a late afternoon he went for a short drive, or went walking, riding, swimming, and sometimes all three, spending an hour before dinner in vigorous exercise. At dinner, often he met a multitude. If he was a bit weary he directed the conversation, primed this man to tell a story, that woman to talk, but kept the dinner table from breaking into stagnant pools. It was one big powwow—that Presidential dinner table in the Roosevelt day. Generally he did the talking, ate well but not gluttonously, and by nine o'clock had dismissed the casual guests and probably picked out two or three. These he took to his library and with them wrangled over the day's passing problem. He was a swift, greedy reader, reading by pages rather than by sentences, yet always absorbing the gist of any matter. He read widely—current literature, Greek classics, biology, the physical sciences, besides following many curious, winding bypaths of literature that led into odd places. He discovered once that Senator Quay made a hobby of Icelandic sagas. Roosevelt crammed up on the subject, invited Quay to dinner, and the two jabbered away for hours, never mentioning the big fundamental differences that had

arisen between them. Having charmed Quay and acquired his
respect, Roosevelt found it easier than before to conquer Quay in
the political matter between them. He must have slept soundly and
with deep refreshment, for often after an eighteen-hour day he was
up and about at six. But with all his splendid vigor, time was not
frittered away. It was directed with a rather indomitable purpose
to the day's work—the thing in hand—the goal of the hour that he
was seeking. He did not win because he was all-wise, Jove-like and
morally thrice armed. His victories came to a great extent because
of the boundless might of his physical body, wherein his brain was
as well trained as his legs or arms, and as tightly in leash as the
corn sheller of a stomach which ground his food into blood and
energy. This knight was no pale dreamer who came to the dark
tower of American politics, dominated it, and set it free. He ruled
not because he was brave and wise and kind, though he was all
three, but because his courage, his wisdom, and his heart were
hitched to a dynamo, which gave him a sort of imperial authority.

There was no fight in prospect in the spring of 1904, and so the
Republican National Convention, opening in Chicago on June 21,
was the first Republican National Convention held in forty years
wherein everyone could get a seat. Empty seats might be had for
the asking the first day, and when the convention opened, hundreds of delegates' seats were vacant on the floor of the Coliseum.
The fighting interest was lacking in the spectacle. Roosevelt was in
control at the Republican machine. He had put rings in the noses
of the holy cattle of the little temples and had assembled the herd,
docile if not happy, in the great arena to nominate him. But they
came without enthusiasm. The cheering was mechanical. When
Roosevelt's name was first mentioned in a polite period by Mr.
Elihu Root, temporary chairman of the convention, the pande-
monium of applause lasted exactly one minute. The name of
Hanna got exactly one minute in the same speech, and a minute
was doled out to McKinley. Evidently the claque was doing its
cheering by the day and not by the piece; for it refused to put an
extra second of lung work on any name to give the performance
finish and the verisimilitude of joy. The only burst of pure felicity
came from the convention to greet Joe Cannon, who stood in
Washington, even in Roosevelt's first term, as the type of old-fash-

ioned "honest politician," whom the President's enemies openly worshiped as their political god. After three days of dreary platitudes from suppressed and subdued orators and favorite sons of the various states, ex-Governor Black, of New York, who disliked Roosevelt instinctively and also for cause, and who had attacked the President covertly at a public dinner two months before, was called upon as the titular leader of the party from Roosevelt's home state to place Roosevelt's name before the convention as a Presidential candidate. Black nominated Roosevelt in an electric fountain of rhetorical icicles. The speech may have thrilled the country—for them Roosevelt was a people's President—but the enthusiasm in the Coliseum hall was only a stage picture. One almost wondered who was the costumer. The galleries cheered heartily, for Chicago admired the President. The politicians on the floor of the convention had to do something, so for twenty long, weary minutes they turned loose and cheered like mummers suddenly turned in upon a wedding feast. When they felt that the amenities of the occasion had been satisfied, when they felt that it would not make "talk" for them to quit, the mummers eased into silence. Senator Mat Quay, at St. Louis eight years before, got a larger demonstration when he ran against McKinley than Roosevelt got at the Chicago convention that nominated him unanimously.

But the people were for Roosevelt, and the politicians obeyed the popular mandate. Roosevelt secured his nomination by working openly upon the Republican organization in the country. He threw pretense aside. He assembled the platform. He chose the officers of the convention and he put his secretary, Mr. Cortelyou, in as chairman of the Republican National Committee to conduct the campaign. He assumed full responsibility and asked the people to be his witness that it was his job. He probably picked Charles Fairbanks, of Indiana, as the Republican candidate for Vice-President. Of course overnice people objected to the Roosevelt manner. They preferred the punctilios of hypocrisy which certain other Presidents had felt constrained to use under the rules of the political game. Such bald[2] candor as Roosevelt's had not been seen in the White House since Jackson's time. Roosevelt

---

[2] His enemies called it brazen.

succeeded because in all his demands of the party he asked for no improper thing. There was his strength. He had moral sense as well as moral courage. His moral sense kept him from tripping. The politicians of the old order and the high caste in his first Presidential years felt that Roosevelt's audacity was a sign of weakness, forgetting that audacity for the right is golden, and that mere impudence, for the sake of winning, is brass.

In three years, Roosevelt had overcome and bound the defenders of the citadel of privilege and had occupied the dark tower himself in his own name. He did not wantonly destroy privilege with a sweep of his hand. He could not have done so. But he had implanted in the popular heart a faith in a new kind of democracy. The lesson to the Republican National Convention of 1904 was rather briefly this: that in the United States political institutions were safe. The party system, when turned over to spoilsmen, makes government merely an agency of priests of prosperity; but the same system is always at hand to serve the decent government when the people, properly led, know how to use government for the ends of justice. And more than this, the convention made it plain that though the party system had bred corrupt men and held them in power because the rank and file of the party sanctioned questionable leadership, when a brave, honest man like Roosevelt rose, strong enough and wise enough to use the party machinery for good ends, then the party system worked as easily and effectively for good ends as for bad ends. So at the close of his first term, his accidental term, Roosevelt functioned with his highest value as an example. It was not what he did, not even what he said, but how he said his say and did his work that counted. It was worth infinitely more to America to have the picture of Roosevelt, triumphing over the Republican machine, stand at the head of the nation where the eyes of young men might see him, than it was to have prosperity and protection maintained, or to have the trusts brought to time, or the currency established upon a sound basis. Roosevelt was valuable to his country in that day, not because he stood for prosperity, and he did stand for prosperity after a fashion, but because he was a flaming prophet of justice, a Jeremiah enthroned! . . .

Theodore Roosevelt began the contest for the so-called Roosevelt policies when he delivered his Inaugural Address in March, 1905. The address was a challenge. He was no longer McKinley's successor. He was a militant liberal, ready to take the liberal leadership of the world, to join the movement which was interested not in policies looking toward the accumulation of wealth, but rather policies which were looking to government as an agency of human welfare, which should enact laws and form a new tendency in the world—a tendency moving toward the equitable distribution of wealth. This policy regarded prosperity as an incident of life, emphasizing justice in human relations before prosperity. This policy appealed to the farmer, to the merchant, to the small manufacturer outside of the trust, to labor in its upper levels, to skilled labor, the railroad brotherhoods, and to the country banker and the professional man.

The Roosevelt policies found their most cordial welcome in the Middle West, their bitterest enemies in New York and New England. The South cheered for Roosevelt, but did not follow him politically. When Roosevelt announced his policy, the holders and supporters of what he termed "aggrandized wealth," "militant capital" turned upon him with righteous indignation. He had, indeed, departed from the ways of the fathers. He was trying to point his country to a new highway, to a new destination. He was following Bryan rather than McKinley. And throughout the land a furor arose. After all, those who lived in the citadel of privilege were by no means confined to Wall Street, Beacon Street, and the homes of the investment bankers. Roosevelt's stand was revolutionary, and every conservative mind was shocked at his pronouncement.

One must remember, in considering this Roosevelt pronouncement, that the wave of Populist protest had submerged even if its force had not subsided. Prosperity had come to the land and blessed it. Only a man of indomitable power could have turned America in that hour from the business of accumulating wealth to a consideration of the equitable distribution of wealth. And how he went at it! He took the Congress that was elected with him and tried to hammer it into a usable instrument. The Congressional leadership was frankly against the Roosevelt policies. Cannon,

Speaker of the House, and Nelson Aldrich, official leader of the
Senate, were openly, bitterly, cynically against Roosevelt and his
program. Which fact did not ruffle him. When he found a Senator
or a member of the House of Representatives difficult to handle,
when, in the discussion of a problem, Senators raised factitious
questions and would have befuddled the issue, Roosevelt, under
his black slouch hat, clicking his white teeth, partly in rage, partly
in joy, and partly from nervous exultation at the thought of
combat, went out over the land into the districts of men who
opposed him, preaching his doctrines, lending the prestige of the
Presidential office to the lever of his logic. And so America moved
upward. His method in dealing with Congressmen was direct,
generally courteous, and always forthright. He loved intrigue of a
harmless sort, but used it for amusement rather than gain. His
Machiavellian strain was grafted upon his sense of humor. But his
sheer brute strength and awkwardness won battles for him rather
than his finesse and cunning. For four years he fought the good
fight in the White House—precious years, fighting years, crammed
full of eighteen battle hours a day. But always his contests were led
by a man who could laugh. Roosevelt never giggled; he chuckled,
and was not above a guffaw, and loved a roaring belly laugh. Yet
one must not forget that he was a Harvardian, a person of
erudition who knew about music, painting, sculpture, history,
poetry—the softer, finer things of life; one who had been reared
observing the amenities—the son of a philanthropist, born indeed
with the silver spoon in his mouth. And if he railed and preached
in Gargantuan laughter, it was not the raucous clamor of a vacant
mind. And so day after day, month after month, for four busy
years, Roosevelt in the dark tower fought to let in the "light and
leading" of liberalism.

Now the Roosevelt policies were not confined to the list which
Roosevelt made. These were largely legislative. But his attitude as
an administrator also was sufficiently marked to make a policy.
The legislative program and the administrative attitude were in
truth an attack upon the citadel of privilege, nothing less and
scarcely more. It was, after all, as an agitator that Roosevelt found
his greatest usefulness, as an agitator against the unsocial attitude

of a wicked and perverse generation—the rulers of the land, indeed the rulers of the world; for the liberal movement of America was going neck and neck with the liberal movement in Europe. Morley, Asquith, Lloyd George in England, the Socialists in Germany, Clemenceau in France, Nitti in Italy were men of a common purpose. And Roosevelt in America, while he won victory after victory in Congress and established justice in a score of bureaus and in every department, his victories and his administrative establishments were preachments of a world-wide creed of liberalism, first object lessons in justice. He was the Moses who was teaching us the new ten commandments. Speaker Joseph Cannon sneered at him as one who had discovered the ten commandments. But the dullness of Cannon and his kind, in not perceiving that there must be a new ten commandments for every new order, made overthrow of the Cannon-Aldrich leadership in Congress inevitable.

The actual list of achievements of Roosevelt in his second term, viewed as a legislative or administrative program, is not imposing; viewed as a crusade for justice it is a revolution. He made men see that the crafty imitation of honorable conduct which the political and financial rulers of the land were often simulating was treason to the social order. He would have swept away the loaded dice of contemporary commerce and instituted at least the vision of a square deal. He applied to the problems of the day a keen, sometimes offensive sanity, a sturdy impatience at unjust traditions, an aggression which startled and finally overcame the well-fed prosperous alliance between politics and business by arousing the popular conscience.

The Roosevelt policies provided for the conservation of the natural wealth of the land; the honest branding of food and drugs; the establishment and construction of the Panama Canal; the establishment of a Department of Commerce and a Department of Labor; the promotion of peace through world organization backed up with a rather militant preparedness ("speak softly and carry a big stick" epitomized his idea of foreign relations); the restoration of competition in industry; the regulation of the railroads; a more scientific attitude toward the tariff.

This list is not the catalogue of the achievements of a revolutionist; but, backed by continual preachment for righteousness hurled defiantly at the nation as the jeremiad of a prophet, this program aroused emotion, got into the common will of the common people, and produced a new spiritual attitude, revolutionary, dynamic. Roosevelt found America in 1901 spiritually mud. He left it marble. . . .

. . . to say that Theodore Roosevelt was merely the sower who went forth to sow seems so little to say, so inadequate a figure to describe the tremendous personality that arose from his store of spiritual energy. The man was gigantic. In his generation he was unique. Men who lived with him died without seeing his kind again. He vitalized everything he touched. For thirty years he maintained a friendship with Henry Cabot Lodge, a friendship that knew no faction or politics. For in factional politics they were not agreed. Lodge was not a great personality, but he had keen perspicacity. "Thin soil highly cultivated" was Tom Reed's characterization of Lodge. Yet Lodge, a New England Brahmin, emotionless, ageless, circumscribed and circumspect, cried out in the Senate—where he stood among the scribes and Pharisees of his kind—when Roosevelt passed:

"Greatheart has gone!"

Greatheart he was—passionate, brave, generous, kind, and wise —a great heart that revived to righteousness a nation that was fattening in greed, languishing in iniquity. Greatheart he was, untouched by the years until he died; always young, ardent, with the merry heart which maketh a glad countenance; always haloed with that divine madness which makes for a gorgeous but charmed audacity. He stalked through the world, a Greatheart indeed, who made his little day a great epoch!

STUART P. SHERMAN

✪

Roosevelt and the National Psychology

I

Mr. Roosevelt's great and fascinating personality is part of the national wealth, and it should, so far as possible, be preserved undiminished. Since his death those who have spoken of him have observed somewhat too sedulously the questionable maxim, *De mortuis nihil nisi bonum.* To say nothing but good of a great man is generally fatal alike to biographical vivacity and to truth. In this case it is a serious detraction from that versatile and inexhaustible energy which Lord Morley admired when he declared that the two most extraordinary works of nature in America were Niagara Falls and the President in the White House. "He made," says William Hard with the intensity of one catching breath after the close passage of a thunderbolt, "he made Theodore Roosevelt the most interesting thing in the world," and he made "the world itself momentarily immortally interesting." That touches the heart of the matter: it explains comprehensively why his friends loved and his enemies admired him. It leaves him with his aggressive definiteness, his color, and his tang. Mr. Roosevelt, as he proudly insisted and as he admirably painted himself in many a capital chapter of

"Roosevelt and the National Psychology" is reprinted with the permission of Charles Scribner's Sons from *Americans*, pages 256–287, by Stuart P. Sherman. Copyright 1922 Charles Scribner's Sons; renewal copyright 1950 by Ruth Sherman. This selection was first published in *The Nation*, November 8, 1919.

his *Rough Riders* and his hunting and exploring books, was
stained with the blood and sweat and dust of conflict. No image
presents him whole that lacks a dash of the recklessness which
appears in Frederick MacMonnies' vaulting trooper and a touch of
the ruthlessness hinted by the fiercely clenched fist in a well-known
photograph of him pacing the deck of the flagship with "Fighting
Bob" Evans. He lived and died fighting, and he gave a thousand
proofs that the keenest joy he knew was the joy of battle. No
memorial so little preserves him as a whitewashed plaster bust.
Better than all the eulogies pronounced in public places I suspect
he would have relished the tribute paid to him in private conversation by one of our distinguished visitors from abroad. "It may be,"
he said, "that Mr. Wilson possesses all the virtues in the calendar;
but for my part I had rather go to hell with Theodore Roosevelt."
Mr. Wilson, he implied, might get off in a corner somewhere with
Saint Peter and Colonel House, and arrange something of the
highest importance to the heavenly host; but all the cherubim and
seraphim of healthy curiosity would be leaning over the impassable
gulf to see what Mr. Roosevelt would do next.

It is because such notes as these recall the most interesting man
of our times, "the great Achilles whom we knew," that I have
heard and read with a certain languor the conventional tributes
evoked by his death, and, more recently, have gone through the
posthumous biographies without entire satisfaction. Excepting Mr.
G. S. Viereck's saucy apology for being a pro-German, the cue of
recent writers has been canonization. Mr. MacIntire, for example,
prefaced by General Wood, has written a purely "inspirational"
narrative with a conquering hero ready for the moving-picture
screen or a Henty novel or a place on the juvenile bookshelf beside
The Boys' King Arthur. As a specimen of its critical quality, I
select the following passage, with the suggestion that it be read in
connection with the report of the federal Commission on the
Packers: "One shudders to think of what fate would have befallen
the United States if the monopolies which Roosevelt curbed while
he was President had been allowed to flourish until this era of
revolution." The first three volumes of *Roosevelt, His Life, Meaning, and Messages* are a collection of important speeches, articles,

and messages arranged by William Griffith; the fourth volume by Eugene Thwing is a rapid biographical compilation, journalistic, readable, and concluding with the happy thought that if the meaning of Roosevelt's life is fully appreciated we shall find in the next generation of Americans "a veritable race of moral giants." Mr. Lewis' book, for which Mr. Taft supplies an introduction, is, of course, a work of quite another order. For the earlier period it is almost as entertaining as the *Autobiography,* and for the latter years, particularly for the history of the Progressive movement, in which the author was an important participant, it is an independent authority and an animated and agreeable one with many small intimate strokes of appreciation. Mr. Lewis candidly announces that he considers his subject too near for "impartial judgment," and he lives up to his declaration most loyally, contending that practically everything Roosevelt said and did was exactly the right thing to say and do.

The eulogists and biographers claim rather too much, and one could wish that they would take a little more pains to harmonize their favorite facts. In order to illustrate the power of mind over matter, they all foster the tradition of Roosevelt's sickly youth. But Mr. MacIntire speaks of him in the New York Assembly as "this puny young chap" at just the period in which Mr. Thwing, after a reference to his "puny voice and puny hand," exhibits him knocking out the slugger Stubby Collins and mopping up the floor with "several" others. There is a similar discrepancy with regard to his linguistic attainments. Roosevelt himself testified that he was "lamentably weak in Latin and Greek"; but Mr. Thwing asserts that he was "a scholar of the first rank in the classics." One observer describes his conversational French at a luncheon in the White House as voluble, but regardless of accent and grammar; but Mr. Thwing says that "the savants of the Sorbonne heard him address them in as flawless French as they themselves could employ." Mr. MacIntire credits Roosevelt with the message ordering Dewey to sail into the port of Manila; Mr. Lewis says it has been established that Secretary Long sent it. Mr. Thwing makes him the discoverer and namer of the River of Doubt; Mr. Lewis represents him as only the explorer of that river which in his honor was renamed Teodoro by the Brazilian government. When there is a difference with regard to verifiable facts, Mr. Lewis appears generally to be right. In the total estimates, however, there is no significant difference; the biographers agree that Roosevelt was "our typical American," and possessed every important virtue that we admire.

When the critical biographer arrives he will re-examine this total estimate. Perhaps he will be challenged to re-examination by a certain passage toward the end of Mr. Lewis' book: "In the year 1918, a friend referred to the year 1921 as the year when he (Roosevelt) would again enter the White House. He had been in one of his jocular moods, but he immediately became very serious. 'No,' he said, 'not I. I don't want it, and I don't think I am the man to be nominated. I made too many enemies, and the people are tired of my candidacy.' " Mr. Roosevelt knew "the people." When he said, "I made too many enemies, and the people are tired of my candidacy," he admitted what none of the biographers concedes, the waning of his star, his perception that he could no longer, as in 1904, say "We believe" with strong confidence that he was uttering the convictions of the overwhelming majority of his countrymen. Both he and "the people" had changed, but the people had changed more profoundly than he in ways which I shall attempt to indicate by sketching an answer to three questions. First, what were the dominant aspects of the national character at about the time of Mr. Roosevelt's advent in public life? Second, what significant alterations in the national psychology did he produce in the period during which his personality was most heartily accepted as an incarnation of the national character? Third, how and to what extent has his national representativeness diminished?

II

Mr. Roosevelt did not emerge conspicuously on the national horizon till late in the nineties. The preceding decade appears to have contained extraordinarily little to kindle the imaginations of spirited and public-minded young men. There had been no war since the youth of their fathers. The government pursued a policy of somber rather than "splendid" isolation. The country offered its imposing attractions chiefly to the big businessmen. Captains of industry flourished like the green bay tree. For diversion there was riotous striking in the Carnegie Steel Works at Homestead; but the state militia put it down. In 1893 there was a financial panic; but it blew over. In 1894 Coxey led an army of the unemployed to Washington; but it dispersed like the chorus of a musical comedy amid general laughter. The Columbian Exposition, at the opening of which Chauncey Depew assisted, was on the whole a symbol of a period of unexampled material prosperity in commerce, agriculture, and manufactures. In 1896 William McKinley, son of an iron manufacturer and author of a tariff bill designed to protect the farmers from the plain people as the manufacturers had already been protected, was elected President under the skillful management of Mark Hanna, wholesale grocer, coal and iron merchant, later United States Senator. Mr. Roscoe Thayer remarks in his life of Hay that the most representative American in the third quarter of the century was P. T. Barnum; and the methods and ideals of Mark Hanna as political manager he compares to the methods and ideals of Barnum. From the popular magazines, reflecting current standards of success, the aspiring youth learned that by frugality and industry he might become as rich as Andrew Carnegie or John D. Rockefeller or as noble and distinguished as Chauncey Depew. The plutocratic era lacked—outside the field of business—ideas, imagination, animating purpose.

While the national mind was absorbed in business why should young men born to wealth and social position strive to thrust themselves in between the captains of industry and their political representatives? Possessing at the start the objects of the race, why should they contend? Politics was generally described as dirty and uninspiring; why should they subject themselves to its soil and fatigue? How some of them were answering such questions, Jacob Riis revealed in his life of Roosevelt:

They were having a reunion of his [Roosevelt's] class when he was Police Commissioner, and he was there. One of the professors told of a

student coming that day to bid him good-bye. He asked him what was
to be his work in the world.

"Oh!" he said, with a little yawn, "really do you know, professor, it
does not seem to me that there is anything that is much worth
while."

III

Then came the impact upon the national character of the Rooseveltian personality, persuaded that there are a hundred more
interesting things than making money, all "worth while": hunting
grizzlies, reforming, exploring, writing history, traveling, fighting
Spaniards, developing a navy, governing men, reading Irish epics,
building canals, swimming the Potomac with ambassadors, shooting lions, swapping views with kaisers, organizing new parties, and
so on forever. Under the influence of this masterful force the
unimaginative plutocratic psychology was steadily metamorphosed
into the psychology of efficient, militant, imperialistic nationalism.
When Roosevelt heard of the young man to whom nothing seemed
much worth while, he is said to have struck the table a blow with
his fist, exclaiming: "That fellow ought to have been knocked in
the head. I would rather take my chances with a blackmailing
policeman than with such as he." Mr. Riis remarks, "This is what
Roosevelt got out of Harvard." But clearly he didn't get it out of
Harvard. He found it—this wrath at the sluggard—in his own
exuberant temperament. Most of his biographers foolishly insist
that he had no extraordinary natural endowment. The evidence is
all otherwise, indicating a marvelous physical and mental energy
and blood beating so hot and fast through brain and sinew that he
was never bored in his life. He never felt the ennui or the horrid
languor of men like Hay and Henry Adams. He had such excess of
animal spirits that, as everyone knows, he was accustomed, after
battling with assemblymen or Senators, to have in a prizefighter to
knock him down.

Whatever delighted him he sought to inculcate upon the American people so that Rooseveltism should be recognized as synonymous with Americanism. Mr. Lewis is at some pains to point out

that in his private life he was an old-fashioned gentleman and invariably dressed for dinner. The fact is mildly interesting, but its public influence was absolutely negligible. Rooseveltism can never be interpreted to mean dressing for dinner. Practically he was a powerful aider and abettor of the movement to banish the word "gentleman" from the American vocabulary, except as a term of contempt. He was ostentatious about his friendships with Mike Donovan, Fitzsimmons, Sullivan, and Battling Nelson, just as he was about his pursuit of the big game of North America, because he loved the larger vertebrates and wished to implant an affection for them in the national mind. In his sports he can hardly be called a typical American; the typical American cannot employ the champion pugilists, nor follow the Meadowbrook hounds, nor hunt elephants with a regiment of bearers. These are the sports of emperors and rajahs and the sporting sons of multimillionaires. Still Mr. Roosevelt took them up and journalized them in behalf of a strenuous athletic ideal for the nation. A powerful animal himself, he gloried, day in and day out, in the fundamental animal instincts and activities, reproductive and combative, the big family and the big stick, the "full baby carriage" and "hitting hard and hitting first"; and he preached them in season and out of season.

I will give two illustrations. On his return from slaughtering elephants in Africa, he stopped off in Berlin to tell the Germans about the world-movement. That was in 1910; and perhaps the Germans were then almost as well informed with regard to the world-movement as Mr. Roosevelt. But in those days his exuberance was very great; for it had been two years since he had sent a message to Congress, and he found relief for his pent-up energies in bestowing advice all the way around the European circuit. Accordingly he solemnly warned the Germans that one of "the prime dangers of civilization has always been its tendency to cause the loss of virile fighting virtues, of the fighting edge." At the same time he marked it as a reassuring sign of our modern period that there were then larger standing armies than ever before in the world. These words seemed to his German hearers so fitly spoken that they then and there made Mr. Roosevelt a doctor of philosophy. He lectured also at the Sorbonne, finding a text in a novel of

Daudet's in which the author speaks of "the fear of maternity which haunts the young mother." The country in which that is generally true, cried Roosevelt to that country of declining birth rate, is "rotten to the core." "No refinement of life," he continued, "can in any way compensate for the loss of the great fundamental virtues; and of these great fundamental virtues the greatest is the race's power to perpetuate the race."

Roosevelt's mental exuberance may be suggestively measured in this fashion. Mark Twain, when he got under way, was a fairly voluble talker. But Mark Twain was silent and overwhelmed in the presence of Rudyard Kipling. Kipling, then, had a certain flow of ideas. But Kipling was silent and overwhelmed in the presence of Roosevelt. I quote Roscoe Thayer:

I have heard Mr. Rudyard Kipling tell how he used to drop in at the Cosmos Club at half past ten or so in the evening, and presently young Roosevelt would come and pour out projects, discussions of men and politics, criticisms of books, in a swift and full-volumed stream, tremendously emphatic and enlivened by bursts of humor. "I curled up on the seat opposite," said Kipling, "and listened and wondered, until the universe seemed to be spinning round and Theodore was the spinner."

IV

Roosevelt quickened the pace of national life by his own mental and physical speed. His special contribution, however, was not the discovery but the direction of strenuousness. The captains of industry had been strenuous enough. He found a new object for physical and mental energy on the grand scale. More than any other man of his time he made political eminence a prize of the first order by his own unequivocal preference of public service and glory to private opulence and ease. The exigencies of his later political life associated him indeed with what a Western humorist has described as the "high-low-brows"; he consorted with publicans and sinners; he broke bread with bosses and malefactors of great wealth; he played up the prizefighters and the cowboys; he hurled epithets at Byzantine logothetes and college professors: so that one almost forgets that he began his career distinctly on the "highbrow" side as a "silk-stocking" reformer, supported by the vote of the "brownstone fronts," foremost of the pure-principled purposeful young "college men in politics" in an era of sordid greed and corruption. But in the days when he was assemblyman at Albany, police commissioner, and civil service reformer, men did not speak of him nor did he speak of himself as a "practical politician." In those days there was a certain bloom on the fruit that he reached for; and he did not disdain to speak of himself as a "practical idealist." In that role he delighted even fastidious disciples of Charles Eliot Norton's fastidious school; and he exercised a wonderfully tonic influence upon well-bred young men of his generation.

His first great service was to his own prosperous class, to young men of means in college, to the "intellectuals" generally. He did not preach against wealth. He held, like the philosopher Frank Crane, that "men who get $20,000 a year and up are the most valuable citizens of the nation." On the other hand, he maintained, like that journalistic sage, that the man who inherits a million and spends his days playing bridge and changing his trousers is "a cootie on the body politic." To fortune's favored sons he declared the responsibilities of wealth and he taught the right uses of leisure. In the vein of Carlyle and Kipling he preached against an idle, pleasure-seeking life as not merely undesirable, but contemptible. He preached the gospel of work for every man that comes into the world, work to the uttermost of his capacity; responsibility for every advantage and every talent; ignominy and derision for the coward and the shirker and the soft-handed overfastidious person who thinks public life too rough and dirty for his participation. Writing of machine politics in 1886, he said, rather fatalistically: "If steady work and much attention to detail are required, ordinary citizens, to whom participation in politics is merely a disagreeable duty, will always be beaten by the organized army of politicians to whom it is both duty, business, and pleasure, and who are knit together and to outsiders by their social relations."

But in 1894 he put the bugle to his lips and summoned the more intelligent class of "ordinary citizens" to arms:

The enormous majority of our educated men have to make their own living. . . . Nevertheless, the man of business and the man of science, the doctor of divinity and the doctor of law, the architect, the engineer and the writer, all alike owe a *positive duty* to the community, the neglect of which they cannot excuse on any plea of their private affairs. They are bound to follow understandingly the course of public events; they are bound to try to estimate and form judgments upon public men; and they are bound to act intelligently and effectively in support of the principles which they deem to be right and for the best interests of the country. . . . If our educated men as a whole become incapable of playing their full part in our life, if they cease doing their share of the rough, hard work which must be done, and grow to take a position of mere dilettanteism in our public affairs, they will speedily sink in relation to their fellows who really do the work of governing, until they stand toward them as *a cultivated, ineffective man with a taste for bric-à-brac* stands toward a great artist. When once a body of citizens becomes thoroughly out of touch and out of temper with the national life, its usefulness is gone, and *its power of leaving its mark on the times is gone also.*

I have italicized in this passage the characteristic threefold appeal: the straightforward statement of duty, the craftily constructed contemptuous phrase for the dilettante, the quiet but significant reference to the rewards of virtue. In Roosevelt's heart there sang lifelong the refrain of Tennyson's ode on the Duke of Wellington, "The path of duty is the way to glory"; and he made it sing in the ears of his contemporaries until the blasé young man of the Yellow Nineties became unfashionable, yielding his place to the Man Who Does Things. This alteration of the national psychology was of profound importance. It marked the difference between a nation headed for decadence and a nation entering upon a renaissance; and Roosevelt's service in bringing it about can hardly be overvalued. Some appraisers of his merits say that his most notable achievement was building the Panama Canal. I should say that his most notable achievement was creating for the nation the atmosphere in which valor and high seriousness live, by clearing the air of the poisonous emanations of "superior" people:

Let the man of learning, the man of lettered leisure, beware of that queer and cheap temptation to pose to himself and to others as the cynic, as the man who has outgrown emotions and beliefs, the man to whom good and evil are as one. The poorest way to face life is to face it with a sneer. . . . There is no more unhealthy being, no man less worthy of respect, than he who either really holds, or feigns to hold, an attitude of sneering contempt toward all that is great and lofty, whether in achievement or in that noble effort which, even if it fails, comes second to achievement. . . . The man who does nothing cuts the same sordid figure in the pages of history, whether he be cynic, fop, or voluptuary.

Preaching duty and meditating on glory, Roosevelt came up through the dull nineties as the apostle of "applied idealism"; and all good men spoke well of him. He seemed to be striking out a new and admirable type of public man; well-bred but strenuous, ambitious but public-spirited, upright but practical and efficient— the idealist who gets things done which everyone agrees ought to be done. But few men guessed the height and depth of desire in this fighter of legislative crooks, this reformer of metropolitan police, this advocate of the merit system; and no one knew what his ideas and temperament would do to the national life if he became its acknowledged leader. In 1898 came the Spanish War, then the Governorship of New York, the Vice-Presidency in 1900, and a year later Roosevelt was in the saddle. These events swiftly disclosed the wider horizon of his mind and the scope of his ambition for himself and for America. The war with Spain brought him forward as the Seminole War brought forward Andrew Jackson; and his personality was immensely responsible for the effect of that "incident" upon the national character.

V

Mr. Roosevelt was an admirer of Thucydides, but he was a much less philosophical historian; for he says that the war with Spain was "inevitable," and leaves his readers to explain why. The small jingo class whose veins perennially throb with red blood and national honor fought, of course, to avenge the blowing-up of the Maine. The mass of the plain people with their perennial simple-hearted idealism were persuaded that they were going in to set Cuba free, even after they discovered that they had also gone in to subjugate the Philippine Islands. Mr. J. A. Hobson, the English economist, says:

Not merely do the trusts and other manufacturing trades that restrict their output for the home market more urgently require foreign markets, but they are also more anxious to secure protected markets, and this can only be achieved by extending the area of political rule. This is the essential significance of the recent change in American foreign policy as illustrated by the Spanish War, the Philippine annexation, the Panama policy, and the new application of the Monroe doctrine to the South American States. South America is needed as a preferential market for investment of trust "profits" and surplus trust products: if in time these States can be brought within a Zollverein under the suzerainty of the United States, the financial area of operations receives a notable accession.

There is an absence of rose-pink altruism from this last explanation which should commend it to the *Chicago Tribune;* but Roosevelt, though the *Tribune's* chief hero, would certainly have rejected it for an interpretation at once more personal and more political.

It is fairly plain that this war, which he had done his utmost to prepare for and to bring about, was first of all an opportunity for a man of his strenuous leisure class with fighting blood and fighting edge to win personal distinction. He himself speaks of his baptism of fire as his "crowded hour of glorious life"; and throughout his narrative of the exploits of his regiment—"My men were children of the dragon's blood"—he exhibits a delight in fighting that reminds one of the exuberant praise of "glorious battle" uttered early in the late war by the colonel of the Death's Head Hussars. He is as proud of personally bringing down his Spaniard as of slaying his first lion. He played his daring and picturesque part in a way to rehabilitate military glory in the national mind. But for the astonishing skill with which he wrung the last drop of dramatic interest from his troop of college men and cowboys the reverberations of the affair would soon have died away in the popular consciousness. He made the deeds of the Rough Riders a popular classic like Lexington and Bunker Hill. His little war did as much to kindle as Mr. Wilson's big war did to quench the military spirit; for Mr. Wilson went in with the grim determination of a chief of police, and Mr. Roosevelt with the infinite gusto of a big game hunter. His little war, as he himself declared, made him President.

In office, he did not sicken of power as did the Washingtonians of whom Henry Adams speaks. With the vast influence of his position he sought to mold the national mind and feelings into the likeness of his own. He sought to make the national mind virile, daring, imaginative, aggressive, and eager for distinction in the world. He preached to the nation as if it were a rich man of leisure with a splendid opening, made by his war, for the practice of the strenuous life. He set the example by magnifying his own office, concentrating power, teaching the public to look to the federal government as the controlling, dynamic, and creative center of American life. His measure for the regulation of monopolies, his seizure of the Canal Zone, his irrigation acts, his reservation of public lands all exemplify in one way and another his aversion from the spirit of *laissez faire,* his passion for identifying the state with the man who does things. In domestic affairs this policy generally estranged the "big interests" and won the support of the "plain people." In foreign affairs the big interests supported him, but the plain people were first dazzled, and then astonished, and then a little perplexed. The plain people do not understand foreign affairs.

President McKinley, by instinct and upbringing a domestically-minded statesman, had indeed begun to speak in a resigned way of manifest destiny with regard to our newly acquired island possessions. He could hardly do otherwise, for this was the midsummer time of the imperial enthusiasm of the "Anglo-Saxons." These were the days of Rhodesian dreamers; Kitchener was fighting in Egypt; Roberts was fighting in South Africa; and in 1899 Mr. Kipling struck up his famous chant: "Take up the white man's burden, send forth the best ye breed." And so McKinley gravely recognized our manifest destiny in the Far East. Yet John Hay

says that he was called in by McKinley to discuss foreign affairs
not more than once a month, but that as soon as Roosevelt was in
office he was called upon every day. It was Roosevelt first who
embraced manifest destiny with the joy of an enkindled political
imagination. It was he that resolutely sought to waken the expan-
sive energies of the nation and to give it the fighting edge and the
will to prevail in the impending conflicts of the powers. It was he
that tirelessly went up and down the land declaring that the
imperialistic tendencies developed by the Spanish War were tokens
of national virility and that the responsibilities of the new foreign
policy were glorious opportunities for men of the heroic mood
imbued with the new Rooseveltian Americanism.

If we are to mark his place in the spiritual history of the times,
we must clearly understand the temper which, at the turn of the
century, he brought into our era of atrocious international conflicts. Nowhere, perhaps, did he declare more eloquently the gospel
of militant imperialistic nationalism than in his address on "The
Strenuous Life," delivered before the Hamilton Club of Chicago in
1899:

> The timid man, the lazy man, the man who distrusts his country, the
> over-civilized man who has lost the great fighting virtues, the ignorant
> man and the man of dull mind, whose soul is incapable of feeling the
> mighty lift that thrills "stern men with empires in their brains"—all
> these, of course, shrink from seeing the nation undertake its new
> duties. . . . The army and navy are the sword and shield which the
> nation must carry if she is to do her duty among the nations of the
> earth. . . . The twentieth century looms before us big with the fate of
> many nations. If we stand idly by, if we seek merely swollen slothful
> ease and ignoble peace, if we shrink from the hard contests where men
> must win at hazard of their lives and at the risk of all they hold dear,
> then the bolder and stronger peoples will pass us by, and will win for
> themselves the domination of the world. Let us, therefore, boldly face
> the life of strife. . . . Above all, let us shrink from no strife, moral
> or physical, within or without the nation—for it is only through
> strife, through hard and dangerous endeavors, that we shall ultimately
> win the goal of true national greatness.

That the sentiments and principles here expressed sound very
familiar to us today is not, I fancy, because most of us have been

reading Roosevelt's addresses of the Spanish War period, but because we have been reading the utterances of the Pan-Germans whom Roosevelt himself in 1910 was adjuring not to lose the fighting edge and whom he was congratulating on the size of European military establishments as a sign of health and virility. Retrospectively considered, his solicitude for the fighting edge of the Germans reminds one of the matador in Blasco Ibáñez' *Blood and Sand,* who, it will be remembered, prays for a "good bull." With the essentials in the religion of the militarists of Germany, Roosevelt was utterly in sympathy. He believed that if you kept your fighting edge keen enough no one would seriously question your righteousness. The only significant difference in objects was that while they invoked the blessing of Jehovah upon Pan-Germany he invoked it upon Pan-America, meaning the United States and her dependencies, protectorates, and spheres of influence—and the Pan-America of his dream made Mittel-Europa look like a postage stamp. The highest point of his working upon the national mind, the point at which his powerful personality most nearly succeeded in transforming the national character from its original bias, was that in which he made it half in love with military glory, half in love with empire-building, half in love with the sort of struggle which was preparing in Europe for the domination of the world.

VI

The American leader of militant imperialistic nationalism fell at the end of his last great fight, a fight which, it may be soberly said, he had done his utmost both immediately and remotely to prepare for and to bring about. All his friends and many who were not his friends give him credit for the immediate preparation. But few of his friends claim or admit his profounder part in the preparation of the stage for the conflict, the will of the combatants, the conditions of the struggle, the prizes of victory. The preparation runs far back to the days when he began to preach the strenuous life in the flush of the Spanish War, to the days when he dangled before our eyes "those fair tropic islands," to the days when he boasted that he had taken Panama and let Congress debate after the act. In the

stunning clash of militant imperialistic nations, a clash which was
the "inevitable" goal of his lifelong policy, as it is that of every
imperialist, he towered above his fellow citizens, constantly and
heroically calling to arms. His countrymen rose, but not for his
battle. They fought, but not for his victory. Time and events with
remorseless irony made him the standard-bearer and rallying point
for an American host dedicated to the destruction of his policy of
militant imperialistic nationalism abroad and at home. He said
"Belgium," he mentioned Germany's transgressions of law; and his
countrymen cheered and buckled on their armor. But if, during the
war, he had dared to exhort them, as in the earlier time, "to face
the life of strife for the domination of the world," they were in a
mood to have torn him in pieces. In that mood they fought and
won their war. Highly as they valued his instrumental services, the
principles on which they waged it and the objects which they
sought drew them away from Roosevelt and toward Lincoln and
Washington.

At the present time it is obvious to everyone that a faction of his
old friends, incorrigibly born and bred in militant imperialistic
nationalism, are making a fight over his body to wrest from the
simple-hearted idealistic plain people the fruits of victory. Gloomy
observers—too gloomy, I think—declare that the fruits are already
gone. The exponents of nationalistic egoism and selfishness will
win some partial and temporary triumphs in this as in other
countries. In the immediate future the memory of Roosevelt will
be the most animating force among our American Junkers. There
will be an attempt to repopularize just those Bismarckian characteristics of their hero which made him so utterly unlike Lincoln—
his moral hardness, his two-fistedness, the symbolic big stick. But
his commanding force as chief molder of the national mind is over.
He must take his rank somewhere among the kings and kaisers in
competition with whom he made his place in the spiritual history
of his times. He can never again greatly inspire the popular liberal
movement in America. The World War has too profoundly discredited the masters of *Weltpolitik* in his epoch. It has too
tragically illuminated the connections between the cataclysm and
the statecraft and militaristic psychology behind it. He was a

realist with no nonsense about him; but all the realists of the period are now under suspicion of being unrealistic in that they ignored the almost universal diffusion of "nonsense" or idealism among mankind. When Mr. Roosevelt fell out with "practical" men, he almost invariably strengthened his position with the plain people. It was when he offended their "nonsense"—as in his vindictive and ruthless onslaughts upon his successor and upon his great rival, and in his conduct of the Panama affair—that they began to doubt whether he had the magnanimity, the fairness of mind, the love of civil ways requisite to guide them toward the fulfillment of their historic destiny. He developed a habit of speaking so scornfully of "overcivilization" and so praisefully of mere breeding and fighting as to raise the question that he himself raised about Cromwell, whether he had an adequate "theory of ends," and whether he did not become so fascinated with his means as frequently to forget his ends altogether.

Take the ever-burning matter of militarism. His apologists, like those of the Kaiser, all declare that he loved peace; and one can quote passages to prove it. I will quote a beautiful passage from his speech in Berlin in 1910: "We must remember that it is only by working along the lines laid down by the philanthropists, by the lovers of mankind, that we can be sure of lifting our civilization to a higher and more permanent plane of well-being than ever was attained by any preceding civilization. Unjust war is to be abhorred. . . ." I pause to ask whether anyone thinks this remark about working on the lines of philanthropists and lovers of mankind is characteristic Rooseveltian doctrine. I now quote the rest of the passage: "But woe to the nation that does not make ready to hold its own in time of need against all who would harm it. And woe thrice over to the nation in which the average man loses the fighting edge." I stop again and ask whether anyone thinks that is *not* characteristic Rooseveltian doctrine? Why does the second of these sentences sound perfectly Rooseveltian and the first absolutely not? Because into the first he put a stroke of the pen, into the second the whole emphasis of his character. The first is his verbal sop to the idealist; the second is his impassioned message to his generation. By his use of rhetorical balance he gives a superficial appearance of the mental equivalent; but by his violent and infallible emphasis he becomes the greatest concocter of "weasel" paragraphs on record. In time his hearers learned to distinguish what he said from what he stood for, the part of his speech which was official rhetoric from the part that quivered with personal force.

He said, it is true, that "mere fervor for excellence in the abstract is a great mainspring for good work"; but in practice he night and day denounced in the most intolerant language those who exhibited mere fervor for excellence in the abstract, and even those who sought excellence by other ways than his. He professed love for the plain people; but the Progressive episode looks today, so far as he was concerned, like a momentary hot fit and political aberration of a confirmed Hamiltonian, regarding the plain people not so much socially as politically, not so much as individuals as a massive instrument for the uses of the state and the governing class. He said that he had a regard for peace but he made plain that he loved and valued war; and he denounced everyone else who said a good word for peace, he reviled every type of pacifist so mercilessly as to rouse suspicion as to whether he really cared a rap for the *object* of the pacifists. He expressed approval of arbitration; but he invariably followed up such expressions with an assertion that the only effective arbitrator is a man in shining armor. He avowed a desire for international order, but his imagination and his faith did not rise to a vision of other ways of attaining it than the ways of Alexander and Caesar—by the imperial dominion of armed power; and he denounced other modes of working for international order so bitterly as to raise a doubt as to his regard for the object. He admitted, like many of his followers, a faint and eleventh-hour respect for the abstract idea of a league of nations; but he led in raising such a thunder of opposition to the only league within sight and reach that he weakened the hands of the American framers, and he raised a question as to what he meant in the old days by his fiery declamation against those who "make the impossible better forever the enemy of the possible good."

Mr. Roosevelt has attained satisfactions which he thought

should console fallen empires: he has left heirs and a glorious memory. How much more glorious it might have been if in his great personality there had been planted a spark of magnanimity. If, after he had drunk of personal glory like a Scandinavian giant, he had lent his giant strength to a cause of the plain people not of his contriving nor under his leadership. If in addition to helping win the war he had identified himself with the attainment of its one grand popular object. From performing this supreme service he was prevented by defects of temper which he condemned in Cromwell, a hero whom he admired and in some respects strikingly resembled. Cromwell's desire, he says,

was to remedy specific evils. He was too impatient to found the kind of legal and constitutional system which would prevent the recurrence of such evils. Cromwell's extreme admirers treat his impatience of the delays and shortcomings of ordinary constitutional and legal proceedings as a sign of his greatness. It was just the reverse. . . . His strength, his intensity of conviction, his delight in exercising powers for what he conceived to be good ends; his dislike for speculative reforms and his inability to appreciate the necessity of theories to a practical man who wishes to do good work . . . all these tendencies worked together to unfit him for the task of helping a liberty-loving people on the road to freedom.

★

Roosevelt I

Roosevelt's reaction to World War I must occupy a large part of
any adequate account of him, for that reaction was probably more
comprehensively typical of the man than any other business of his
life. It displayed not only his whole stock of political principles,
but also his whole stock of political tricks. It plumbed, on the one
hand, the depths of his sagacity, and on the other hand the depths
of his insincerity. Fundamentally, I am convinced, he was quite
out of sympathy with, and even quite unable to comprehend the
body of doctrine upon which the Allies, and later the United
States, based their case. To him it must have seemed insane when
it was not hypocritical, and hypocritical when it was not insane.
His instincts were profoundly against a new loosing of democratic
fustian upon the world; he believed in strongly centralized states,
founded upon power and devoted to enterprises far transcending
mere internal government; he was an imperialist of the type of
Cecil Rhodes, Treitschke and Delcassé.

But the fortunes of domestic politics jockeyed him into the
position of standing as the spokesman of an almost exactly
contrary philosophy. The visible enemy before him was Wilson.
What he wanted as a politician was something that he could get
only by wresting it from Wilson, and Wilson was too cunning to

yield it without making a tremendous fight, chiefly by chicane—whooping for peace while preparing for war, playing mob fear against mob fear, concealing all his genuine motives and desires beneath clouds of chautauqua rhetoric, leading a mad dance whose tune changed at every swing. Here was an opponent that more than once puzzled Roosevelt, and in the end flatly dismayed him. Here was a mob-master with a technique infinitely more subtle and effective than his own. So, lured into an unequal combat, the Rough Rider got bogged in absurdities so immense that only the democratic anesthesia to absurdity saved him. To make any progress at all he was forced into fighting against his own side. He passed from the scene bawling piteously for a cause that, at bottom, it is impossible to imagine him believing in, and in terms of a philosophy that was as foreign to his true faith as it was to the faith of Wilson. In the whole affair there was a colossal irony. Both contestants were intrinsically frauds.

When, soon after his death, I ventured in a magazine article to call attention to Roosevelt's philosophical kinship to the Kaiser,[1] I received letters of denunciation from all parts of the United States, and not a few forthright demands that I recant on penalty of lynch law. Prudence demanded that I heed these demands. We live in a curious and often unsafe country. Haled before a Roosevelt judge for speeding my automobile, or spitting on the sidewalk, or carrying a jug, I might have been railroaded for ten years under some constructive corollary of the Espionage Act. But there were two things that supported me in my contumacy to the departed. One was a profound reverence for and fidelity to the truth, sometimes almost amounting to fanaticism. The other was the support of the eminent Iowa right-thinker and patriot, Professor S. P. Sherman. Writing in the *Nation,* Dr. Sherman put the thing in plain terms. "With the essentials in the religion of the militarists of Germany," he said, "Roosevelt was utterly in sympathy."[2]

Utterly? Perhaps the adverb was a bit too strong. There was in the man a certain instinctive antipathy to the concrete aristocrat

---

[1] "Roosevelt and Others," *Smart Set,* March 1920, pp. 138–144.
[2] "Roosevelt and the National Psychology," *Nation,* November 8, 1919 [reprinted on pp. 33–51].

and in particular to the aristocrat's private code—the produce, no doubt, of his essentially bourgeois origin and training. But if he could not go with the Junkers all the way, he could at least go the whole length of their distrust of the third order, the undifferentiated masses of men below. Here, I dare say, he owed a lot to Nietzsche. He was always reading German books, and among them, no doubt, were *Also sprach zarathustra* and *Jenseits von Gut und Böse*. In fact, the echoes were constantly sounding in his own harangues. Years ago, as an intellectual exercise while confined to hospital, I devised and printed a giveaway of the Rooseveltian philosophy in parallel columns—in one column, extracts from *The Strenuous Life;* in the other, extracts from Nietzsche. The borrowings were numerous and unescapable. Theodore had swallowed Friedrich as a farmwife swallows Peruna—bottle, cork, label and testimonials. Worse, the draft whetted his appetite, and soon he was swallowing the Kaiser of the *Garde-Kavallerie*-mess and battleship-launching speeches—another somewhat defective Junker. In his palmy days it was often impossible to distinguish his politico-theological bulls from those of Wilhelm; during the war, indeed, I suspect that some of them were boldly lifted by the British press bureau, and palmed off as felonious imprudences out of Potsdam. Wilhelm was his model in *Weltpolitik,* and in sociology, exegetics, administration, law, sport and connubial polity no less. Both roared for doughty armies, eternally prepared—for the theory that the way to prevent war is to make all conceivable enemies think twice, thrice, ten times. Both dreamed of gigantic navies, with battleships as long as Brooklyn Bridge. Both preached incessantly the duty of the citizen to the state, with the soft pedal upon the duty of the state to the citizen. Both praised the habitually gravid wife. Both delighted in the armed pursuit of the lower fauna. Both heavily patronized the fine arts. Both were intimates of God, and announced His desires with authority. Both believed that all men who stood opposed to them were prompted by the devil and would suffer for it in hell.

If, in fact, there was any difference between them, it was all in favor of Wilhelm. For one thing, he made very much fewer speeches: it took some colossal event, such as the launching of a dreadnought or the birthday of a colonel-general, to get him upon his legs; the Reichstag was not constantly deluged with his advice and upbraiding. For another thing, he was a milder and more modest man—one more accustomed, let us say, to circumstance and authority, and hence less intoxicated by the greatness of his high estate. Finally, he had been trained to think not only of his own immediate fortunes, but also of the remote interests of a family that, in his heyday, promised to hold the throne for many years; and so he cultivated a certain prudence, and even a certain ingratiating suavity. He could, on occasion, be extremely polite to an opponent. But Roosevelt was never polite to an opponent; perhaps a gentleman, by what pass as American standards, he was surely never a gentle man. In a political career of nearly forty years he was never even fair to an opponent. All his gabble about the square deal was merely so much protective coloration. No man, facing him in the heat of controversy, ever actually got a square deal. He took extravagant advantages; he played to the worst idiocies of the mob; he hit below the belt almost habitually. One never thinks of him as a duelist, say of the school of Disraeli, Palmerston and, to drop a bit, Blaine. One always thinks of him as a glorified bouncer engaged eternally in cleaning out barrooms— and not too proud to gouge when the inspiration came to him, or to bite in the clinches, or to oppose the relatively fragile brass knuckles of the code with chair legs, bung-starters, cuspidors, demijohns and ice picks.

Lawrence Abbott and William Roscoe Thayer, in their official lives.[3] made elaborate efforts to depict their hero as one born with a deep loathing of the whole Prussian scheme of things. Abbott even went so far as to hint that the attentions of the Kaiser, during Roosevelt's historic tour of Europe on his return from Africa, were subtly revolting to him. Nothing could be more absurd. Sherman, in the article I have mentioned, blows up that nonsense by quoting from a speech made by the tourist in Berlin, a speech arguing for the most extreme sort of militarism in a manner that must have made even some of the Junkers blow their noses dubiously. The

---

[3] Abbott, *Impressions of Theodore Roosevelt* (New York, 1920); Thayer, *Theodore Roosevelt, an Intimate Biography* (New York, 1920).

disproof need not be piled up; the America that Roosevelt dreamed of was always a sort of swollen Prussia, truculent without and regimented within. There was always a clank of the saber in his discourse; he could not discuss the tamest matter without swaggering in the best dragoon fashion. Abbott gets into yet deeper waters when he sets up the doctrine that the invasion of Belgium threw his darling into an instantaneous and tremendous fit of moral indignation, and that the curious delay in the public exhibition thereof, so much discussed afterward, was due to his (Abbott's) fatuous interference—a *faux pas* later regretted with much bitterness. Unluckily, the evidence he offers leaves me full of doubts. What the doctrine demands that one believe is simply this: that the man who, for mere commercial advantage and (in Frederick's famous phrase) "to make himself talked of in the world," tore up the treaty of 1848 between the United States and Colombia (*geb*. New Granada), whereby the United States forever guaranteed the "sovereignty and ownership" of the Colombians in the Isthmus of Panama; that this same man, thirteen years later, was horrified into a fever when Germany, facing powerful foes on two fronts, tore up the treaty of 1832, guaranteeing, not the sovereignty, but the bald neutrality of Belgium—a neutrality already destroyed, according to the evidence before the Germans, by Belgium's own acts.

It is hard, without an inordinate strain upon the credulity, to believe any such thing, particularly in view of the fact that this instantaneous indignation of the most impulsive and vocal of men was diligently concealed for at least six weeks, with reporters camped upon his doorstep day and night begging him to say the very thing that he left so darkly unsaid. Can one imagine Roosevelt, with red fire raging within him and sky rockets bursting in his veins holding his peace for a month and a half? I have no doubt whatever that Abbott, as he says, desired to avoid embarrassing Wilson—but think of Roosevelt showing any such delicacy! For one, I am not equal to the feat. All that unprecedented reticence, in fact, is far more readily explicable on other and less lofty grounds. What really happened I presume to guess. My guess is that Roosevelt, like the great majority of other Americans, was *not* instantly and automatically outraged by the invasion of Belgium. On the contrary, he probably viewed it as a regrettable, but not unexpected or unparalleled device of war—if anything, as something rather thrillingly gaudy and effective, a fine piece of virtuosity, pleasing to a military connoisseur.

But then came the deluge of Belgian atrocity stories, and the organized campaign to enlist American sympathies. It succeeded very quickly. By the middle of August the British press bureau was in full swing; by the beginning of September the country was flooded with inflammatory stuff; six weeks after the war opened it was already hazardous for a German in America to state his country's case. Meanwhile, the Wilson administration had declared for neutrality, and was still making a more or less sincere effort to practice it, at least on the surface. Here was Roosevelt's opportunity, and he leaped to it with sure instinct. On the one side was the administration that he detested, and that all his self-interest (e.g., his yearning to get back his old leadership and to become President again in 1917) prompted him to deal a mortal blow, and on the other side was a ready-made issue, full of emotional possibilities, stupendously pumped up by extremely clever propaganda, and so far unembraced by any other rabble-rouser of the first magnitude. Is it any wonder that he gave a whoop, jumped upon his cayuse, and began screaming for war? In war lay the confusion of Wilson, and the melodramatic renaissance of the Rough Rider, the professional hero, the national Barbarossa.

In all this, of course, I strip the process of its plumes and spangles, and expose a chain of causes and effects that Roosevelt himself, if he were alive, would denounce as grossly contumelious to his native purity of spirit—and perhaps in all honesty. It is not necessary to raise any doubts as to that honesty. No one who has given any study to the development and propagation of political doctrine in the United States can have failed to notice how the belief in issues among politicians tends to run in exact ratio to the popularity of those issues. Let the populace begin suddenly to swallow a new panacea or to take fright at a new bugaboo, and almost instantly nine-tenths of the masterminds of politics begin to believe that the panacea is a sure cure for all the malaises of the republic, and the bugaboo an immediate and unbearable menace to all law, order and domestic tranquillity.

At the bottom of this singular intellectual resilience, of course, there is a good deal of hard calculation; a man must keep up with the procession of crazes, or his day is swiftly done. But in it there are also considerations a good deal more subtle, and maybe less discreditable. For one thing, a man devoted professionally to patriotism and the wisdom of the fathers is very apt to come to a resigned sort of acquiescence in all the doctrinaire rubbish that lies beneath the national scheme of things—to believe, let us say, if not that the plain people are gifted with an infallible sagacity, then at least that they have an inalienable right to see their follies exe- cuted. Poll-parroting nonsense as a matter of daily routine, the politician ends by assuming that it is sense, even though he doesn't believe it. For another thing, there is the contagion of mob enthusiasm—a much underestimated murrain. No man is so re- mote and arctic that he is wholly safe from that contamination; it explains many extravagant phenomena of a democratic society; in particular, it explains why the mob leader is so often a victim to his mob.

Roosevelt, a perfectly typical politician, devoted to the trade, not primarily because he was gnawed by ideals, but because he frankly enjoyed its rough-and-tumble encounters and its gaudy rewards, was probably moved in both ways—and also by the hard calculation that I have mentioned. If, by any ineptness of the British press agents and tear-squeezers, indignation over the inva- sion of Belgium had failed to materialize; if, worse still, some gross infringement of American rights by the English had caused it to be forgotten completely; if, finally, Wilson had been whooping for war with the populace firmly against him—in such event it goes without saying that the moral horror of Roosevelt would have stopped short at a very low amperage, and that he would have refrained from making it the center of his polity. But with things as they were, lying neatly to his hand, he permitted it to take on an extraordinary virulence, and before long all his old delight in German militarism had been converted into a lofty detestation of German militarism, and its chief spokesman on this side of the

Atlantic became its chief opponent. Getting rid of that old delight, of course, was not easily achieved. The concrete enthusiasm could be throttled, but the habit of mind remained. Thus one beheld the curious spectacle of militarism belabored in terms of militarism—of the Kaiser arraigned in unmistakably *kaiserliche* tones.

Such violent swallowings and regurgitations were no novelties to the man. His whole political career was marked, in fact, by performances of the same sort. The issues that won him most votes were issues that, at bottom, he didn't believe in; there was always a mental reservation in his rhetoric. He got into politics, not as a tribune of the plain people, but as an amateur reformer of the snobbish type common in the eighties—by the *Nation* out of the Social Register. He was a young Harvard man scandalized by the discovery that his town was run by men with such names as Michael O'Shaunnessy and Terence Googan—that his social inferiors were his political superiors. His sympathies were essentially antidemocratic. He believed in strong centralization—the concentration of power in a few hands, the strict regimentation of the nether herd, the abandonment of platitudes. His heroes were such Federalists as Morris and Hamilton; he made his first splash in the world by writing about them and praising them. Worse, his daily associations were with the old Union League crowd of high-tariff Republicans—men almost apoplectically opposed to every movement from below—safe and sane men, highly conservative and suspicious men, the profiteers of peace, as they afterward became the profiteers of war. His early adventures in politics were not very fortunate, nor did they reveal any capacity for leadership. The bosses of the day took him in rather sportively, played him for what they could get out of him, and then turned him loose. In a few years he became disgusted and went West. Returning after a bit, he encountered catastrophe: as a candidate for Mayor of New York he was drubbed unmercifully. He went back to the West. He was, up to this time, a comic figure—an antipolitician victimized by politicians, a pseudo-aristocrat made ridiculous by the mobmasters he detested.

But meanwhile something was happening that changed the whole color of the political scene, and was destined, eventually, to give Roosevelt his chance. That something was a shifting in what might be called the foundations of reform. Up to now it had been an essentially aristocratic movement—superior, sniffish and anti-democratic. But hereafter it took on a strongly democratic color and began to adopt democratic methods. More, the change gave it new life. What Harvard, the Union League Club and Godkin's *Nation* had failed to accomplish, the plain people now undertook to accomplish. This invasion of the old citadel of virtue was first observed in the West, and its manifestations out there must have given Roosevelt a good deal more disquiet than satisfaction. It is impossible to imagine him finding anything to his taste in the outlandish doings of the Populists, the wild schemes of the pre-Bryan dervishes. His instincts were against all that sort of thing. But as the movement spread toward the East it took on a certain urbanity, and by the time it reached the seaboard it had begun to be almost civilized.

With this new brand of reform Roosevelt now made terms. It was full of principles that outraged all his pruderies, but it at least promised to work. His entire political history thereafter, down to the day of his death, was a history of compromises with the new forces—of a gradual yielding, for strategic purposes, to ideas that were intrinsically at odds with his congenital prejudices. When, after a generation of that sort of compromising, the so-called Progressive party was organized and he seized the leadership of it from the Westerners who had founded it, he performed a feat of wholesale englutination that must forever hold a high place upon the roll of political prodigies. That is to say, he swallowed at one gigantic gulp, and out of the same Herculean jug, the most amazing mixture of social, political and economic sure cures ever got down by one hero, however valiant, however athirst—a cock-tail made up of all the elixirs hawked among the boobery in his time, from woman suffrage to the direct primary, and from the initiative and referendum to the short ballot, and from Prohibition to public ownership, and from trust-busting to the recall of judges.

This Homeric achievement made him the head of the most tatterdemalion party ever seen in American politics—a party composed of such incompatible ingredients and hung together so loosely that it began to disintegrate the moment it was born. In part it was made up of mere disordered enthusiasts—believers in anything and everything, pathetic victims of the credulity complex, habitual followers of jitney messiahs, incurable hopers and snufflers. But in part it was also made up of rich converts like Roosevelt himself—men eager for office, disappointed by the old parties, and now quite willing to accept any aid that half-idiot doctrinaires could give them. I have no doubt that Roosevelt himself, carried away by the emotional hurricanes of the moment and especially by the quasi-religious monkeyshines that marked the first Progressive convention, gradually convinced himself that at least some of the doctrinaires, in the midst of all their imbecility, yet preached a few ideas that were workable, and perhaps even sound. But at bottom he was against them, and not only in the matter of their specific remedies, but also in the larger matter of their childish faith in the wisdom and virtue of the plain people.

Roosevelt, for all his fluent mastery of democratic counter-words, democratic gestures and all the rest of the armamentarium of the mob-master, had no such faith in his heart of hearts. He didn't believe in democracy; he believed simply in government. His remedy for all the great pangs and longings of existence was not a dispersion of authority, but a hard concentration of authority. He was not in favor of unlimited experiment; he was in favor of a rigid control from above, a despotism of inspired prophets and policemen. He was not for democracy as his followers understood democracy, and as it actually is and must be; he was for a paternalism of the true Bismarckian pattern, almost of the Napoleonic pattern—a paternalism concerning itself with all things, from the regulation of coal mining and meat packing to the regulation of spelling and marital rights. His instincts were always those of the property-owning Tory, not those of the romantic liberal. Even when, for campaign purposes, he came to terms with the liberals his thoughts always ranged far afield. When he tackled the trusts the thing that he had in his mind's eye was not the restoration of competition but the subordination of all private trusts to one great national trust, with himself at its head. And when he .attacked the courts it was not because they put their own prejudices before the law but because they refused to put *his* prejudices before the law.

In all his career no one ever heard him make an argument for the rights of the citizen; his eloquence was always expended in expounding the duties of the citizen. I have before me a speech in which he pleaded for "a spirit of kindly justice toward every man and woman," but that seems to be as far as he ever got in that direction—and it was the gratuitous justice of the absolute monarch that he apparently had in mind, not the autonomous and inalienable justice of a free society. The duties of the citizen, as he understood them, related not only to acts, but also to thoughts. There was, to his mind, a simple body of primary doctrine, and dissent from it was the foulest of crimes. No man could have been more bitter against opponents, or more unfair to them, or more ungenerous. In this department, indeed, even so gifted a specialist in dishonorable controversy as Wilson seldom surpassed him. He never stood up to a frank and chivalrous debate. He dragged herrings across the tail. He made seductive faces at the gallery. He capitalized his enormous talents as an entertainer, his rank as a national hero, his public influence and consequence. The two great lawsuits in which he was engaged were screaming burlesques upon justice. He tried them in the newspapers before ever they were called; he befogged them with irrelevant issues; his appearances in court were not the appearances of a witness standing on a level with other witnesses, but those of a comedian sure of his crowd. He was, in his dealings with concrete men as in his dealings with men in the mass, a charlatan of the very highest skill—and there was in him, it goes without saying, the persuasive charm of the charlatan as well as the daring deviousness, the humanness of naïveté as well as the humanness of chicane. He knew how to woo—and not only boobs.

The appearance of such men, of course, is inevitable under democracy. Consummate showmen, they arrest the wonder of the mob, and so put its suspicions to sleep. What they actually believe is of secondary consequence; the main thing is what they say; even more, the way they say it. Obviously, their activity does a great deal of damage to the democratic theory, for they are standing refutations of the primary doctrine that the common folk choose their leaders wisely. They damage it again in another and more subtle way. That is to say, their ineradicable contempt for the minds they must heat up and bamboozle leads them into a fatalism that shows itself in a cynical and opportunistic politics, a deliberate avoidance of fundamentals. The policy of a democracy thus becomes an eternal improvisation, changing with the private ambitions of its leaders and the transient and often unintelligible emotions of its rank and file. Roosevelt, incurably undemocratic in his habits of mind, often found it difficult to gauge those emotional oscillations. The fact explains his frequent loss of mob support, his periodical journeys into Coventry. There were times when his magnificent talents as a public comedian brought the proletariat to an almost unanimous groveling at his feet, but there were also times when he puzzled and dismayed it, and so awakened its hostility.

I have a notion that he died too soon. His best days were probably not behind him, but ahead of him. Had he lived ten years longer, he might have enjoyed a great rehabilitation, and exchanged his old false leadership of the inflammatory and fickle mob for a sound and true leadership of the civilized minority. For the more one studies his mountebankeries as mob-master, the more one is convinced that there was a shrewd man beneath the motley, and that his actual beliefs were anything but nonsensical. The truth of them, indeed, emerges more clearly day by day. The old theory of a federation of free and autonomous states has broken down by its own weight, and we are moved toward centralization by forces that have long been powerful and are now quite irresistible. So with the old theory of national isolation: it, too, has fallen to pieces. The United States can no longer hope to lead a separate life in the world, undisturbed by the pressure of foreign aspirations. Roosevelt, by whatever route of reflection or intuition, arrived at a sense of these facts at a time when it was still somewhat scandalous to state them, and it was the capital effort of his life to reconcile them, in some dark way or other, to the prevailing platitudes, and so get them heeded. Today no one seriously maintains, as all Americans once maintained, that the states can go on existing together as independent commonwealths, each with its own laws, its own legal theory and its own view of the common constitutional bond. And today no one seriously main-

tains, as all Americans once maintained, that the nation may safely
potter on without adequate means of defense. However unpleasant
it may be to contemplate, the fact is plain that the American
people, during the next century, will have to fight to maintain their
place in the sun.

Roosevelt lived just long enough to see his notions in these
directions take on life, but not long enough to see them openly
adopted. To the extent of his prevision he was a genuine leader of
the nation; and perhaps in the years to come, when his actual ideas
are disentangled from the demagogic fustian in which he had to
wrap them, his more honest pronunciamentos will be given canoni-
cal honors, and he will be ranked among the prophets. He saw
clearly more than one other thing that was by no means obvious to
his age—for example, the inevitability of frequent wars under the
new world system of extreme nationalism; again, the urgent necessity, for primary police ends, of organizing the backward nations
into groups of vassals, each under the hoof of some first-rate
power; yet again, the probability of the breakdown of the old
system of free competition; once more, the high social utility of the
Spartan virtues and the grave dangers of sloth and ease; finally, the
incompatibility of free speech and democracy. I do not say that he
was always quite honest, even when he was most indubitably
right. But insofar as it was possible for him to be honest and exist
at all politically, he inclined toward the straightforward thought
and the candid word. That is to say, his instinct prompted him to
tell the truth, just as the instinct of Wilson prompted him to shift
and dissimulate. What ailed him was the fact that his lust for glory,
when it came to a struggle, was always vastly more powerful than
his lust for the eternal verities. Tempted sufficiently, he would
sacrifice anything and everything to get applause. Thus the statesman was debauched by the politician, and the philosopher was
elbowed out of sight by the popinjay.

What he stood most clearly in opposition to was the "superior"
pessimism of the three Adams brothers—the notion that the public
problems of a democracy are unworthy the thought and effort of a
civilized and self-respecting man—the same error that lies in wait
for all of us who hold ourselves above the general. Against this

suicidal aloofness Roosevelt always hurled himself with brave effect. Enormously sensitive and resilient, almost pathological in his appetite for activity, he made it plain to everyone that the most stimulating sort of sport imaginable was to be obtained in fighting, not for mere money, but for ideas. There was no aristocratic reserve about him. He was not, in fact, an aristocrat at all, but a quite typical member of the upper bourgeoisie. The marks of the thoroughbred were simply not there. The man was blatant, crude, overly confidential, devious, tyrannical, vainglorious, sometimes quite childish. One often observed in him a certain pathetic wistfulness, a reaching out for a grand manner that was utterly beyond him. But the sweet went with the bitter. He had all the virtues of the fat and complacent burgher. His disdain of affectation and prudery was magnificent. He hated all pretension save his own pretension. He had a sound respect for hard effort, for loyalty, for thrift, for honest achievement.

His worst defects were the defects of his race and time. Aspiring to be the leader of a nation of third-rate men, he had to stoop to the common level. When he struck out for realms above that level he always came to grief: this was the "unsafe" Roosevelt, the Roosevelt who was laughed at, the Roosevelt retired suddenly to cold storage. This was the Roosevelt who, in happier times and a better place, might have been. Well, one does what one can.

✪

The Progressive Mind in Action

. . . The Progressive movement, in the years before 1912, came to be symbolized in a national way by three leaders: Bryan, Roosevelt and La Follette. Bryan, however, showed repeatedly that he couldn't win through to office; he could only run, stir up a fuss and fall back. His value was that of ambassador of the rural crowd. Roosevelt and La Follette, on the other hand, had genius for politics as well as agitation; they were elected to office on the basis of their expressed ideas.

Each man had his own type of courage; each had a magnificent will. Their backgrounds, however, were as different as homespun is from silk. La Follette was a born democrat; Roosevelt came closer to the English ideal of the disinterested gentleman in politics—which implies disinterestedness within a class orbit, of course. It was no aberration that dictated Roosevelt's genuine detestation of Thomas Jefferson. And if Roosevelt never referred to the people as a "great beast" in public, he was not one to suffer fools in denim shirts gladly. La Follette, in contrast, had a mystical faith in "the people"; he belived that, provided there was plenty of light, the common man would find his own way. The superior population of Wisconsin was excuse enough for his credo.

Roosevelt, born in New York in 1858 of the still dominant

Knickerbocker caste, was always able to live on inherited wealth; money was of no more importance to him than it was to his Manichean college mate, Boies Penrose. Freedom from economic worry caused him to take the kid-gloved reformer attitude in exaggerating the importance of abstract morality as divorced from fundamental necessities; never having been tempted, he couldn't understand temptation. This mistake of assuming the relevance of the ten commandments to be constant, even in a jungle society, was never made by La Follette, who, nevertheless, was as exacting in his standards of morality in public office as Roosevelt. La Follette, in fact, demanded much more than Roosevelt of public servants. But he did not expect the "Big Bill" Haywoods and the 'Gene Debses to maintain the amenities of Knickerbocker society in the midst of imperative economic warfare.

Roosevelt's inheritance bred in him a certain philosophical irresponsibility. He was not interested in ideas—which is to say that he was a careerist, a showman of his own personality. He might have gone the way of so many of his fellows; he might have dabbled in the law, done a little hunting, followed the migrations of the social seasons. His showmanship might have been limited to chasing the fox with superior skill; it might have been circumscribed by yachting at Newport or on Long Island Sound. But a weak body, shaken in youth by recurrent spasms of asthma, and weak eyes that rendered him unfit for baseball or football caused him to rebel against his physical heritage in such a way that he exalted a certain synthetic primitivism; he must climb mountains, jostle with cowboys on the roundup, meet the "bad men" on their own ground and on their own terms. He must turn his back on the playing fields of the polite world; and with the need of this primitivism went a corresponding rejection of polite values. "I'll make my body," he told his father. And when somebody objected that politics was too vulgar a business for the Knickerbocker patrician, he answered that "if this were so it merely meant that the people I knew did not belong to the governing class, and the other people did—and that I intended to be one of the governing class."

By stepping out of his social context, Roosevelt was forced to make a game of life. His background of inherited wealth, with its assumed concomitant of noblesse oblige, engendered in him, it is true, a certain feeling of responsibility; but it was never whole souled. Since he was making a gift of his life to the commonwealth, since he was playing a game, there were privileges he might assume, laurels he might demand for the victory. He was making a career; the career should make him.

And so, at crucial moments, consistency, proclaimed philosophical principle, the assumptions he made at beginning points and in his books on ideals went casually by the board. "Get action," he said, "do things; be sane, don't fritter away your time; create, act, take a place wherever you are and be somebody; get action." But (so a philosophically responsible person might ask) action for what? . . . Do what things? . . . Be sane in what way, and for what reason? . . . Employ your time how, and to what end? . . . Create what? . . . Take a place for what program? . . . Be somebody to what good? . . . Isn't all this admonition to place and action simply another and more febrile way of keeping up with the Joneses?

Indeed, if one makes a thorough scansion of Roosevelt's career, the exhortation to strenuous living, the eternal harping upon activity, the crashing words and writhing visage all seem a little pathological. Action becomes a drug, Roosevelt just an American version of the Rimbaud myth. "The great game [of life] in which we are all engaged" comes down to a childish pirouetting over a void—and Roosevelt was always afraid to look into the void. This is the very negation of spiritual courage.

How different it is with La Follette! It was never "get action" with him, never "take a place and be somebody." It was "put through a specific railroad or income tax law, and you will find action enough on your hands." "Create a railway rate and valuation board, and you won't have any time to fritter away." "Don't mind whether they call you insane or not if you are certain you are not compromising your principles." Refuse to take a place unless it is for some specific end." "Create a progressive movement within the Republican party and you will find you are somebody."

La Follette was words and deeds in close tandem; Roosevelt

was words—and an occasional deed for the sake of the record, or to save face. La Follette was a man who sought to make strict economic analysis the basis of his laws; he never talked without facts, the best available facts, and the University of Wisconsin faculty came, characteristically enough, to replace the lobby in his home state. But Roosevelt was, confessedly, "rather an agnostic in matters of economics"; the tariff bored him. With all his interest in cultural and scientific matters, he never understood the spirit of the laboratory—which was the one hope of the Progressive, or Liberal, movement.

Certainly Roosevelt had no realistic definition of government, no philosophical grasp of the nature of politics. Politics, by definition, is primarily the organization by legislation and control of the means of life; it is based pretty largely on economic desires and it reacts upon economics in turn. An "economic agnostic" has no more business running for legislative or executive office than an ibis has at the North Pole. But Roosevelt, the "agnostic" ("I do not know"), never had any hesitation about injecting himself into the forefront of the political fight. Like so many Americans who were still confusing the imperatives of the stomach with the voice of God, he conceived of politics as a sphere for the dramatics of Protestant morality. The result was a vast confusion about standing at Armageddon (with Boss Bill Flinn of Pittsburgh) and battling for the Lord (who was on the side of the biggest slush fund). And the worst of it is, Roosevelt was perfectly sincere about his Armageddon stuff at the moment of utterance. He may, as Medill McCormick said, have understood the "psychology of the mutt," but it was a subconscious understanding, soaked in at the pores. If Roosevelt had only understood the springs of his activity one would be justified in calling him a demagogue, but one would never be justified in calling him unintelligent.

Opinions differ on Roosevelt. But even his firmest friends admit a certain weakness in fundamentals; they see his primary value as the sort of person who "sits on the bulge," curbing excesses on the part of labor, on the one hand, and capital, on the other. Roosevelt dramatized the antithesis of "predatory wealth" and "predatory poverty"; he couldn't see, this man who administered "antiscorbutics to socialism," that predaciousness cannot be eliminated until the simpler antithesis of wealth and poverty has been reduced to a synthesis. Gilson Gardner, one of the wisest of tired radicals, sums up the Roosevelt tightrope act in a pithy paragraph. "More honesty," he offers as the Roosevelt credo; "By George, they mustn't do it. The rich must be fair and the poor must be contented—or, if not contented, at least they must be orderly. I will tell them both. No restraining of trade by the great corporations and no rioting by the toiler. Give me the power and I will make them behave." The ideal may be laudable. But just what class of people is there left *to delegate the power?* A middle class? Yes, for a while, but a middle class cannot exist permanently in a dynamic society that is creating "great corporations" that need restraining. The "great corporations" must be blotted out or made one corporation beyond the pale of manipulation for private profit. This, Roosevelt never could bring himself to realize. He had too many nice friends who were part of the corporation system.

.   .   .   .   .

On January 6, 1919, Roosevelt died—and is it too much to say that the "moral" age in American politics died with him? Bryan, it is true, would live to face the cameras at Dayton, Tennessee, but he had gone into political eclipse at Baltimore in 1912. La Follette would linger on to lead his forlorn hope in 1924, but that would be the final gasp of an agrarian idealism in the days of the New Era. And Wilson, though still nominally a liberal, would or could do nothing in his last days in the White House to stop the Red witch-hunting of his Attorney General, A. Mitchell Palmer.

The Roosevelt myth grew apace after his death. For ten years the memory of the looming teeth, the impetuous "By George," the emphatic "I've done nothing that wasn't absolutely right and proper" would continue to bemuse the commentator. Joseph Bucklin Bishop, Charles Willis Thompson, Owen Wister, all of whom wrote from close acquaintance, were blinded by the remembered brilliance of the sun itself.* Hermann Hagedorn suffered, and

* Chamberlain refers here to Joseph B. Bishop [ed.].

still does, from the delayed adolescence acquired from the Roosevelt of Spanish War days. Lord Charnwood's biography, representing the English point of view, sounded as if it had been written by the British press bureau—as, indeed, in a way, it was. But at the end of a decade a change for the more wholesomely astringent was felt. Thomas Beer, in his *Hanna,* sniffed about teeth and spectacles like a cat inspecting a new house—and objectivity was thereby born. In his autobiography Lincoln Steffens waved away the myth that had grown up around T.R. as a police commissioner. With the best will in the world, Steffens still could not avoid giving the impression that Roosevelt's accomplishment in Mulberry Street was mainly pictorial—a faint prefiguration of Smedley Butler's adventures among Philadelphia's vice rings. And Walter Millis, in *The Martial Spirit,* uttered some second thoughts about Las Guasimas which should have occurred to others long before.

All this was preliminary. But in 1931 came two biographies of the man that attempted to give him in sum. The first, by Walter McCaleb, was excellent for two reasons: it attempted to tell the truth about the Panama Canal steal; and it set forth the facts about the Panic of 1907, in which Roosevelt was played for a sucker by Gary and Frick, whose representations resulted in the swallowing by United States Steel of its biggest rival, the Tennessee Coal and Iron Company. The second, by Henry Pringle, is a more complete job. But both biographies suffer from an unwillingness on the authors' parts to think things through. When Dr. McCaleb comes to the war years he is himself blinded by the sun, and his book dissolves into dubious rhetoric. Mr. Pringle, too, has a hard time making up his mind about the war. Neither one tackles the tremendous three-cornered fight that went on, under the phrases and flag-waving, between the factions of Woodrow Wilson (which looked to the community of nations within an international league), of La Follette (which believed in putting home houses in order before attempting a world synthesis), and of Roosevelt, who believed in *la gloire,* and the "big stick," and antiwar pacts only when all the nations should become as civilized as the United States of America.

The curious thing about Dr. McCaleb and Mr. Pringle is their return to the opinions of Roosevelt held by his saner contemporaries. The little vanities of T.R., the bullyragging and bulldozing, the mercurial uncertainty of the man were quite apparent to Harry Thurston Peck early in the muckrake decade. "His courage," Peck wrote, "was of the French, rather than of the Anglo-Saxon type. It was allied with a certain nervousness which could perform the most daring deeds if they were deeds of action, but which became restive and almost uncontrollable when patience and grim endurance were demanded." Here we have the complete antithesis to La Follette painted before the Wisconsin Senator had become a national figure. Peck, echoing his contemporaries, was particularly struck by Roosevelt's use of the personal pronoun. He tells an amusing, though probably apocryphal story: "In writing one of his earlier books he used . . . 'I' so frequently that his publishers were compelled to order from a type-foundry a fresh supply of that particular letter." Peck quoted, too, a story about Theodore Roosevelt and John Hay. The charming Hay, diplomat to his finger tips, remonstrated gently with Theodore for using the word "big" too frequently in one of his early messages. "Big," said Theodore, with visible annoyance, "is a good strong Anglo-Saxon word! I like to use such words as that." Yet Roosevelt, the lusty, was unable to appreciate Lincoln's harmless fondness for smutty jokes in which good strong Anglo-Saxon words predominated. The masculinity of Roosevelt, in truth, was always a little febrile, the courage likely to waver. Even the Booker T. Washington luncheon incident at the White House, for which Roosevelt has been praised or damned many times with no half-tones, seemed, to Peck, an example of Dutch courage. Roosevelt, Peck surmised, was "afraid of being thought afraid" to ask the Negro to lunch. And blocs could make T.R. back down. When H. C. Evans, a pensions commissioner, angered the G.A.R. by exposing frauds in the pension legislation, Roosevelt, fearing the loss of the soldier vote, removed him from office by "promoting" him. McKinley, a weaker man than Roosevelt in many ways, had not done this; in fact, he had staunchly refused to touch Evans' job. The facts that Evans was "promoted" and that an equally honest man was put in his place do not compensate for the lack of courage shown by Mc-

Kinley's successor. But, on the credit side of the ledger, Peck was careful to note that Roosevelt ". . . brought in, as it were, a stream of fresh, pure, bracing air from the mountains to clear the fetid atmosphere of the national capital."

This admiration for the "pure, bracing air," coupled with a sane analysis of Roosevelt's essential character, is part of the attitude toward the apostle of the strenuous life which both Pringle and McCaleb rehabilitate. No one in his right mind would condemn T.R. in toto. One cannot, upon a full review of a remarkable life, remain either a Roosevelt idolator, or—if one warms to wistfulness—a Roosevelt hater. Roosevelt had his physical courage, no one doubts that. His romanticizing of the wilderness will always have its appeal. His admiration for soldiers (Cromwell, Moltke), his love of war for its own sake, his family affections, his childlikeness, his flashing humor, his social charm, his bullying, his willingness in an explosive moment to call a man guilty before he had been proved guilty, his wistful hedging-away from the problems of an afterlife, and, finally, his lack of inwardness will always combine to make a fascinating study in personality. But more than any of these characteristics, the one that most stands out is the Rooseveltian inability to think things through. Roosevelt scored heavily against Woodrow Wilson when he struck off the phrase "weasel words." But no one knew the uses of weasel words better than T.R. himself, as La Follette has conclusively shown in his autobiography in the section that reviews Roosevelt's public statements as a Progressive. . . .

Roosevelt was always willing, at any time, to contradict himself, by word or deed, if by contradiction he could further his career. His friends will be quick to say, "No, no." But there are so many major issues on which he shifted ground at the precise moment when his career was involved that charity balks at the attempt to find excuses. He became a Progressive when the Republican party threatened to become Progressive—but it should not be forgotten that he fought La Follette in Wisconsin in 1904, and he was willing to enter a "gentleman's agreement" with Nelson Aldrich not to disturb the McKinley home policies if he could have a free hand in the conduct of foreign affairs. He reversed himself on free trade early in his career. This would be understandable as a natural growth—only Roosevelt never had any real conviction on the tariff, one way or another. His attitude, when President, was "Let Taft change the tariff when I'm gone"; but when Taft compromised with Aldrich and the Bourbons of the Senate, Roosevelt lapsed into an unholy rage. He denounced the "corrupt" Blaine; but when Blaine was nominated, in 1884, the willing worker in the vineyard decided that Cleveland, the friend of civil service reform, was the real instrument of Satan. And when Blaine became Harrison's Secretary of State, Roosevelt was quite willing to play up to him for a job.

Again, though Roosevelt admitted his agnosticism in the realms of economics, he contradicted his expressed friendship for the frontiersman by echoing his smart friends in denunciation of Bryan. Altgeld he refused to meet; he was afraid he might be compelled to fire on the Illinois "anarchist" some day at the head of a battalion. Yet Altgeld was one of the first of the "Progressives"—if the word is to have any meaning at all. Free silver might have been a nostrum (and the discovery of the cyanide process for extracting gold cheaply from ore makes it seem so in retrospect), but Roosevelt didn't think the matter out for himself in 1896—he took Mark Hanna's word for it. Yet the deflation of the post-Civil War period had meant grinding poverty for the sons of the frontier whom "Colonel" Roosevelt invited to storm San Juan Hill with him. On labor, the Progressive knight showed himself to have no grasp of the situation. His decisions as an Albany assemblyman were those of a young Goo-goo out of Edith Wharton's *Age of Innocence*. He opposed a bill in 1882 requiring New York and Buffalo to pay laborers two dollars a day. At a later period he made the statement that if he, instead of Wilson, had been President he would not have signed the Adamson eight-hour bill. His apologists suggest it may have been the Wilson-hater speaking here—but it is no apology that a man allows personal hatreds to come between himself and professed humanitarian principles.

Roosevelt could always take a high moral tone; he repeatedly showed himself on the side of righteousness, even though humanity might, at times, go hang. But even in the matter of morality, expediency altered cases. The young Governor of New York State temporized on the Erie Canal frauds. As President, Roosevelt was perfectly willing to use party machinery to dictate Taft's nomination, yet in 1912 he called Elihu Root a thief for exercising the same prerogative in throwing out the Roosevelt delegates. When John Hay negotiated the Hay-Pauncefote Treaty, Roosevelt didn't like it, and argued that a government had the right to abrogate a treaty in a "solemn and official manner." But when Colombia refused to accept the Hay-Herran Treaty, Roosevelt quickly doubled on his tracks and denounced the Bogotà "dagoes," as he called them, for "breach of faith." And as for arbitration, he could urge it at Christiania before the Nobel Prize committee in 1910, and later denounce Taft for suggesting a treaty for arbitration with France. France, it seemed, was not sufficiently "civilized" to be treated with.

But perhaps the most damaging giveaway of Roosevelt's pretensions to morality involved the invasion of Belgium. H. L. Mencken has shown, in an essay* that was written immediately after Roosevelt's death while the flood of eulogy was at its height, that Roosevelt had no immediate experience of shock when the Germans tore up the "scrap of paper" and marched through Luxembourg and across the Belgian frontier. The moral reaction didn't reach Oyster Bay until the temper of the country had changed; Roosevelt simply shifted to meet the demands of public opinion. His course, after the *Outlook* article that "explained" and justified the invasion of Belgium, was vacillating to the extreme—and well might Roosevelt vacillate in view of his own "ethical" trampling of Colombia in 1903!

All the chopping and changing, the roaring invocations to morality and the sudden descents to political bargaining, simply prove to me that Roosevelt was a surface swimmer—not so brave a man as Grover Cleveland, and neither so honest as Boies Penrose on the one hand, nor as La Follette, on the other. He was, it is clear, the perfect *representative* of the middle class of prewar America. His class philosophy, however, was inchoate—in no way so clearly formulated as La Follette's. Indeed, on the score of possessing an articulate middle-class, democratic philosophy, La

* Reprinted on pp. 52–65 [ed.].

Follette deserved to be the leader of the middle-class movement. But the most conspicuous attribute of the middle class of 1900–1909 was its confusion; it had delusions about rising into the plutocracy, and yet it feared being forced into the ranks of labor. It wanted to curb the trusts, yet it wanted to leave an opening at the top—the good old American right to succeed! Therefore it was in the dilemma of Mrs. Facing-Both-Ways. La Follette saw this, Lincoln Steffens saw this, and both labored to make clear the vitiating nature of the desire and the fear. But Roosevelt perfectly represented the confusion, as his attitude toward the trusts shows. Mr. Dooley summed it up when he put words into Roosevelt's mouth: " 'Th' thrusts,' says he, 'are heejous monsthers built up be th' enlightened intherprize iv th' men that have done so much to advance progress in our beloved country,' he says. 'On wan hand I wud stamp thim unher fut; on th' other hand, not so fast.' "

The result of equivocation on Roosevelt's part, and on the part of those he represented, is that the middle sort of man now finds himself, more than ever before, between the upper fascist millstone and the nether stone of communism. Had La Follette's views been heeded, had industrial development been halted at the single corporation, had the combination of corporations been prevented in John Sherman's time or in Roosevelt's (impossibilist dream though it may be), the vision of a middle-class democracy of farmers and shopkeepers and small manufacturers, all obeying the laws of trade formulated at Manchester, might have been made a reality.

What were the accomplishments of Theodore Roosevelt as a statesman? There was the matter of forcing England and Germany to back down in Venezuela. Good evidence exists to show that Roosevelt exaggerated his use of the "big stick" in bringing this incipient conflict to a peaceful conclusion. But Roosevelt was always shaking the big stick—a stick which often, as Gilson Gardner says, turned out to be a "stuffed club." In his early years Roosevelt was an unmitigated jingo. He believed that an occasional war was a good thing for "the moral fiber of the nation"—a view that has been adapted to the current depression. He wrote to Lodge, in 1895, when the earlier Cleveland controversy was raging about Venezuela: "I most earnestly hope that our people won't weaken in any way on the Venezuela matter. The antics of the bankers, brokers and Anglo-maniacs generally are humiliating to a degree. . . . As for the editors of the *Evening Post* and the *World*, it would give me great pleasure to have them put in prison the minute hostilities began. . . ."

The young jingo is to blame for the present embarrassing possession of the Philippine Islands by the United States. He and Henry Cabot Lodge cooked up the attack on Manila before hostilities in 1898 had begun. The order which eventually sent Dewey to the Philippines was issued by Assistant Secretary of the Navy Roosevelt one day after Secretary Long had gone home to sleep—and Long never quite dared countermand it. It would make him look like a fool! But at the time it was issued McKinley had not given a thought to the Philippines, and most Americans didn't know of their existence. Before the Spanish-American War came to provide Roosevelt with his taste of glory in the field, the young fire-eater was spoiling for a fight with England. "We would take Canada," he wrote to Henry Cabot Lodge. All that the full martial program of the fledgling Roosevelt contained was the annexation of Canada, the abolishing of all European powers from the Western Hemisphere, and the taking of Cuba, Porto Rico, Hawaii and the Philippines. Peace advocates were mollycoddles. A big navy was needed to police the world in the interests of American morality. If this is "world-mindedness," give us La Follette's "Little American" program any day. Even when Roosevelt's "world-mindedness" was of the peaceful sort, he blundered into war traps. There was the Moroccan crisis, for instance; here Roosevelt, through Henry White, helped France to complete the encirclement of Germany which led to the Great War. And the "taking of Panama," after the comic-opera intrigue which featured the wily William Nelson Cromwell—who made lobbying one of the Seven Lively Arts—and the connivance of Roosevelt himself, might have led to bloodshed if the "revolution," carried out under the guns of American ships, hadn't gone off without a hitch.

Roosevelt's domestic achievements were more ethical than the Panama intrigue. But his two administrations were more talk than effort; Taft's "progressive record" is fully as clean as Roosevelt's own. The coal-strike compromise of 1902 was an undoubted temporary feather in the Rough Rider's hat; yet, after all, it merely settled *one* coal dispute—as Harlan and Bell counties and both bituminous and anthracite Pennsylvania are still with us to testify. The Elkins Rebate Law was good, but the Hepburn Act—as we have seen—was only an indication that a fight against railroad abuses had started. The Hepburn Act was in reality a victory for the "crafty Aldrich," since it limited rate-making to fixing maximum charges after complaint had been made, and offered no provision for valuation. The so-called modified "broad court" review clause played into the very hands of the judges whose decisions Roosevelt wanted subject to "recall" in 1912. Conservation and the beginnings of pure-food legislation were the great Roosevelt accomplishments. One might also include the Alaska boundary settlement, the Russo-Japanese War arbitration, the appointment of Justice Holmes to the Supreme Court (it is amusing that the Holmes decision in the Northern Securities case nettled Roosevelt considerably), and the creation of the Department of Commerce and Labor.

But didn't T.R., whose first term resounded to the war whoops of "trust-busting," do *something* about certain particular trusts? Well, there were 149 trusts in 1900, representing $4 billion in approximate capitalization. When Roosevelt went out of office, there were 10,020 trusts with a capitalization of virtually $31 billion, 70 per cent of which was estimated as pure water. And Roosevelt was only nominally victorious in the Northern Securities case by which he set such store. The dissolution decree did not by any means restore competition between the two Northwestern railroads—the Northern Pacific and the Great Northern. The order of the Supreme Court had been phrased so that the bond issue floated against the two companies remained intact. Charles G. Dawes compared the issue to a stepladder with one leg in one road and the other in another road. And Philander C. Knox, Roosevelt's "crackerjack" Attorney General, had permitted the decree to be so written. The dissolution wording actually enabled James J. Hill to squeeze E. H. Harriman out of the control of the Northern

Pacific, since the original stock was not returned to those who had come in on the holding company scheme. Harriman got as much value as he had turned over to the Northern Securities Company, but it was split between Northern Pacific and Great Northern securities. He had a majority control in neither railroad when the dust cleared away. The ultimate dissolution of the oil and tobacco trusts was to come in Taft's time, but the letter has been more altered than the spirit, and the results have been barren. The existence of the "power trust" today is a commentary on the effectiveness of the whole cloudy program of the prewar trust-busting.

A final estimate of Roosevelt, I think, will be that expressed by Senator Aldrich: he was the greatest politician of his time. Not, mind you, the greatest statesman—not even by the test of action, which John Carter makes the one test of statesmanship. And no one has succeeded in endowing Roosevelt with economic sense; the judgment of Gardner, that he kept himself an economic moron in order to remain in politics, must stand. So let him rest—as a great politician and an astounding, charming, effervescent character. But what an ironic role to be played by a moralist!

✪

T.R.

The profound truth about triumphant Republicanism toward the turn of the century is that it could not produce statesmen able to control the industrialization of the country. Its Presidents were inadequate and its Governors and Congressmen were either pawns or, at best, upright men who were tolerated in the party because they were ineffectual. The real political rulers of the country were of the stamp of Roscoe Conkling, Tom Platt, Marcus A. Hanna, Boies Penrose—men of personality and strength, "boss" proto-types of the rude industrial conquistadors whom they represented. Praiseworthy men of the quality of Samuel J. Tilden and Grover Cleveland, who were possessed of character and honesty, were in the minority among the "sound" citizens, and they had little understanding of the forces of evil they desired to fight. Tilden led the prosecution of Tweed, but he was not to be found among the opponents of monopoly. Love of honesty and fairness did not prevent Cleveland from breaking the Pullman strike, when it came; and his other decisions were no less colored by class bias: reverence for private property under all conditions was to him a first principle—and Cleveland was a Democrat.

Yet the common man's dissatisfaction during the past years had not been fruitless. Victories in civil service reform, the propaganda

---

Reprinted from Louis Filler, "T.R.," *Crusaders for American Liberalism* (New York: Harcourt, Brace, 1939), pp. 60–70. Reprinted by permission of the author.

of third parties, the organizing campaigns of labor, the mounting power of the Socialist party and other radical groups—these had operated along with other social processes to leash ruthless individualism. So far had opposition to the predatory capitalist progressed that, by the time of the muckrakers, any President of the United States who dared to order troops to fire on strikers would have had revolutionary disturbances on his hands. Times had indeed changed. It was well for industrial peace that Theodore Roosevelt now appeared to dull the edge of labor's bitter feeling.

Calumny followed every President, no matter how drab or mediocre, but in the case of Theodore Roosevelt it reached unprecedented proportions. He was charged with every conceivable crime by gossip-mongers and the extreme reactionary press. He was so openly accused of being a drunkard that he felt constrained to fight the allegations in the open himself. Throughout his campaigns against "the malefactors of great wealth," as he called them, it was generally whispered, among the highest circles of righteousness, that he was insane. To certain influential persons he was an incendiary who was ruining America, and every weapon that might be used to discredit him was justifiable. For conservatives sensed revolution, or at least genuine reform—which was just as bad—and Roosevelt, far from applying force to it, was trying to conciliate it. When contrasted with McKinley, in particular, Roosevelt appeared a prophet of doom to those who clung to the old economic traditions.

Roosevelt was generally held responsible for the appearance of the muckrakers and identified with them, despite the fact that he himself in anger gave them their opprobrious name. A hundred apologists for him have been unable to disentangle him from apparent kinship with the exposers he despised. How incongruous is the notion of his muckraking connections appears from the evidence. Still, it had its logic. It assumed that he had indicted only the "sensational fringe" of the reformers; but that the best of them were literary equivalents of the Roosevelt who wielded the "big stick."

Each year Roosevelt becomes less impressive in retrospect, and it is unlikely that he will ever resume the stature he enjoyed in his days of triumph. If Roosevelt dominated his era, it was only in the sense that he formed the most outstanding figure for attack and defense. The great social developments of the time made less sensational news. The growth of organizations which represented the diverse needs of a new and complex social order—consumers' leagues and associations for furthering child-labor legislation, social research, housing improvement, and the like—these were not widely publicized. Before anyone was aware of it they were functioning and mature. Labor groups of the modern variety were organized and energized without any assistance from Roosevelt. As for the muckrakers, who formed the very pivot upon which all this social activity swung, they were consistently described in derogatory terms by Roosevelt and those whom he particularly represented.

To show that in these years popular victories—municipal reform, pure-food and social legislation, the exposure of infamy in business and finance, the triumphs of labor, and the rest—involved Roosevelt only incidentally is not to explain the role he actually played. That role is best suggested by a review of the opinions of Roosevelt that were then current.

Roosevelt was seen in three characters. The partisan, purely political opinion of Republicanism and Democracy, both party-bound, was to praise or blame him according to one's political affiliation. The more thoughtful dissident party members, Socialists, muckrakers, and political independents saw a man of mixed qualities. The Roosevelt Cult, to whom the Master's every word was sacrosanct, said "God bless him" whenever they thought of him. These three schools of opinion have passed into history; nothing remains of the passion which marked their differences. It has been the task of Mark Sullivan, who in his day was part muckraker and part cultist, and who subscribed to men of both parties, to weave tenderly the best tribute[1] that all the factions together could have prepared for T.R.—a more substantial tribute, at any rate, than the cultists could have prepared by themselves.

[1] In the first several volumes of *Our Times* (New York: Charles Scribner's Sons, 1927–1935).

Of all the cultists none was more sincere than Jacob Riis, whose voice of praise was not to be at all embarrassed by the good-natured or vicious fun which the cynics made of him. Roosevelt was to him true Americanism incarnate. For Riis was a naïve sentimentalist who had brought with him from Denmark something of the simplicity and idealism of the Scandinavian fairy tale. At the same time he was a journalist and a man of action who abhorred the dirt and grime of New York City, and was not afraid of confronting the Mauve Decade, which he was otherwise incapable of judging, with it. He lectured and wrote persistently of the dark corners of life in the East Side, and accomplished certain reforms. "The most useful citizen of New York," Roosevelt called him, and there was much truth in that descriptive phrase. For Riis, unprofound and unsophisticated, was the typical successful reformer of that time, thoroughly of New York, with no understanding of the nation as a whole and no conception of national policy. The West was still the Far West to him; Populism was not so much a political credo as a violent aberration of Western ignorance; for him social maturity lay in the direction of New York civilization. He had no respect for the "yellow" press, no understanding of such individuals as Henry George, whom he considered beneath discussion. On the other hand, he could not help seeing that despite the best efforts of conservative reformers, social inequalities continued to produce unrest and to rouse the sections of the country against one another. Something, Riis concluded, had to be done.

And here was Theodore Roosevelt to do it, a shining young knight in the habiliments of chivalry, emerged from among the machine politicians! It was enough for Riis, who hated politics and did not care to acquaint himself with its realities, that Roosevelt spoke vigorous words and got things done. For him, Roosevelt was little less than perfect and he followed the man's career with frank delight. As the 1904 election approached, Riis was set to writing an informal biography of his friend and idol. Never was a political tract written with greater sincerity than *Theodore Roosevelt, The Citizen*. It was full of loyalty and conviction that could not have been bought at any price: the biographer, although older than his subject, was never able to discuss him in any other terms than those of reverence.

It was significant that Roosevelt should have had so selfless an admirer as Riis: the very fact described the radicalism which Roosevelt professed better than a hundred essays. Riis innocently gave the game away, for he was out of the running, old-fashioned, of secondary importance when the muckraking era came; his work was done. The plain truth was that Roosevelt typified the new young man who was succeeding the old in politics. The new young man understood that labor could no longer be ignored, and that the West had to be conciliated, and that the inequalities among farmers and workingmen and capitalists required a new approach, concrete proposals, action. The new young men made no windy appeals to abstractions: that had been the failure of their fathers, who had merely talked while the country was carved up according to the practical plans of industrialists and promoters. Among the newcomers Beveridge, from Indiana, had a quasi-Lincolnian dream of equal justice and imperial glory. La Follette of Wisconsin was gathering forces behind him for a revolution in state politics. In Oregon, U'Ren was building a reform machine that could fight the lumber and railroad interests on major issues; Hiram Johnson was doing the same in California. The Senate and the House of Representatives, with these men up and coming, had a day of wrath ahead.

Roosevelt, too, had his principles, and they included first and foremost a strong desire for law and order. Law and order meant two parties, not three. And so, although Roosevelt knew that Blaine, "the plumed knight," was no chief to follow because of his known traffic with corruptionists, he went along with "the party," that is, the Republican party, on the candidacy of Blaine in 1884. He went along not with the cold, financial calculations of a Munsey but with sound and fury. Did this compromise make any difference to Riis? It simply proved to him that Roosevelt was not only a man of ideals but a practical man, a man who knew how to compromise at the proper time:

When Mr. Roosevelt's term [that is, in the legislature] was out [wrote Riis], he had earned a seat in the National Council of his party. He went to Chicago in 1884 as a delegate to the convention which nominated Blaine. He was strongly in opposition, and fought hard to prevent the nomination. The outcome was a sore thrust to him. Some of his associates never forgave him that he did not bolt with them and stay out. Roosevelt came back from the far West, where he had gone to wear off his disappointment, and went into the fight with his party. His training was bearing fruit. . . . He did not join in the revolution; the time had not come, in his judgment, to take the isolated peak.[2]

The time never did come—a fact that was more apparent to those who did face the need for doing so squarely than to those who did not. Men took isolated peaks because of bold and personal analyses which they dared to make of social situations. There was never any danger that the Roosevelt who, in his history of New York, could write thus of the tragic draft riots, would ever feel called upon to stand alone:

The troops and the police were thoroughly armed, and attacked the rioters with the most wholesome desire to do them harm; . . . a lesson was inflicted on the lawless and disorderly which they never entirely forgot. Two millions of property had been destroyed and many valuable lives lost. But over 1,200 rioters were slain—an admirable object lesson to the remainder.[3]

Riis approved every word of these remarks. He himself had witnessed the riots of 1877 and remembered the deeds of the striking workers with abhorrence. The question never crossed his mind whether there might have been provocation on both sides, provocation of which he had no inkling.

Roosevelt was absolutely honest in his passion for law and order; and that passion masked his political opportunism. Behind his hearty enthusiasm and earnest argumentativeness there was a shrewd political climber whom Riis was incapable of seeing. Roosevelt made a principle of party loyalty to the extent of holding on to Republicanism in its worst phases—its Hanna and Morgan phases. Riis himself quit the Democrats in order to

[2] Jacob Riis, *Theodore Roosevelt, The Citizen.* By permission of The Macmillan Company, publishers.
[3] Quoted in *Theodore Roosevelt, The Citizen.* By permission of The Macmillan Company, publishers.

support Roosevelt, and loudly voiced his "dream" that after
Roosevelt had finished his "labors" in Washington he should sit
"in the City Hall in New York as Mayor of his own city. . . .
That year I would write the last chapter of my 'battle with the
slum,' and in truth it would be over." Roosevelt, he was certain,
would crush Tammany and eradicate the slums of New York—
Roosevelt a Mayor, after having tasted kingship! Riis was indeed
naïve.

How principled Roosevelt was in the alliances which dictated
his policies we can see from his break with the Taft he had been
unable to control. Taft, too, was Republicanism as Roosevelt had
known it—a little less glamorous, a bit more pompous, but
Republicanism. When Taft was renominated for the Presidency,
Roosevelt did not go along, as he had gone along with Blaine. This
time he bolted to the Progressives who, coincidentally, nominated
him for a third term in the White House.

Roosevelt, then, was never the violent radical his enemies called
him; he was still less the father of muckrakers and sponsor of
Socialists. He was certainly less soundly based intellectually than
others of his own time and place and general ideals. Still, he
represented an enormous change from the Eastern politician who
had so long ruled American government. He was, at least, someone to make a hero of, if hero there must be—a correct and
acceptable hero. Roosevelt hunting big game, Roosevelt charging
San Juan Hill, Roosevelt denouncing and exhorting was a forceful
and arresting personality. His career in the New York Legislature,
as civil service commissioner, as reform Commissioner of Police of
New York, and as reform Governor of the state compared well
with the histories of the more venal and unscrupulous politicians
to which the East was accustomed. And this reformer really
reformed. He made principled concessions, it was true; but he
would never have risen if he had not done so. As it was, party
bosses sought to bury him in the Vice-Presidency. Hanna, going to
Washington to witness McKinley's second inauguration, remarked
that he was hurrying to see Roosevelt take the veil. T.R. was
potent political material.

And once T.R. was President, he presaged trouble. He talked

too much; he had too much joy in life. He destroyed all the rubber-stamp dignity that financial America had labored to build up in its figureheads. He had opinions of his own which, to say the least, threatened to interfere with the smooth and usual movement of the politics of state. There was, for example, the affair concerning Booker T. Washington. The Negro leader—no revolutionary figure—had been invited to the White House for luncheon. The occasion had no significance, yet a veritable scream of rage went up with charges that Roosevelt had insulted the entire South. Roosevelt stuck to his guns, realizing perhaps that liberalism was here very much in order. He was, in fact, extraordinarily acute in those matters and rarely made decisions that might really weaken his conservative support. Only three years after, when Maxim Gorki's American visit had been turned into a tragic ordeal by the barrage of lies laid upon him, Roosevelt refused to see the Russian novelist.

Roosevelt was talkative, open, independent, with a gift for vigorous phraseology that was startling and real, and as the times gathered momentum these characteristics stood him in good stead. McKinley would never have been heard amid the clamor of the muckrakers; or, perhaps, he would have been heard as Herbert Hoover was heard when crisis came again to America. T.R. *was* heard. He invited the confidence of the journalists, he fraternized with them, and he won in this way the entire forum of the press.

Roosevelt enjoyed one of his great opportunities when the great anthracite strike broke out in Pennsylvania and he stepped forward to act as mediator. It was a long time since the story of the Molly Maguires had come out of the mines, darkly, as from another and fiercer world. Labor had multiplied, and learned how to behave. The miners had struck in 1900, but Hanna had at that time run to the mine owners and forced a truce so that the disturbance would not interfere with McKinley's re-election. Conditions, however, had grown worse, and in May of 1902 the miners had struck again. Their plight could have been appreciated by less than passionate liberals. So certain was it that they could hold public sympathy that John Mitchell, who was no radical and who looked more like clergyman than labor leader, offered to arbitrate the case. The operators, however, wanted nothing to do with him or his union. They would not recognize the union and they had no intention of raising wages, reducing hours, or providing for the honest checking of coal mined. So the strike dragged on, and winter suffering seemed imminent not only for the strikers but for the city folk who needed coal. The miners having won the sympathy of the public with their excellent organization and discipline, an aroused public now demanded that the strike be settled and justice administered. As the situation stood, the strikers were in position to win; their opponents could win only with the help of strike-breaking government troops—if the public would stand for such intervention.

It was at this moment that Roosevelt stepped in. The operators were outraged and horrified, declaring that this was proof positive that the man was a radical. Riis and others like him spread the word far and wide that the country at last had a great President who could do things. Yet Roosevelt's actual achievement in the affair reveals facts that look neither like the charges of the mine owners nor the praises of Riis. Roosevelt first sent Hanna to George F. Baer, the leader of the operators, with a plea for conciliation. Baer was adamant: he would not give an inch to the union. There was a time-wasting and futile conference in Washington on October 3. Roosevelt then sent Secretary of State Root to New York to plead with Morgan for arbitration. What followed is not too clear. It is said that Roosevelt was determined to send troops to the mines and see that coal was sent out under government supervision, and that he had in preparation an order for the sending of such troops. It has been said that Morgan, under this threat, gave in to Root's pleas. It is possible that Roosevelt convinced Morgan of the senselessness of standing out against public opinion. In any event, the strike ended. There was arbitration and the award included several concessions to the miners but no union recognition.

Whatever labor thought of Roosevelt—and he was called a demagogue from many sides—there was no question as to what the conservatives would now make of him. The country rang with the sensation he had created. But today it is quite impossible to make startling and absorbing his role in the great strike. The sensation can only be "recaptured" as Mark Sullivan "recaptured" it by a furious concentration upon Roosevelt, upon what Roosevelt said, and said he said. Our retrospective interest is in the strike itself, in its demonstration of a power and maturity in labor organization which, unfortunately, did not fulfill itself at that time.

Much more original was T.R.'s unexpected prosecution of the Northern Securities Company. The company had come into the world heralded like the United States Steel Corporation a little while before. It was the fruit of a sudden battle in which Hill and Harriman, the great railroad magnates, had become embroiled. These two, backed by Kuhn and Loeb on the one hand and by Morgan on the other, suddenly began to struggle for monopoly of the Western railroads. The violence of the struggle threatened to precipitate a national crisis. To save themselves, the combatants finally called the battle off, and a compromise was agreed upon. The Northern Securities Company was organized, representing a division of shares which kept Harriman and Hill still strong and still enemies.

The company was a gigantic trust, one of the most ambitious of the Morgan projects. When Roosevelt, through his Attorney General, struck at it and demanded its dissolution, it seemed as though the trusts, which had been multiplying so quickly since the beginning of the new century, had met a David at last. Roosevelt was actually doing what Bryan and the Populists had promised to do; Roosevelt was a sort of Populist! Again the country echoed with his name, and arguments concerning him waxed hot. Roosevelt was evidently no bluffer: he had the prosecution pushed to a conclusion, and the Northern Securities Company was dissolved. What more could any radical ask?

And yet, seen in perspective, the suit dwindles in significance. Roosevelt never carried out the promise it implied: of the several thousand trusts in the land only the merest fraction received the Rooseveltian rebuff. Several of the most important suits, as we shall see, did not originate with Roosevelt; on the contrary, he served, with full consciousness of what he was doing, as a brake upon the activities of more militant antitrust fighters.

Of the Northern Securities case a number of pointed remarks

can be made. Before the suit the company was in the public consciousness as a vivid reminder of the nerve-shaking duel between Hill and Harriman; it foretold future trouble in the railroad councils; it was known to be seriously overcapitalized; its formation impressed people as a truculent gesture on the part of the big financial interests involved. The prosecution of the case was therefore an obvious necessity and did not require particularly radical motives. Morgan himself was less outraged by the government's action than were some of the smaller fry in the business. Morgan was said to have remarked mildly that abrupt counteraction had not been needed; if he had known that the President was against the combine, he would have been glad to talk things over. At best the suit against the Northern Securities Company was a pledge of further action, further prosecutions under the Sherman antitrust laws—a pledge Roosevelt did not keep.

One could view Roosevelt as a product of social forces. One could show that he had been reared amid wealth and was both cultured and virile; that he was likely, therefore, to dislike brutality and coarseness either from labor or from capital. His ideal would be a kind of benign but firm capitalism that would strive to render justice and make sure, at the same time, to keep all classes in correct order. But Roosevelt was also very much an individual, with a mind of his own, with personal ideals concerning national welfare. He sponsored the Reclamation Act with real enthusiasm. The Newlands Act of 1902 set aside the proceeds of the sale of public lands in sixteen states for use in the development of irrigation. Such measures were due, were demanded, for the bitter competition among the lumber barons and mine operators was laying waste expanses of territory which it had seemed would require hundreds of years to develop, let alone exploit. The nation's soils, too, were being impoverished and eroded away. The long, sad story is being told only now of how the national resources were being squandered.[4] Government intervention was

---

[4] *Holy Old Mackinaw,* by Stewart H. Holbrook (New York: Macmillan, 1938), one such story, tells vividly how the great trees fell, a billion feet a year. With the donkey engine, the highball, and the double-cut bandsaw the lumberjacks did work that had been better left undone.

necessary if physical debilitation of the nation was to be checked.

And so again Roosevelt was a radical and a leader of radicalism. The Newlands Act, it was true, took only a step in the direction of control; it left loopholes for recalcitrant capitalists. Roosevelt took not one step toward reclaiming for America any of the numberless acres of which the nation had been brazenly robbed. The muckrakers, not Roosevelt and his followers, were those who told the American people about those facts.

There was a Rooseveltian Era; there was, at the same time, a Muckraking Era, and this was more solidly based in social conscience. From it stemmed the reforming zeal that was to leaven future American politics. The crux of muckraking was the realistic analysis of the deeper maladjustments of society. Future crusaders for pure-food laws would turn for guidance to the muckrakers rather than to the Roosevelt caucus which passed the compromise measures which we shall soon examine. Labor experts, too, turned to the muckrakers for their information, rather than to Roosevelt's National Civic Federation which was a poor substitute for a labor department. Foreign-policy experts were not likely to turn to the hero of San Juan for light on peace, nor to the man who sent the American fleet about the world as the emblem of American culture, nor even to the arbiter of the Russo-Japanese War.

Roosevelt's mark was, however, inevitably upon all the agitation and reform that attended muckraking and Progressivism. He balanced himself upon that movement; he even managed to represent it at Armageddon. He was, in fine, the Average Man: ambitious, well-to-do (as the Average Man hoped to be), enthusiastic, wordy. Whether the Average Man was poor or rich, Roosevelt's illusions were his. Roosevelt was therefore bound to influence the ideas and achievements of men who were more bold than he, more sincere and principled, who dared to see and think what he could not.

Roosevelt was a promise rather than a fulfillment. The excitement that attended him was mainly the excitement of anticipation. But there was never any danger that T.R. would do more than he promised: he was settled and complete; he did no more than he meant to do. Detached observers who have looked back on the Rooseveltian Era for light to cast on the present and future wonder

at the storm and controversy that attended so much of T.R.'s
career. But when they examine the records carefully, they are
likely to become aware of a gleam of teeth and a flash of glasses
symbolizing something intensely dynamic and explaining in part
the hold that T.R. had on the citizenry. If he warranted no more
than Riis was able to make of him, he warranted, surely, no less.
Even those muckrakers who anticipated least from him, who had
fewest reasons to accord him wholehearted admiration recognized
this.

✪

Rough Rider

The life of Theodore Roosevelt, it has been said, was the dream of every typical American boy: he fought in a war, became President, killed lions, and quarreled with the Pope.[1] In many respects, he was youth's own hero because he never grew sedate. In 1904, the year of his triumphant election to a second term in the White House, Roosevelt's favorite Englishman, Cecil Spring Rice, was writing: "You must always remember that the President is about six." On his forty-sixth birthday that October, Roosevelt received a message of congratulation from Elihu Root: "You have made a very good start in life, and your friends have great hopes for you when you grow up."[2] Roosevelt's world, like the world of adolescence, was a place of high adventure, swagger, conspiracies with a touch of melodrama, fierce loyalties and equally fierce hates. And, sometimes, a boy's will was the wind's will—blowing and veering unaccountably. To politics he became what Buffalo Bill had been to the big top. But in his whole life of sixty years there was never a dull moment. He established a family tradition: that under a Roosevelt administration, whatever its faults, ennui is banished from public affairs.

[1] Henry F. Pringle, *Theodore Roosevelt: A Biography* (Blue Ribbon Books, 1931), p. 101.
[2] *Ibid.*, pp. 4, 490.

In 1906, in the "Log Cabin to White House" series for young readers, that veteran dime novelist Edward S. Ellis brought out *From Ranch to White House: The Life of Theodore Roosevelt.* "He was heavily handicapped at the beginning," wrote our trusty author. "He was born into a 'blue blood' family without the necessity of toiling for a living." But as a nearsighted and asthmatic boy he refused to be pampered. He swung dumbbells and took boxing lessons. At Harvard "one of his first steps . . . was to seek out a Sunday School in which he could do work for his Master"; learning that one of his pupils had blacked the eye of a bully who had pinched the boy's sister, Roosevelt "took out a dollar bill and handed it to the astonished lad with the remark, 'You did right.'" Shocked, the authorities of this Episcopal Sunday school dismissed the young teacher, who went over to a Congregational church—where, we gather, muscular Christianity was more admired. This legend is not wholly accurate; the chief reason for Roosevelt's retirement from his Sunday-school class was his refusal to subscribe to Episcopalian doctrines.[3] Equally untrue is Ellis' assertion that Roosevelt's first race in politics was for the United States Congress, against "the dainty aristocrat William Waldorf Astor." (Whereupon, it is said, "the defeated Astor shook the dust of his country from his feet, and sailed for Europe, where he has lived ever since"—a rather startling sequence, that would place upon Roosevelt's shoulders the responsibility for the present Lady Astor, the policies of the *London Times,* and other transatlantic phenomena.)

As a matter of fact, Roosevelt was elected to the New York Legislature in 1881 against a Democratic opponent named Dr. W. W. Strew, some nine years before Astor's expatriation. But Roosevelt's strenuous Americanism, in days when other blue bloods were being pierced by what Henry James called "the sharp outland dart," lent a spirit of truth to the myth. To his generation, Roosevelt seemed to be the first American since the spoils system began who brought inherited wealth and background into the hurly-

[3] Edward S. Ellis, *From Ranch to White House* (1906), p. 17; and Pringle, p. 39.

burly of politics. He lent a forgotten prestige to public life. In an age when the leisure class was devoted either to making money, with the Vanderbilts, or to the nerveless disillusion of Henry Adams, Roosevelt proved that there were scores of things more exciting than making money—reform, ranching, hunting, fighting, building ships and canals, travel, exploration, even reading Tacitus —while boredom was a personal disgrace. And, as the late Stuart Sherman remarked, "Whatever delighted him he sought to inculcate upon the American people so that Rooseveltism should be recognized as synonymous with Americanism."[4]

.   .   .   .   .

Roosevelt's Papers, as preserved in the Library of Congress, show no such outpouring of hopes and fears, of heart-throbs from the humble, as do the Bryan Papers. Here and there we find a letter like one in the fall of 1898 from Mrs. W. S. Miller of Atoka, Indian Territory: "What advice would you give to young boys about chewing tobacco—you are the Idol of every small boy in the country. A word from you now would be worth all the lectures on this subject till the end of time." Rare indeed is a message such as Roosevelt received from New York City in 1900, when he was Governor, written on a yellow ruled sheet torn from a copybook:

> Thursday June 21st
> West Side Italian School
> Grade 2 B
>
> You are a good gentleman to us. Your are nice.
> You have a pretty looking face. I love you.
>
> Your girl
> Rosie Biorno

There are a few letters from city boys who want to go out West and live on a ranch, and ask Mr. Roosevelt's advice. And there are a great many from Rough Riders, telling of children named for him, asking for jobs, or requesting help in trouble. "A bugler in your Regiment in Cuba, has been arrested upon a charge of shoplifting at Wanamaker's . . ." "Unable to work I held up a

4 Stuart P. Sherman, *Americans* (1922), p. 267.

Gambler, and was sentence to Yuma, Ariz. Territorial Prison
. . . I beg to have your aid . . . Mr. Roosevelt you know every
one of your men loved you when you were Captain and expect
your love in return, how well I remember the battle we had in
Elcaney by the big Block House on the little river half a mile from
the town, and how easily we won the Battle, by having you at our
head, to lead us on." Major W. H. H. Llewellyn sent more or less
regular bulletins: "I have the honor to report, that Comrade
Ritchie, late of Troop G, is in jail in Trinidad, Colorado on a
charge of murder . . . that Comrade Webb, late of Troop D, has
just killed two men at Bisbee, Arizona. Have not yet received the
details of our comrade's trouble . . . but understand that . . .
he was entirely justified in the transaction." Roosevelt, telling his
men good-by in September, 1898, with perhaps less grandeur than
the farewells of Washington and Lee, had warned them against the
backwash of strenuousness: "Don't get gay and pose as heroes.
Don't go back and lie on your laurels, they'll wither."[5]

His own laurels were still burgeoning. Elected to the Vice-
Presidency in 1900, he found himself President the next September,
after McKinley's assassination. Here and there, conservatives
gloomed over "this crazy man" in the White House. The great
public, however, was delighted to share in the family spectacle of
the Roosevelts, including "Princess Alice" and the five children of the President's second marriage. Their clothes and
sports, Alice's daring cigarettes and her marriage in the White
House to Mr. Nicholas Longworth held the people enthralled.
Some grew excited, in the South indignant, when the new President invited Booker T. Washington to his dinner table. The
President's tennis drew much comment, on the whole more favorable than that attendant later upon Taft's golf—which seemed a
more plutocratic game. Roosevelt's boxing lessons from Mike
Donovan also captivated a public used to fat, sedentary men in the
White House. Later, Donovan wrote a book called *The Roosevelt
That I Know,* and testified: "Had he come to the prize ring,
instead of to the political arena, it is my conviction he would have

[5] Hermann Hagedorn, ed., *The Works of Theodore Roosevelt* (1926), XI,
154–155.

been successful. The man is a born fighter." A memory that often played Roosevelt false in the direction of goals he wanted, but failed to reach, convinced him that he had once been lightweight champion at Harvard.[6] According to impartial accounts, as a boxer Roosevelt had pluck but not much skill; legend however has magnified his ability. But on occasion he startled the public by a real exhibition of stamina. One of his last acts in office, early in 1909, was to ride horseback one hundred miles over rough Virginia roads, in order to shame grumblers in the army over his recent order that all stout officers be able to ride a certain stated distance.

Roosevelt's theme song, played in the Cuban war, in swings around the country and on campaign, and at the inaugural parade in 1904, was "There'll Be a Hot Time in the Old Town Tonight." Big business began to wonder if there were not something ominous in that lyric pledge, but the people loved it as an index to the man whose exuberance was speeding the tempo of public life in the United States. He was a man of pure action, preaching a less selfish gospel of work than that of the success cultists. One worked for patriotism, for the state—and in the 1900's the specter of fascism had not arisen to haunt this doctrine. His scorn for the slacker, the cynic, and the "cultivated, ineffective man with a taste for bric-à-brac" served as a tonic to that generation. The first Boy Scouts would soon listen with awe to his advice: "Don't flinch, don't foul, hit the line hard!" While the adult public delighted in his apothegm, that he said was "A West African proverb: 'Speak softly and carry a big stick.' " The most famous demonstration of the latter saying, if not of the former, occurred near the close of his first term, in the taking of Panama. The building of a canal across the isthmus he regarded, with undoubted wisdom, as a national necessity. But his methods caused some criticism. Informally he called the Latin Americans "dagoes," remarking that "we may have to give a lesson to those jack-rabbits." He gave a benign wink to Panama, which revolted from Colombia on a prearranged date, while the American navy stood by. "I took Panama without consulting the Cabinet," Roosevelt wrote breezily

[6] Pringle, p. 35.

in his *Autobiography,* which appeared in 1913. At the University
of California in 1911 he had recalled: "I took the canal zone and
let Congress debate, and while the debate goes on the canal does
also." Biographers have noted that this speech cost the United
States $25 million. It so shocked the idealistic stratum of public
opinion that, when Wilson became President, a treaty was drafted
offering Colombia this sum and an apology. Furious, Roosevelt
and his friends blocked this treaty. Not until 1921 was the sum
paid, without the apology, in order to smooth the way for Colom-
bian oil concessions in which the Harding Cabinet was interested.[7]
Certainly, in comparison with the motives of Albert B. Fall, those
of Theodore Roosevelt appeared not too unsavory—and his
seizure of the Canal Zone did no damage to his popular repute.
Americans felt, with some truth, that Roosevelt's personality and
acts were making the United States into a first-class power.

Here and there one heard demur at the new militancy of
America. In 1902 Ernest Crosby, pacifist and Tolstoian, published
a book called *Captain Jinks, Hero.* Jinks, having fought for his flag
in the "Cubapines," yearns to be the perfect soldier. But in trying to
convince himself that, on command, he would shoot his wife, he
worries himself into an asylum where he is last seen playing with
lead soldiers. Such criticism naturally focused upon the bellicose
man in the White House, "as sweet a gentleman," wrote Colonel
Henry Watterson, "as ever scuttled a ship or cut a throat." More
genially, McLandburgh Wilson wrote:

> Our hero is a man of peace,
> Preparedness he implores;
> His sword within its scabbard sleeps,
> But mercy! how it snores.

That Roosevelt loved moments of fondling the big stick, such as
sending the navy round the world, cannot be denied. But Roosevelt in office was less the fire-eater than Roosevelt the private
citizen. He was not unmindful of responsibility, and did everything
in his power to quench the jingoes of America and Japan in 1906,
when hard feelings over immigration laws led to war talk. And, as

[7] *Ibid.,* pp. 315–332.

the arbiter of Japan's war with Russia, he was the first American to receive the Nobel Peace Prize. For all his emphatic motions toward imperialism, as toward reform, Roosevelt often arrested his hand in the midst of a gesture. Even in ordering the public printer to adopt simplified spelling, he added that if the changes were not popularly approved they would be abandoned—disclaiming his intention "to do anything far-reaching or sudden or violent, or indeed anything very great at all.[8] He liked to deliver thumping opinions upon any subject that crossed his mind—including birth control versus the "full baby carriage," divorce, the novels of Dickens and Zola, the private life of Gorki, and nature-faking— for, as he once said, "The White House is a bully pulpit." And he also loved power. But he was saved from being a dictator, political or moral, because he either took the popular side of an old issue or else listened anxiously for the public's reaction whenever he committed himself on a new one. He could be as angry as a later Roosevelt over what he regarded as interference between himself and the people, chiefly from the courts, but to the murmurs of the ground swell he hearkened almost timorously. "No man values public opinion or fears it as much as Theodore Roosevelt," wrote a shrewd politician, spying out the field for Standard Oil in 1905. "No man seeks popularity as much as he. Mild reproof or criticism of his policy would nearly paralyze him. Today he hears only the cries of the rabble and thinks it is public sentiment."[9] Rightly, the public never looked upon his toothy grin as the baring of dictatorial fangs, but took to their hearts the "Teddy bear," symbol of his ferocious playfulness.

His election to the Presidency in 1904, "in his own right," by a majority of two and a half million, vastly heightened his self-confidence. (His only error, in that moment of exuberance, was in disavowing any future plans for a third term: "under no circumstances will I be a candidate for or accept another nomination." In 1912 he had to eat these words.) He had been "dee-lighted" by the campaign and the thunderous applause that reached his ears—

[8] *The New York Times,* September 3, 1906.
[9] J. C. Sibley to J. D. Archbold, March 7, 1905, Clapp Committee, II, 1588.

except, as he told Lodge, that he was irked by the "outrageous lie that I had been kissing babies." Mr. Dooley in an aside remarked that a baby kissed by Roosevelt knew it had been kissed, and would bear the honorable scars for life—that in fact a generation would grow up among us looking like German university graduates. Whether a kisser of babies or not, Roosevelt was a born politician. He had found his ancestors, Dutch, Scotch, English, Welsh, and Huguenot, so useful in stumping for votes, that a popular anecdote claimed he had instinctively greeted a Jewish caller with a crushing handshake, "Congratulations! I am partly Jewish, too."

And the people were enchanted, too, when he stood up in his carriage and waved to admirers on the way to his inauguration. His frank delight in the presence of Rough Riders on this stately occasion, and the fact that he bent his knees in time to the band playing "There'll Be a Hot Time in the Old Town Tonight" were equally reassuring. Roosevelt had created a character, and lived up to it with winning consistency. And the crowd, as Samuel G. Blythe noted, "cheered the flag and cheered the Rough Riders, and felt that America was indeed a country which had licked Spain with . . . facile ease, and that they, being component parts of it, were not half bad themselves." The nubbin of the Roosevelt cult was seized upon by one of his old New York police captains: "It was not only that he was a great man, but, oh, there was such fun in being led by him."[10] Somebody compared his irresistibility to that of a circus parade led by a steam calliope.

Roosevelt never tried to conceal his opinion that Bryan was a kindly but cheap demagogue—to Roosevelt's eyes, not unlike Thomas Jefferson. But with the passing years Roosevelt came more and more to adopt Bryan's dreams, and, as Bryan could not do, to realize them in action. When at the Gridiron Dinner of 1905 a debate between them was proposed, one member of the club cried out, "What's the use? They're both on the same side."[11]

[10] Quoted by Mark Sullivan, *Our Times* (1926), III, 71. The *Baltimore News,* March 4, 1905, contains an interesting analysis of Roosevelt's popularity as compared with that of Andrew Jackson, Clay, and Cleveland.
[11] A. W. Dunn, *Gridiron Nights,* p. 154; cited Pringle, p. 368.

Roosevelt launched the trust-busting era, and so successfully stig-
matized "malefactors of great wealth" that for the next generation
very rich men had to hire public relations counsels, like the late
Ivy L. Lee, to whitewash them with human interest stories about
dimes given to small boys and millions to churches and medicine.
Roosevelt's attacks undoubtedly enhanced the endowment of many
colleges and universities, including his own alma mater Harvard. A
moderately rich man himself, Roosevelt had none of the venera-
tion for a Brahmin caste felt by most of the self-made Presidents
from Grant through McKinley. Moreover, in the coal strike of
1902, after dealing with George F. Baer and other thick-witted
industrialists, Roosevelt saw that his future adversaries were more
foolish than fearsome. With no very clear program in view, but a
sincere wish to gain popular approval, Roosevelt set forth to
correct certain crying abuses. He attacked the railroads for their
discriminatory rates and secured passage of the Hepburn Act in
1906; he had a measure of success in enforcing the Sherman Act
against huge industrial combines like Northern Securities, and in
threatening Standard Oil; he did much for public health in reforming the meat-packing industry and sponsoring the Pure Food and
Drugs Act; and he helped the cause of Western land conservation
and irrigation. But he was careful time and again to veer to the
right, to praise "real conservatism." And in 1906 he tried to call a
halt to sensational exposure of graft in high places by his lecture
"The Man with the Muck-Rake," with strangely little perception
that the muck was worse than the rake. As a liberal, Theodore
Roosevelt was a house divided.

Nevertheless, Wall Street and the railroads began to curse him.
In words reminiscent of those later hurled at Theodore Roosevelt's
fifth cousin, Jim Hill of the Northern Pacific wrote bitterly: "It
seems hard . . . that we should be compelled to fight for our
lives against the political adventurers who have never done anything but pose and draw a salary." The rich looked upon him
reproachfully as a traitor, and the self-made charged him with
having no conception of the practical rules of the game. So long as
he had confined himself to preaching the Darwinian philosophy of
imperialism, with its stress upon the survival of the fittest, they had

no quarrel with him. Now they began to fear that a radical was at the helm. They breathed a sigh of relief in March, 1909, when he quitted the White House. Roosevelt, who always loved the larger vertebrates, had picked genial and able William Howard Taft as his successor. And though Taft owed his nomination and election to the still potent magic of "T.R.," Wall Street was reassured. Taft's face, as well as his waistline, promised that the strenuous age was over.

Roosevelt's announcement that he was bound for Africa to hunt big game was one more fillip to his adoring public. Within a few weeks' time he received more souvenirs than had been given to any President before. There were rifles and cameras, walking sticks and shooting sticks, kits and mosquito netting, and innumerable toy elephants and lions. Potteries sold the public a vast number of toby jugs showing Roosevelt's grinning bespectacled face, a gun at his side, and the handle of the jug shaped like an elephant's trunk. (From the portraiture of toby jugs, it is said, "mug" came to mean face.) Roosevelt's had come to be the best-known face in the world. In an age of cartoons it was the caricaturist's answer to prayer—so compact, mobile, expressive. A later decade would see it carved, pince-nez effect and all, upon the cliff of Mount Rushmore, as the companion of Washington, Jefferson, and Lincoln. The five-cent stamp also would send his image on foreign-borne mail throughout the world. Meanwhile, his face was remarkably popular on cigar labels—ranging from a brand called "TR" to one captioned "U. S. Bouquet," featuring him alongside his peers Washington, Jefferson, and Lincoln. That Roosevelt himself never used tobacco in any form did not matter. . . .

Roosevelt's big-game hunt was a great success. King Edward VII, sharing perhaps the jealousy of those who lack the fluency and journalistic verve of the Roosevelts, remarked to Spring Rice that it was "a great pity" the ex-President sold his experiences in advance to *Scribner's* Magazine for $50 thousand. But, before Roosevelt's grand tour was over, King Edward was dead and Roosevelt as representative from the United States had a decorously jolly time among the kings and maharajas at his funeral. Pageantry had a habit, it seemed, of dogging Roosevelt's steps.

Wherever he went interesting things happened, and he kept Germany, France, and Italy excited with his speeches and controversies. He was the mad American of that generation. In June, 1910, he came home to find a great naval parade being held in his honor, a medal struck, and immense grandstands erected at the Battery. "Certainly the first citizen of the world today," wrote Major Archie Butt. Roosevelt was not so sure. After getting his bearings he commented a few months later: "I think that the American people feel a little tired of me, a feeling with which I cordially sympathize."[12] But like Buffalo Bill he could never resist farewell appearances. Soon he was touring the country, making speeches to say "I stand for the Square Deal," and daring to ride in an airplane at St. Louis while thousands held their breath.

The Square Deal was lightly tinged with a paternal socialism of which Roosevelt himself was hardly aware—the result partly of his revulsion against the blandness of Taft, and partly from a Roosevelt habit of growing imperceptibly more radical after years of keeping an ear to the grass roots. His feud with Taft, like his growing bitterness toward Woodrow Wilson, cost him something in prestige. It revealed a subconscious rivalry in Roosevelt's spirit, a lack of generosity toward those who came after him. Again, it was the fatal flaw springing from his lack of magnanimity. His postponement of announcing his candidacy as a leader of the Progressives left La Follette's aspirations to wilt on the vine. "I do not wish to put myself in the position where, if it becomes my plain duty to accept, I shall be obliged to shirk such duty because of having committed myself," he said.[13] The bolt of the Bull Moose faction made him of course a drafted candidate, as he had foreseen. Prone to be as gloomy about the future, in private, as he seemed optimistic in public, Roosevelt anticipated defeat. Nonetheless he began a brisk campaign, advocating recall of judicial decisions, social welfare legislation, farm relief, workmen's compensation, health insurance in industry, heavier taxes upon wealth, and limited injunction in labor disputes. Enemies, like Frank I. Cobb in the *New York World,* said Roosevelt sponsored "the state

[12] Joseph B. Bishop, *Theodore Roosevelt and His Times* (1920), II, 390.
[13] *Ibid.,* II, 307–308.

of mind that wants a Little Father, that wants Federal interference with every form of human industry and activity."[14] A great surge of popular sympathy went out to Roosevelt in October, 1912, when on his way to speak in Milwaukee he was shot in the breast by a fanatic. "I will make this speech or die," Roosevelt told friends who tried to rush him to the hospital. "It is one thing or the other." In this spirit of quixotic courage the speech was made; the country rang with applause. Here was the great Roosevelt tradition. The wound was superficial, but Roosevelt's campaigning days were almost over. In the November election he surpassed Taft, but fell before Wilson and "the New Freedom." A later day would see the Square Deal and the New Freedom fused as the New Deal.

Once more, in the spring of 1913, the hunter left for the hills. Roosevelt plunged into the jungles of Brazil to explore the River of Doubt. With an injured and abscessed leg, and stricken with tropical fever, Roosevelt made another of his Boy Scout gestures, at once so absurd and so appealing. "I want you . . . to go ahead," he said to his son Kermit. "We have reached a point where some of us must stop. I feel I am only a burden to the party." Of course he was not abandoned to die, but brought home, never to be physically fit again. . . .

The world of Woodrow Wilson went to war in an idealistic mood, not in intellectual sympathy with the imperialism of Roosevelt. After that war came a mood of disillusion and cynicism that was even more alien to his spirit. During the economic depression he faded rapidly as a symbol, the Square Deal which he never had a chance to attempt being forgotten in a widespread impression that he was merely a "warmonger." Both conservatives and liberals were apt to shelve his claims to supreme herohood, while keeping a sentimental fondness for the most picturesque American of his generation. The final appraisal of Theodore Roosevelt is yet to be made, with his virtues of strength and courage, his vast energy and consuming patriotism, and his generally beneficent effect upon American life set over against a few flaws that are so obvious as almost to disarm criticism. Although he and Bryan were both, in a sense, immature, and sprang from an America

[14] *New York World,* January 2, 1912.

which seemed to have grown younger and more awkward since Washington's and even Lincoln's time, it is clear that Roosevelt had a far better head than Bryan. He undoubtedly left a deeper impress than Bryan was able to do, upon the ways of American leadership. In his legend there was something more heroic. He was our last great American on horseback—as an epic bronze statue of him on a charger, unveiled before the American Museum of Natural History in New York, on Roosevelt's birthday in 1940, bears witness.

In 1921 . . . Arthur Vandenburg submitted to some fifty "representative Americans" the query, "Who in your opinion is the greatest American?" A clear majority—ranging from Samuel Gompers to Edison, from John Spargo to John D. Rockefeller, Jr.—unequivocally voted for Lincoln. A substantial minority— including most Democratic leaders and such members of Wilson's Cabinet as Lansing, Josephus Daniels, Newton D. Baker, and Franklin D. Roosevelt (cautiously eliminating "the great names from 1850 on," which "cannot be considered final")—chose George Washington. These results are such as one might expect. Likewise, some said the three greatest were "Washington, Lincoln, and Cleveland," "Washington, Lincoln, and Roosevelt," or "Washington, Lincoln, and Wilson." A good many echoed the judgment of William Allen White: "If I were speaking of the most typical American, it would be Theodore Roosevelt. But he is not our greatest American, nor does he approach the American ideal so nearly as Lincoln." Said Professor Charles M. Andrews, Yale's distinguished American historian: "If you are searching for the most typical American . . . I should name Roosevelt." More boldly wrote Henry C. Wallace, agricultural journalist of Des Moines and father of Henry A. Wallace: "I say without hesitation that in my opinion Theodore Roosevelt is best entitled to be called The Greatest American, because he exemplified in his own life the qualities we value most in an American citizen." An equally strong partisan, Gifford Pinchot, declared:

I believe that Roosevelt could have done everything Washington did and a good many things that Washington could not have done. That leaves Lincoln and Roosevelt. Between the two I confess I am in doubt. Roosevelt, I think, could not have played the part that Lincoln did in humanizing the relations between the North and South. Lincoln, I think, as a pure, intellectual force did not equal Roosevelt, nor could he in my judgment have grasped great international problems with the clear definition which so remarkably characterized Roosevelt's mind in action. My answer must be Lincoln or Roosevelt; which, I do not know.

Similarly, Professor Van Tyne of the University of Michigan, after polling his class in American history on . . . Vandenburg's question, reported 119 votes for Lincoln, 57 for Roosevelt, 18 for Wilson, 10 for Washington, 4 for Franklin, 1 each for Jefferson, Bryan, and Edison.[15] (College students are prone to vote for the more contemporaneous.) Qualities of cheerful aggressiveness, energy, decisiveness, love of adventure and daring, and a basic honesty and simplicity were doubtless those which caused Theodore Roosevelt to seem, if not the greatest American, then perhaps the most typical.

The verdict of 1921 was probably more enthusiastic toward Roosevelt than that of a decade later. His present standing, as a national symbol, is difficult to gauge. But if America ever enters upon another era of expansion, of taking up the Anglo-Saxon's burden in Latin America or the Orient, his legend will be burnished anew. Whether he will become *the* Roosevelt of American hero worship depends upon our future national policies.

[15] Arthur H. Vandenburg, *The Greatest American: Alexander Hamilton* (1921), Part I.

✪

Theodore Roosevelt:
The American as Progressive

The progressive movement . . . is summed up in the character
and personality of Theodore Roosevelt. There is reason enough for
this, for in the campaign of 1912 Roosevelt gave progressivism the
best dramatization of its rather confused career, but there may also
be detected some of the irony that seems to be a special fondness
of history. Roosevelt was a force in his time, and lent the
rebellious elements of his day the color and energy of a flamboyant
leadership, but he remains in the American mind for reasons that
have little or nothing to do with progressivism.

One of the secondary Americans, properly belonging in the
lesser hierarchy reserved for such figures as William Jennings
Bryan, the hero of San Juan Hill escaped Bryan's fate largely
because he was that hero, became President, shot lions and tigers,
and because the ultimate tragedy of his life, which came when
Woodrow Wilson would not grant him permission to serve in the
War of 1914–1918, is a tragedy only by special definition, with
none of the burlesque overtones that marked the Dayton monkey
trial.

In the historical balance, however, the scales are nearly equal—
Bryan's Democratic populism against Roosevelt's Republican pro-

gressivism; the Great Commoner against the Rough Rider; the cross of gold against the big stick. Both were actors, both were gifted with the quality of leadership, both led broad popular movements against entrenched privilege—and both failed. That Roosevelt's failure is never recalled by most Americans, while that of Bryan is attached like a stigma to his memory, is also traceable to the Dayton monkey trial. Roosevelt, whose greatness was attributed by one admirer to his understanding of the "psychology of the mutt," never permitted himself to be made ridiculous; Bryan, in his insistence that Eve was indeed created from Adam's rib, was too sincere to be that fortunate. The portrait of Bryan that most Americans remember is the one done in mercury by H. L. Mencken. The image of Roosevelt is the one created by himself.

It is this, the way in which whatever issues he happened to represent were submerged in his own personality, that makes him one of the guideposts to the present century. With Roosevelt there is marked the beginning of twentieth-century personalism in American government. There had been leaders in America before, and the history of Europe may be written in terms of personal leadership, but during the past in America there had always been a program, or at least a fairly definite attitude toward a program, associated with the man. In the election of 1800, when the victory of Jefferson and his Democratic-Republicans blocked the dangerous monarchial trends of the Federalists, men voted for Jefferson because he was Jefferson, "The People's Friend." Along with these emotional ballots, however, they cast their votes for what he represented. Those who went down with his opponent did likewise.

Daniel Webster, in a later era, was bluntly specific on the point. "If you approve my principles, elect me," he said. "If you disapprove, reject me." And in the famous contest of Lincoln and Douglas, one of the most dramatic clashes of personality in American life, there was also a debate of principles. Lincoln would not have had it otherwise.

After the coming of the Industrial Revolution, however, and the growth of mass democracy accompanied by an increasing ambiguity in political platforms, this stressing of principles tends to disappear. The first signs of modern personalism in government begin to be apparent with the election of General U. S. Grant. In the career of Theodore Roosevelt it takes on the form that characterizes it as one of the distinguishing features of the twentieth century. Roosevelt came to the Presidency by a combination of accidents, the ambitions of Mark Hanna and the trajectory of an assassin's bullet happening to coincide at a particular moment in time; but for the rest of his political career he was to run on a platform that had been reduced to the strict simplicity of two initials: T.R. With him, more emphatically than at any time in the past, the American government came to be symbolized by an individual—just as it would later come to be even more notably symbolized by another Roosevelt in an era when the English system was personalized by Winston Churchill, and Stalin, Hitler and Mussolini gave the color and dominance of their own characters to the dictatorships over which they ruled. . . .

Distressing though it may be for those whom William James christened the "tender-minded" to think so, it is not unlikely that almost everything that happens in modern politics is eventually based on instincts and emotions. The sum total of these instincts and emotions, in moments of inflammation, make up that herd instinct or mass drunkenness that sometimes takes possession of whole peoples. But mass drunkenness, of itself, cannot be a prime mover in politics because, as Bertrand Russell has said, it cannot determine what the final action of the mass will be. This was proved during the early days of the Russian Revolution. It is here that leadership comes into play. But neither can leadership of itself determine the final result in politics. There is always an interplay of forces. The mass influences leadership, leadership influences the mass. It is only when the articulated ambitions of the former begin to coincide with the unarticulated ambitions of the latter that some kind of decision is reached. The will of Lenin plainly did not represent the whole will of the Russian people. It was representative of enough of their will, however, to make possible the necessary identification. The same thing may be said of Hitler in his relation to the people of Germany.

This is why the arguments of those critics who quarrel with

Theodore Roosevelt for not setting the nation on a more revolutionary path fall of their own lack of weight. If revolution was what the country wanted, instead of reform, it could have followed the Socialist, Eugene V. Debs, or, if not Debs, the more truly progressive Robert M. La Follette. The progressive movement was not directed against the American system, with its promise of personal success, but against the monopolistic combines which threatened to nullify that promise. It was the middle-class belief (which in the United States may be considered almost synonymous with the general belief) in the Puritan verities of thrift and enterprise and individual success that was most offended. All the values implicit in the philosophy of moral materialism seemed at stake.

The men and women who followed Theodore Roosevelt were not at all anxious to repudiate the profit system: they were merely angry and outraged with those who had made too good a thing out of the profit system. The American reverence for bigness was for the moment shaken. As one small businessman after the other was gobbled up, as the railroads squeezed the farmer, as it became shockingly clear that government of the people, for the people and by the people was turning into government of the corporations, for the corporations and by the corporations—to borrow a phrase of the time—bigness, in the form of monopoly, took on the sinister shape of the figure of King Stork. Every trail of crookedness and corruption in government followed by the journalistic muckrakers, every smell that rose from the shame of the cities led straight to the doorstep of Monopoly and Big Business: at the end of every path stood the figure of King Stork. It was the trusts that had poisoned the springs of economic well-being, that pulled the wires of invisible government, that had made a mockery of *laissez faire*. The aroused battalions of the middle class, alarmed as never before, moved forward to attack. In Theodore Roosevelt, whose mind fit its philosophy with a neatness that might have been tailored for the occasion, it found its natural leader. . . .

. . . unlike Carnegie's autobiography, with its mixture of naïveté and self-approval that gives us so many valuable insights into the character of the author, that of Roosevelt is curiously lacking in interest. The picture that comes through is that of a Public Figure who confesses nothing because he imagines he has nothing to confess—not from self-congratulation, which is not one of Roosevelt's more noticeable traits, but rather from a conviction that he understands the motives that lie behind his every act, motives always admirable, always simple to the extreme. Beyond this there are pages and pages of energetic tedium (Roosevelt did not write with a pen; he charged with it), enlivened by a notable collection of forceful platitudes. He is for marriage and exercise, against laziness and graft. He thinks that a man will succeed if he has "the right stuff" in him, will not if he has not. He does not care a rap for power, only for "the use that can be made of the substance." As long as a single copy of the *Autobiography* remains, it may judicially be said, Roosevelt's reputation as the apostle of the obvious is safe.

Nor do any of his other literary compositions manage substantially to shake this reputation. As good a sample of his serious thought as any (with the possible exception of his life of Oliver Cromwell, whom he admired almost as excessively as did Carlyle) are the several essays brought together under the title *History as Literature*. There is a range of intellectual curiosity that commands respect, the stamp of an alert intelligence whose gravest fault lies in its inability to understand that there are certain walls that cannot be breached by mere derring-do, and a literary knowledge some of his critics might envy. The lecture delivered at Oxford in 1910 on "Biological Analogies in History" shows more than a superficial acquaintance with science, "The Search for Truth" reveals an ability to appreciate the ideas of such diverse philosophers as Henri Bergson and William James, and, if in the address delivered at the University of Berlin on "The World Movement" the tendency to think in terms of platitude is more marked, some of his observations, such as "Under modern circumstances the books we read, the news sent by telegraph to our newspapers, the strangers we meet, all tend to bring us into touch with other peoples," were destined to be repeated by other voices to larger audiences during the century.

It is in his lecture on "Citizenship in a Republic," however, delivered at the Sorbonne during the barnstorming tour of 1910, that his claim to the title of apostle of the obvious is most boldly staked; and where, with the brevity imposed by the lecture form, he gives us the essence of his political thought. There is a great appearance of struggle, of mortal intellectual combat, but we soon come to see that most of this noise and display of battle is merely Theodore Roosevelt wrestling with himself—or, more exactly, with his extreme reluctance to come actually to grips with the problem that lies before him.

That Roosevelt was aware of the true nature of the problem is obvious. He knew as well as any man of his generation that the Industrial Revolution had more clearly defined class differences in America, that the movement of society was becoming less fluid, that the chief threat to the democratic idea—this being before the rise of a new and unsuspected threat to democracy in the form of the corporate state—was contained in Marx's philosophy and program of class revolution. Such knowledge, implied by Roosevelt's complaint that the muckraking journalists (whom he christened) were building up revolutionary sentiment, was at the Sorbonne openly confessed.

"There have been," he said, "many republics in the past, both in what we call antiquity and in what we call the Middle Ages. They fell and the prime factor in their fall was the fact that the parties tended to divide along the line that separates wealth from poverty."

Well, if this was so, if this was the lesson of history, what was the answer? If here lay the threat to democracy, how was democracy to meet that threat? The question was an enormous one, and the fourth decade of the century would still find it lying unanswered, but plainly more was demanded than the crying out that such a state of affairs should not exist and the piling of one excellent sentiment upon another. Roosevelt, in these pages, suggests a man who, finding himself faced with a complicated problem in chess, his king in check, tries to improve his position by sweeping the pieces from the board. The most important thing he could find to say was:

The gravest wrong upon his country is inflicted by that man, whatever his station, who seeks to make his countrymen divide primarily on the line that separates class from class, occupation from occupation, men of more wealth from men of less wealth, instead of remembering that the only safe standard is that which judges each man on his worth as a man, whether he be rich or poor, without regard to his profession or his occupation in life. Such is the only true democratic test, the only test that can with propriety be applied in a republic.

Who can possibly quarrel with this? Who can deny that "A good man is a brave man"? Or that "Character must show itself in a man's performance both of the duty he owes himself and the duty he owes the state"? But who, at the same time, can find in this anthology of homilies even an approach to the problem at hand, much less its answer? Roosevelt's reputation as a political thinker has admittedly never been high, but it is still uncomfortable to see him standing on the lecture platform of the Sorbonne and lending the weight of his own evidence to the remark Cecil Spring Rice made of him: "You must always remember that the President is about six."

To find fault with Roosevelt on this score, however, is to fall into the same kind of obviousness we would hold against him. "Full of platitudes," William Howard Taft decided finally, and Robert M. La Follette, in his autobiography, said: "Theodore Roosevelt is the ablest living interpreter of what I would call the superficial public sentiment of a given time, and he is spontaneous in his reactions to it." Yet it was exactly this spontaneous response to public sentiment, the way in which "the psychology of the mutt" found a reflection in his own, that enabled Roosevelt to become the outstanding leader of his time. Had his obviousness of thought not been brought to such a high point of development, were he less a master of saying exactly what the disgruntled citizenry wanted to hear said, he would probably not have become President. . . .

It would be a mistake, however, because of what one of Roosevelt's critics has called his unflagging approval of the ten commandments, to imagine that he brought nothing but evasiveness and platitude to bear upon the problem caused by the impact of the Industrial Revolution upon a political philosophy and system of government that had its origins in an agrarian society. Behind Roosevelt's famous "balanced judgments," often so well balanced that they hang exactly in mid-air meaning nothing at all, there lies a definite, though no less balanced answer to the question *Is democracy possible?* Yes, replied Roosevelt, but there must be reform.

Reform may itself be interpreted as a form of evasiveness, especially by those who are impatient with the democratic process, and it may even be seen as an offshoot of cowardice. Georges Sorel, the prophet of violence who was so deeply to influence Benito Mussolini and others, who found in the principle of violence the basis of a new ethic, was unsparing in his contempt of those whom he always italicized as *worthy progressives*. No recent denunciation of reform improves in any way upon the invective Sorel pours out in his *Reflections on Violence*. "The specious reasoning of these gentlemen—the pontiffs of 'social duty'—supposes that violence may diminish in proportion as the intellectuals unbend to the masses and make platitudes and grimaces in honour of the union of the classes . . . It is enough to make one despair of sociology! If they had any common sense, they would remain quiet instead of devoting themselves to 'social duty.' Etc., etc."

Evasive or not—and it would seem, as an answer, evasive only to those who might find a similar evasiveness in any color not black or white—Theodore Roosevelt found his answer, or had the answer found for him by the progressives, in reform. He worked no miracles with reform, and his period as President was perhaps less productive of important social legislation than that of his successor William Howard Taft, but his answer, in broad outline, was identical with that later to be given by Woodrow Wilson and, later still, Franklin D. Roosevelt.

He had, it may be said, a clearer idea of his hopes, as expressed in a letter wherein he said that the idea toward which he was striving was to bring about a diffusion of wealth so as to avoid "the extremes of swollen fortune and grinding poverty," than of how to translate such hopes into reality. ("I cannot say," he confessed, "that I entered the Presidency with any deliberately planned and far-reaching scheme of social betterment.") He remains, however, the first President of the United States openly to propose that the political authority of the state be used to discipline economics and bring about a wider distribution of wealth—a doctrine that would lie at the heart of Franklin D. Roosevelt's New Deal and find its most violent preachment in the hillbilly text of Huey P. Long.

One of Roosevelt's most explicit statements on political theory, far worthier of him than anything said at the Sorbonne, is to be found in an article, "The Trusts, the People, and the Square Deal," which is included as an appendix to his autobiography. But even here, it is interesting to notice, there is still a certain reluctance to take a clear and forthright stand. Instead of speaking in his own right, Roosevelt quotes from a speech made by Senator Cushman K. Davis in 1886 (Davis being of that earlier progressive school whose best representative was Henry J. Altgeld of Illinois, and whose thought was perhaps best summed up by Simon Patten in *The Premises of Political Economy*), and then adds his own approval—not, however, without introducing a few "balanced judgments" later on. But, in any case, the argument is stated:

When Senator Davis spoke, few men of great power had the sympathy and vision necessary to perceive . . . that it was absolutely impossible to go back to an outworn social status, and that we must abandon definitely the *laissez-faire* theory of political economy, and fearlessly champion a system of increased Governmental control, paying no heed to the cries of the worthy people who denounce this as Socialistic.

This is still the central paragraph of progressive thought; the argument remains relatively unchanged. It has been recast more times than can be counted, as in Franklin D. Roosevelt's dictum that the United States could not go back to "horse-and-buggy days," but nowhere has it been greatly improved upon. Here the main battleground of American politics for the next four decades was staked off. The interminable arguments for and against Woodrow Wilson's New Freedom, for and against Franklin D. Roosevelt's New Deal, all the endless shouting and tumult would be

merely paraphrases and modifications of the arguments for and
against Theodore Roosevelt's Square Deal. "The Sage of Oyster
Bay" was of no great intellectual stature, the word sage having
here a certain malicious content, but his shadow, which was the
accumulated shadow of all the progressives he came to represent,
was to linger across the American landscape when all that remained of his memory was the legend of his personality and tales
of the strenuous life.

Enough has been written of Roosevelt's addiction to the strenuous
life to make any further examination unnecessary—Gamaliel
Bradford, one of the gentlest of scholars, confessed that merely to
think about all that energy made him feel tired. Even when
Roosevelt sat in a rocking chair he went on with his fury of living
and, as John Burroughs recalled, should it happen that a mosquito
needed killing, there was enough force expended to stun a bull
elephant.

But what lay behind all that immense vitality, that furious
celebration of muscular activity, that emphasis upon action that
was to be his battle cry for fifty years? ("Get action . . . don't
fritter away your time; create, act, take a place wherever you are
and be somebody; get action.") Why was he so contemptuous of
the weakling, the timid, the uncertain? Such reasons as Roosevelt
gives us are not altogether convincing. He believed he was the
most honest man in the world, and the most sincere, yet in the end
we come to feel he was always duping himself—or, if not that,
trying to convince some disbelieving part of his mind of things he
suspected were untrue. There is a gap somewhere, a missing
center, the lack of a solid conviction whose absence must always
be covered up by words. The portrait that emerges from Roosevelt's various hymns to the strenuous life, containing enough of a
love of force to be a foreshadowing of the worship of force that
was to become one of the most abnormal fixations of the century
he helped inaugurate, is that of a man playing a part—a man of
aggressive vanity and obdurate will, an ego-centered personality
with a strong inclination toward self-dramatization.

Vanity, generally regarded as a negative quality, is one of the most positive human traits, probably having its roots in nothing more noxious than the normal desire to win the approval of others. (Self-love or narcissism, which is most often taken to be the meaning of vanity, is merely one of its offshoots.) A variable, taking different forms in different men, vanity may range from the self-abnegation of the anchorite, who expresses it by asserting the superiority of his spirit over the temptations of the flesh, to the more energetic ego of those who are determined to leave an indelible impress upon the tracks of time.

It is this latter form of vanity that we come across most frequently in politics. An art only by special definition, a science by no definition at all, politics is yet one of the more important forms of self-expression—one that men frequently turn to when other forms have proved inadequate or unsatisfactory. It is illuminating, even if obvious, that all the outstanding leaders of the twentieth century thus far—Theodore Roosevelt, Woodrow Wilson, Lenin, Mussolini, Hitler, Stalin, Churchill, Franklin D. Roosevelt—also had . . . talents and ambitions in other fields.

Theodore Roosevelt was not ungifted as a writer and had he been more determined in this direction, and perhaps more rebellious against the standards and values of his class, it might not have been impossible for him to find a career in literature rather than politics, and to have become more reconciled to the frail body that made him unhappy as a youth. It was the determination to make over his body into a more adequate instrument, as everyone knows, that led him to embrace the strenuous life. But this determination, the ambition of a sickly boy born into a leisured class that has always emphasized sports in the manner of the English nobility, was clearly rooted in a sense of inferiority too galling for either will or vanity to stand.

One of the most revealing passages of Roosevelt's autobiography is that in which he tells how two boys made life miserable for him on a trip West, and how when he tried to fight them he was made to suffer the further humiliation of being handled with easy contempt. It was then, he tells us, that he made up his mind never again to be put into such a helpless position; when, having become "bitterly conscious that I did not have the natural prowess to hold my own, I decided to supply its place by training." Up to this point he is completely convincing: he wins our agreement as well as our sympathy. There then follows, however, a long paean to muscularity that is a cross between the chatter of a hunt breakfast and the noisier passages of Jack London—a younger contemporary with whom Roosevelt had much in common.

Roosevelt takes himself seriously here, just as he does in all his panegyrics to the strenuous life, but it is hard for us to do so. The picture is too forced, too desperate, too much the anxiety of a man who is fearful of dropping his pretense lest the whole thing tumble before his eyes. Roosevelt the he-man, dressed up as a hunter, seems always stalking the memory of the boy Roosevelt with the frail body: the image of inferiority must be destroyed again and again. There was other, more tangible game—lions, tigers, moose, grizzlies—but even in these exploits Roosevelt lacks conviction. The hunter's emotion is a hard one to communicate—as hard, perhaps, as the emotion of love—and it is probably unreasonable to expect of Roosevelt anything more than the surface record he gives us in *African Game Trails*. The question does arise, however, if he went hunting because he liked to hunt, or whether hunting was part of the game, the very complicated and elaborate game he called the strenuous life.

"Playing a game"—time after time, in his books and correspondence, the phrase repeats itself; always we come across ideas linked to it. "The great game in which we are all engaged," he says in his autobiography, trying to get hold of the meaning of life. "It will be awful if we miss the fun," he remarked when the Spanish-American War broke out. "Get into the game," he advised the Boy Scouts. "Hit the line hard. Play the game for all you're worth."

What we have here, patently, is the most obvious kind of teen-age symbolism. But other than that, because of the persistence of the "playing a game" image and the ideas linked to it, there is the clear suggestion that Roosevelt actually did think of life as a kind of large performance. Crowded though his mind's eye was with his own image, there appears to have been scarcely a moment when he was not acutely conscious of the impression he was making on others.

"How I wish I *wasn't* a reformer, Oh, Senator!" he wrote to Chauncey Depew when he was Governor of New York. "But I suppose I must live up to my part, like the Negro minstrel who blacked himself all over."

Living up to his part as a reformer, he showed an equal brilliance in other roles. The Rough Rider could turn quickly into a naturalist; the big game hunter could shed his soiled garments and put on the academic weeds of a professor of history; the passionate advocate of muscularity could take his ease and discourse on art and belle-lettres. And all the kaleidoscopic changes were made without apparent effort: each part was played with enough authority to convince the paying customers. "No other President of the United States," one admirer sums up, "ever put on such a corking good show."

With this it is easy to agree. The first American representative of twentieth-century personalism in government, the first President of the United States openly to propose a more equitable distribution of wealth, Roosevelt was also the first exponent of twentieth-century Barnumism in American politics. His understanding and appreciation of showmanship was almost as marked as that of the Great Educator. To his histrionic inclinations—the childlike love of dressing up in fancy clothes, the delight in presenting himself to admiring throngs, the joy of hearing his own words—he grafted a talent for press-agentry that enabled him to stamp his initials like a rancher's brand on the maverick hide of his time.

Under the influence of the four great founding fathers of modern journalism, Pulitzer and Hearst, Scripps and Bennett (all of whom had profited by the lessons of Barnum), the press had taken on a new and powerful importance as the prime instrument of mass education—a position later to be challenged only by the motion picture and radio—and Roosevelt was not long in discovering the truth of the newspaperman's maxim that the only politician who does not need publicity is a dead politician. Reporters were never left without copy. If there was no news, Roosevelt "made" news—preaching the gospel of simplified spelling, inviting Booker T. Washington to lunch, delivering himself of opinions on birth control, divorce, the "full baby carriage," the diet of blackbirds and the private life of Maxim Gorki. "The White House," he exclaimed, "is a bully pulpit!"

Having created a character, he knew how to live up to it—when to put on his cowboy clothes, when to wear his Rough Rider suit; when to bellow, when to grin. The voyage of the American fleet around the world, the search for the River of Doubt in South America, the hunting trips in Africa—he understood the publicity value of them all. More important than that, however, in a manner that would have compelled the admiration of the Great Educator, he knew how to exploit them so that his own name always managed to come first.

But his greatest performance, the role he played regularly for twenty years in all the corners of the globe, was that of the high priest of the strenuous life. The English knew of it, the Germans, the French and the Italians, the South Americans and the Japanese. Into it went all his imagination, all his aggressiveness, all his dramatic technique. . . .

. . . if Roosevelt's endless proselyting of the strenuous life, the celebration of energy born of the conflict between an originally weakling body and the aggressive impetus of a swollen will, would eventually cause Georges Sorel and others to call attention to the likeness between his ideas and those of Nietzsche, and to see him as representative of the imperial conqueror, the man on horseback, here again he was but a foreshadowing of the shape of things to come—again he might say, as he said during the campaign of 1912, "After all, was I not a great sounding board?"

In the end, however, for all of this, he comes to seem more like a figure out of fiction than of history—the last hero of the Age of Innocence, a frail boy with thick glasses who wanted to be big and strong and found, in America, the symbol of all he hoped to be. He ended by confusing America with himself, reading into the one the ambitions of the other; but while he never stopped celebrating himself, it is clear that he was also offering up a celebration of America—a country brave and mighty, the opposite of all the sloth and indifference and cynicism he came to abhor, unique and splendid among the nations of the world. Perhaps he misread its character, even as he misread his own, but he never misread the measure of his own devotion. The flow of his invocation often falls into a jingo chant, and in his dreams were visions of golden islands to be invested beyond the seas; but even his imperialism has a certain rhetorical quality: it too was part of the strenuous life. Finding his symbol in America, and America in Theodore Roosevelt, he came to regard himself as its only authentic spokesman—there are times, indeed, when America seems to be the frail near-sighted boy who wanted to be big and strong, and Roosevelt the American dream. He thought of himself in epic terms, and of his life in epic proportions, but both the terms and the proportions were those of a boy. His greatest misfortune, like that of all the heroes of the Age of Innocence, the Horatio Alger protagonists whom in so many ways he closely resembled, was that he never quite grew up. He was the Great Boy among the Presidents, ego-driven and willful, and it was perhaps inevitable that he should come to be remembered as the Boy Scout of the White House—peering through his thick glasses at all the great ambitions that were ultimately to elude his grasp, and blazing, almost unconsciously, trails that others were to follow.

When he called himself a great sounding board, he reached an evaluation that can hardly be improved upon. We can only add that he was a greater sounding board than he knew. For while his legacy to the American inheritance consists of little more than a few phrases and the legend of his personality, the lines of his life are like isobars and isotherms that trace much of the American weather to come. There would be more striking evidences of personalism in government, more lavish exhibitions of political Barnumism, a more emphatic effort in the progressive direction. In each instance, however, it was he who broke the ground and showed the way. And as the century neared its halfway mark, and the various questions he raised still awaited their answers, he would come to take on a larger stature than the one he actually possessed—standing like a portent on the threshold of a new and different world, casting his shadow before.

★

Theodore Roosevelt:
The Conservative as Progressive

> How I wish I wasn't a reformer, Oh, Senator! But I suppose I
> must live up to my part, like the Negro minstrel who blacked
> himself all over!
> —THEODORE ROOSEVELT TO CHAUNCEY DEPEW

I

The coarse, materialistic civilization that emerged in the United
States during the years after the Civil War produced among
cultivated middle-class young men a generation of alienated and
homeless intellectuals. Generally well-to-do, often of eminent family backgrounds, clubmen, gentlemen, writers, the first cluster of a
native intellectual aristocracy to appear since the great days of
Boston and Concord, the men of this class found themselves
unable to participate with any heart in the greedy turmoil of
business or to accept without protest boss-ridden politics. Money-
making was sordid; politics was dirty; and the most sensitive
among them made their careers in other ways. Those who were
less interested in public affairs usually managed to fit themselves
into the interstices of American existence. Some, like Henry
James, escaped abroad or, like his brother William, immersed

---

themselves in academic life. One, Oliver Wendell Holmes, Jr., found sanctuary on the Massachusetts bench and at length rose to the Supreme Court; another, Henry Adams, made a sort of career of bitter detachment. Some who were strong enough to overcome their distaste for business entered it without finding much personal fulfillment and left without regret. Charles Francis Adams, Jr., upon retiring from an unhappy career as a railroad executive, observed that among all the tycoons he had met, "not one . . . would I care to meet again in this world or the next; nor is one associated in my mind with the idea of humor, thought, or refinement."

Conventional politics, on the other hand, offered a choice between merely serving the business class or living off it in a sort of parasitic blackmail.[1] For the more scrupulous this was impossible; in the case of the fastidious Adamses, Brooks and Henry, even the weight of a great family tradition and an absorbing concern with political affairs was not enough to counterbalance distaste. They were, as Henry put it, "unfashionable by some law of Anglo-Saxon custom—some innate atrophy of mind." The era impelled the frustrated politician into scholarship and forced his interest in politics to find wistful expression in the writing of history. Among hardier and somewhat younger souls, however, there appeared the scholar-in-politics, a type represented by Albert J. Beveridge, John Hay, Henry Cabot Lodge, Theodore Roosevelt, and Woodrow Wilson. Such men, though hardly typical politicians, held their noses, made the necessary compromises, worked their way into politics, and bided their time until the social milieu gave them a chance to ride into power. These were the practical men of the breed, men of steady nerves, strong ambition, tenacity, and flexible scruples. The most striking among them was Theodore Roosevelt.

In his *Autobiography* Roosevelt tells how horrified his friends were when he first broached to them his determination to enter politics. "The men I knew best," he recalled, "were the men in the

[1] "No one wanted him," wrote Henry Adams of his own dilemma. "No one wanted any of his friends in reform; the blackmailer alone was the normal product of politics as of business."

clubs of social pretension and the men of cultivated taste and easy life." Politics, they told him, is a cheap affair run by saloonkeepers and horsecar conductors and shunned by gentlemen. "I answered that if this were so it merely meant that the people I knew did not belong to the governing class, and that the other people did—and that I intended to be one of the governing class." And so Roosevelt began at the bottom by joining an organization that met in a spittoon-furnished hall over a barroom, the Jake Hess Republican Club of New York's 21st Assembly District.

The ends for which Roosevelt and his peers entered politics were not mere boodling or personal advancement. Searching for goals that they considered more lofty, ideals above section or class or material gain, they were bent on some genuinely national service, sought a larger theater in which to exercise their statecraft, and looked down with the disdain of aristocrats upon those who, as Roosevelt said, had never felt the thrill of a generous emotion. Adventurers in a sense they undoubtedly were, tired of "that kind of money-maker whose soul has grown hard while his body has grown soft." In an article written for the *Century* when he was only twenty-eight, Roosevelt aired his disgust at rich Americans as a political type:

The wealthier, or, as they would prefer to style themselves, the "upper" classes, tend distinctly towards the bourgeois type, and an individual in the bourgeois stage of development, while honest, industrious, and virtuous, is also not unapt to be a miracle of timid and short-sighted selfishness. The commercial classes are only too likely to regard everything merely from the standpoint of "Does it pay?" and many a merchant does not take any part in politics because he is short-sighted enough to think that it will pay him better to attend purely to making money, and too selfish to be willing to undergo any trouble for the sake of abstract duty; while the younger men of this type are too much engrossed in their various social pleasures to be willing to give up their time to anything else. It is also unfortunately true . . . that the general tendency among people of culture and high education has been to neglect and even to look down upon the rougher and manlier virtues, so that an advanced state of intellectual development is too often associated with a certain effeminacy of character.

But if Roosevelt was in revolt against the pecuniary values of "the glorified huckster or glorified pawnbroker type," it was not from the standpoint of social democracy, not as an advocate of the downtrodden. He despised the rich, but he feared the mob. Any sign of organized power among the people frightened him; and for many years he showed toward the labor movement an attitude as bitter as that expressed in John Hay's anonymously published novel, *The Breadwinners*. The most aggressive middle-class reformers also annoyed him. Until his post-Presidential years, when he underwent his tardy but opportune conversion to radicalism, there was hardly a reform movement that did not at some time win his scorn. His writings are dotted with tart characterizations of "extremists," "radical fanatics," "muckrakers," and "the lunatic fringe." "Sentimental humanitarians," he asserted in his life of Benton, "always form a most pernicious body, with an influence for bad hardly surpassed by that of the professional criminal class."

What Roosevelt stood for, as a counterpoise to the fat materialism of the wealthy and the lurking menace of the masses, were the aggressive, masterful, fighting virtues of the soldier. "No amount of commercial prosperity," he once said, "can supply the lack of the heroic virtues," and it was the heroic virtues that he wished to make central again in American life. His admiration went out most spontaneously to the hunter, the cowboy, the frontiersman, the soldier, and the naval hero. Herbert Spencer, whose ideas were supreme in American thinking during Roosevelt's formative years, taught that Western society was passing from a militant phase, dominated by organization for warfare, to an industrial phase, marked by peaceful economic progress. Roosevelt, whom Spencer would have called atavistic, was determined to reverse this process and restore to the American spirit what he fondly called "the fighting edge." Despite his sincere loyalty to the democratic game, this herald of modern American militarism and imperialism displayed in his political character many qualities of recent authoritarianism—romantic nationalism, disdain for materialistic ends, worship of strength and the cult of personal leadership, the appeal to the intermediate elements of society, the ideal of standing above classes and class interests, a grandiose sense of destiny, even a touch of racism.

It is customary to explain Theodore Roosevelt's personality as the result of compensation for physical inferiority.[2] His sight was always poor, and at length he lost the use of his left eye. As a child he was tormented by asthma and shamed by a puny body of which he grew increasingly conscious. An encounter at the age of fourteen left an inexpugnable mark on his memory. He was riding on a stagecoach to Moosehead Lake when he met two other boys of his own age who teased him beyond endurance; and when he tried to fight back, "I discovered that either one singly could not only handle me with easy contempt, but handle me so as not to hurt me much and yet to prevent my doing any damage whatever in return." Upon coming back to New York he began taking boxing lessons, and his life thereafter was cluttered with the paraphernalia of physical culture—boxing gloves, dumbbells, horizontal bars, and the like. From his Harvard days there survives a picture of him in boxing costume; his muscular arms are folded histrionically across his chest, and on his face there is a fierce paranoid scowl. He was still boxing in the White House at forty-three.

Possibly there is no such thing as a saturation point in such psychological compensations; but if there is, Roosevelt, above all men, should have been able to find salve for his ego. He sparred with professional prizefighters; he rode with cowboys; he led a famous cavalry charge; he hunted Spaniards and big game; he once had the exquisite pleasure of knocking out a tough in a Western barroom; he terrorized an entire police force; he defied a Pope; he

[2] "One can state as a fundamental law that children who come into the world with organ inferiorities become involved at an early age in a bitter struggle for existence which results only too often in a strangulation of their social feelings. Instead of interesting themselves in an adjustment to their fellows, they are continually occupied with themselves and with the impression which they make on others. . . . As soon as the striving for recognition assumes the upper hand . . . the goal of power and superiority becomes increasingly obvious to the individual, and he pursues it with movements of great intensity and violence, and his life becomes the expectation of a great triumph." Alfred Adler, *Understanding Human Nature*, pp. 69, 191.

became President of the United States and waved his fist under J. P. Morgan's nose. If all this was supposed to induce a sense of security, it seems to have failed badly. At the age of sixty he was still waving the flag and screaming for a regiment. One can only suspect that he was fleeing from some more persistent sense of deficiency than that induced by the obvious traumatic experiences of his childhood. He fled from repose and introspection with a desperate urgency that is sometimes pitiable. In 1886, two years after the simultaneous death of his first wife and his mother, he wrote his biography of Thomas Hart Benton in four months, during most of which he was on fourteen- or sixteen-hour ranching schedules and "pretty sleepy, all the time." In this period he poured out seven volumes of history and essays within five years, while active both in politics and on his ranch. "Get action, do things; be sane," he once raved, "don't fritter away your time; create, act, take a place wherever you are and be somebody: get action." A profound and ineluctable tendency to anxiety plagued him. His friends noticed with wonder that Roosevelt, at the time of his engagement to Alice Lee, who became his first wife, lived in a stew of fear lest someone run off with her, threatened acquaintances with duels, and actually smuggled a set of French dueling pistols through the customhouse in preparation for the event. "There were all kinds of things of which I was afraid at first," he confessed in his memoirs, ". . . but by acting as if I was not afraid I gradually ceased to be afraid."[3]

"Manly" and "masterful," two of the most common words in Roosevelt's prose, reflect a persistent desire to impose himself upon others. Such a personal motive, projected into public affairs, easily became transformed into the imperial impulse. It was no mere accident that the Rough Rider's popularity grew most rapidly as a result of his Spanish War service. The depression of the nineties found the American middle classes in an uneasy and fearful mood as they watched the trusts growing on one side and

[3] Roosevelt was writing in particular about his reaction to hunting dangerous game, but the remark may illuminate a larger pattern of behavior. In many cases what the hunter hunts is nothing so much as his own fear; trophies are esteemed because they are evidence of risks undergone and fears surmounted.

the labor and populist movements massing on the other. For them, as for him, a fight served as a distraction; national self-assertion in the world theater gave them the sense that the nation had not lost its capacity for growth and change. The same emotions that made the people so receptive to the unnecessary Spanish War made them receptive to a man of Roosevelt's temperament. Stuart Sherman has suggested also that his popularity was due in large part to the fact that Americans, in the search for money and power that had grown so intense in the gilded age, had lost much of their capacity for enjoyment, and that Roosevelt, with his variety and exuberance and his perpetual air of expectation, restored the consciousness of other ends that made life worth living.[4] "On the whole," the colonel proclaimed in 1899, "we think that the greatest victories are yet to be won, the greatest deeds yet to be done, and that there are yet in store for our peoples and for the causes that we uphold, grander triumphs than have yet been scored."

Roosevelt himself loved the company of rough and aggressive men. Some of the most disarming writing in his *Autobiography* deals with the cowboys and hard characters he knew in the badlands. "Every man," he declared in one of his essays,

who has in him any real power of joy in battle knows that he feels it when the wolf begins to rise in his heart; he does not then shrink from blood or sweat or deem that they mar the fight; he revels in them, in the toil, the pain, and the danger, as but setting off the triumph.

The joy of battle could be found in warfare against primitive and inferior peoples. This feeling was first aroused in Roosevelt by the Indians, whom he saw with the eyes of a cowboy. He took the Western view, he confessed in 1886.

I don't go so far as to think that the only good Indians are the dead Indians, but I believe nine out of every ten are, and I shouldn't like to inquire too closely into the case of the tenth. The most vicious cowboy has more moral principle than the average Indian.

[4] It should be remembered also that his talents as a comedian were by no means slight.

Roosevelt's major historical work, *The Winning of the West,* which was written during his thirties, was an epic of racial conflict in which he described "the spread of the English-speaking peoples over the world's waste space" as "the most striking feature of the world's history." Only "a warped, perverse, and silly morality" would condemn the American conquest of the West. "Most fortunately, the hard, energetic, practical men who do the rough pioneer work of civilization in barbarous lands, are not prone to false sentimentality."

Roosevelt lauded the expansionist efforts of all the nations of Western Europe. In September, 1899, he declared at Akron:

In every instance the expansion has taken place because the race was a great race. It was a sign and proof of greatness in the expanding nation, and moreover bear in mind that in each instance it was of incalculable benefit to mankind. . . . When great nations fear to expand, shrink from expansion, it is because their greatness is coming to an end. Are we still in the prime of our lusty youth, still at the beginning of our glorious manhood, to sit down among the outworn people, to take our place with the weak and craven? A thousand times no!

The Rough Rider was always ready for a foreign war, and did not lack the courage of his convictions; as his most discerning biographer, Henry Pringle, points out, he was a perennial volunteer. In 1886, braced at the encouraging prospect of a set-to with Mexico, he proposed to Cabot Lodge that he organize the "harum-scarum" riders of his ranch into a cavalry battalion. Nine years later, when Cleveland's quarrel with the British over the Venezuela boundary seemed likely to bring war, he was all jingo enthusiasm. Let American cities be bombarded and razed, he somewhat irrelevantly told a reporter for the *New York Sun,* rather than pay a dollar to any foe for their safety. War with England would certainly be followed by the conquest and annexation of Canada—a delightful prospect. "This country needs a war," he wrote to Lodge in December, 1895, and when he was denounced by President Eliot of Harvard as a jingoist, he struck back at "the futile sentimentalists of the international arbitration type" who would bring about "a flabby, timid type of character which eats away the great fighting qualities of our race." A few years later he was pumping hard for the annexation of Hawaii, even at the risk of war with Japan. In June, 1897, as Assistant Secretary of the Navy, he made a classic militaristic speech before the Naval War College in which he dwelt again on his pet theme of the superiority of military to pecuniary values. The most dangerous mood for the nation would be an overpacific, not a warlike mood, he insisted. A wealthy nation "is an easy prey for any people which still retains the most valuable of all qualities, the soldierly virtues." All the "great masterful races have been fighting races."

No triumph of peace is quite so great as the supreme triumphs of war. . . . We of the United States have passed most of our few years of national life in peace. We honor the architects of our wonderful material prosperity. . . . But we feel, after all, that the men who have dared greatly in war, or the work which is akin to war, are those who deserve best of the country.

A war with Spain, he assured a naval officer as the crisis over Cuba grew more acute, would be justified from two standpoints. First, both humanity and self-interest required interfering on behalf of the Cubans and taking another step in freeing America from "European domination." Secondly, there would be "the benefit done to our people by giving them something to think of which isn't material gain, and especially the benefit done our military force by trying both the Army and Navy in actual practice." The hesitancy of big business to launch upon a martial adventure at a time when prosperity was returning won Roosevelt's scorn. "We will have this war for the freedom of Cuba, in spite of the timidity of the commercial interests," he warned Mark Hanna.[5] Not long afterward the war began.

The Spanish War, Roosevelt believed, should be waged as aggressively as possible, and he urged that a flying squadron should be sent through Gibraltar at night to strike against Barce-

[5] "The big financiers and the men generally who were susceptible to touch on the money nerve, and who cared nothing for national honor if it conflicted even temporarily with business prosperity, were against the war," he recalled in his *Autobiography*.

lona and Cádiz. Such counsels were ignored. But it was at Roosevelt's instance and without authorization from his superior, Secretary J. D. Long, that Admiral Dewey launched his attack upon the Spanish fleet in the Philippines. The extraordinary initiative Roosevelt took on this occasion has drawn sharp comment from historians; but to the chief actor himself there seemed nothing exceptionable in it. He never suffered from an overdeveloped sense of responsibility. Some years later he complained to Cecil Spring Rice that "our generals . . . had to grapple with a public sentiment which screamed with anguish over the loss of a couple of thousand men . . . a sentiment of preposterous and unreasoning mawkishness."

Once the fighting began, a desk job was too dull. To the despair of his friends and family—even John Hay, who thought this a "splendid little war," called him a *"wilder werwegener"* for leaving the Navy Department—Roosevelt went off to form a volunteer cavalry regiment, the famous Rough Riders. He chafed under training, fearing that the fighting would be over before the War Department delivered him to the front; but at last the great hour came; the Rough Riders reached Cuba and participated in several actions, including the so-called San Juan charge. Roosevelt was magnificent. "Are you afraid to stand up when I am on horse-back?" he asked some laggards; and many years later he remembered how "I waved my hat and we went up the hill with a rush." "I killed a Spaniard with my own hand," he reported to Lodge with pride—"like a jack-rabbit," was the expression he used to another. At the end came the supreme human profanity of his moment of triumph: the exhortation to "look at those damned Spanish dead!" Less than three years later he became President of the United States.[6]

[6] During his Presidency Roosevelt showed greater restraint in the conduct of foreign policy than might have been expected. Although foreign policy remained a primary interest to him, he did not seek war. His three most significant acts—intervention in the Morocco crisis of 1905, mediation in the Russo-Japanese War, and the intrigue that led to acquisition of the Panama Canal Zone—were marked by considerable noise and a fine show of activity, but no long-range accomplishments from the standpoint of "national interest." His contribution to the settlement of the Morocco crisis, probably

II

It was a tortuous path that took Roosevelt to the executive chair. After serving three highly moral terms as a New York State "reform" assemblyman, he deserted the reform element during the Presidential race of 1884 under Lodge's guidance, and threw his support to Blaine. Two years later he carried the Republican standard in a hopeless contest, the three-cornered New York City mayoralty campaign, in which he ran a weak third to Abram S. Hewitt and Henry George. President Harrison appointed him to the Civil Service Commission in 1889, where his zealous activity on behalf of the merit principle won him a nonpartisan reappointment from Cleveland. In 1895 he returned to New York to become president of the city's Board of Police Commissioners. At length Lodge's influence procured him the Assistant Secretaryship of the Navy under McKinley. He became a popular hero after his derring-do in the Spanish War, and was elected Governor of New York in 1898. There he proved troublesome to the Platt machine; the bosses welcomed a chance to kick him upstairs, and a combination of friends and enemies gave him the Vice-Presidential place on the McKinley ticket in 1900. Reluctant though he was to run for an office that seemed to promise only obscurity, Roosevelt campaigned effectively. His ultimate reward was the Presidency.

Coming into the world under the best stand-pat auspices, Roosevelt had been indoctrinated with a conservatism that could be tempered only by considerable experience. His father, whom he described as "the best man I ever knew . . . a big powerful man with a leonine face, and his heart filled with gentleness for those

---

the most successful of his ventures, gained nothing for the United States and involved a serious risk of inciting animosity. Of his mediation in the Russo-Japanese War, Professor Samuel Flagg Bemis concludes that it "did some harm and no good to the United States." The intrigue with the Panamanian revolutionists, which brought the United States the Canal Zone on Roosevelt's terms—a source of great pride to him—has been condemned by most American historians who deal with it, on grounds of national expediency and international morality. At best it is conceded that he gained some months' time in constructing the canal, at the cost of adding tremendously to the United States' burden of ill will in Latin America.

who needed help or protection," was engaged in the glass-importing business and in banking. He held the conventional views of the big-business Republicans and had no truck with political reforms, although he engaged actively in philanthropies.

At Harvard, where J. Laurence Laughlin was preaching an extreme version of *laissez faire,* Roosevelt recalled that he was exposed to orthodox canons. Beyond this he seems to have had few concrete ideas about economic policy; he admits freely that after twenty years of public life he came to the White House with only a slight background in economics. Given a college assignment on the character of the Gracchi, which could have led him to review one of the great social struggles of antiquity, he displayed, as he puts it, "a dull and totally idea-proof resistance." But the frigate and sloop actions between American and British ships during the War of 1812 fascinated him; his first historical work, begun during his senior year in college, was a loving and highly competent technical account of *The Naval War of 1812*.

Roosevelt's determination to enter politics and become a member of "the governing class" was not inspired by a program of positive aims, but rather by a vague sense of dedication. Beyond a conviction that the pure in heart should participate more actively in politics, a disdain for purely material ends, and a devotion to the national state, one can find little deliberate ideology in the early Roosevelt. He summed up the greater part of his positive faith in a letter to his brother-in-law, Admiral William Cowles, April 5, 1896:

> Although I feel very strongly indeed on such questions as municipal reform and civil service reform, I feel even more strongly on the question of our attitude towards the outside world, with all that it implies, from seacoast defense and a first-class navy to a properly vigorous foreign policy. . . . I believe it would be well were we sufficiently foresighted steadily to shape our policy with the view to the ultimate removal of all European powers from the colonies they hold in the western hemisphere.

One of the best indices of Roosevelt's place in the political spectrum was his attitude toward labor. The mid-eighties and the nineties were punctuated by hard-fought strikes. Since his own city and state were centers of the growing labor movement, he was in constant contact with organized labor pressure.

Early in his tenure in the New York Assembly Roosevelt was appointed to a commission to investigate tenement sweatshops in the New York City cigar industry. Shocked by the filthy conditions he found on his tour of inspection, he supported a bill, then considered dangerous and demagogic by his friends, designed to abolish tenement cigar manufacturing—although he acknowledged the measure to be "in a certain sense . . . socialistic." Subsequently he voted for bills to limit the working hours of women and children in factories and for legislation dealing with industrial safety. Beyond this he would not go. His attitude toward other labor legislation won him a bad reputation in labor circles. His views at this time were well to the right of such liberal capitalists as Abram S. Hewitt and Mark Hanna. Not long after his first year in the legislature he wrote that it had been a bad year "because demagogic measures were continually brought forward in the interests of the laboring classes." Among these "demagogic" measures was one that Roosevelt was instrumental in blocking, requiring the cities of New York, Brooklyn, and Buffalo to pay their employees not less than two dollars a day or twenty-five cents an hour. Objecting to the cost it would impose on New York City, he characterized it as "one of the several score of preposterous measures that annually make their appearance purely for the purposes of buncombe." He also opposed bills to abolish contract convict labor, to raise the salaries of New York City police and firemen, and to improve enforcement of the state's eight-hour law; he indignantly fought a bill to set a twelve-hour limit on the workday of horsecar drivers in street-railway systems.

His next important contact with labor was as New York City's police commissioner. In this capacity he won applause from the labor and reform movements for getting many tenement houses condemned; he made a practice of touring the slums in the enlightening company of Jacob Riis; he began to read in the literature of housing and showed an interest in social work. But he clashed with labor time and again over his method of policing strikes. In 1895 he was quoted in the *Evening Post* as saying:

We shall guard as zealously the rights of the striker as those of the employer. But when riot is menaced it is different. The mob takes its own chance. Order will be kept at whatever cost. If it comes to shooting we shall shoot to hit. No blank cartridges or firing over the head of anybody.

The industrial unrest stirred by the depression of the nineties was a constant torment to Roosevelt. When the notorious Bradley-Martin ball was planned in the midst of the pall of hunger and unemployment that hung over the city, the police commissioner, deeply irritated by the needless provocation the affair would give to the poor, remarked with felicitous irony: "I shall have to protect it by as many police as if it were a strike."

By 1899 Roosevelt had learned that he could assimilate some of the political strength of the labor movement (or other popular movements) by yielding to it in many practical details. As Governor he showed increasing flexibility in dealing with labor. He worked hard to get the legislature to pass a law against sweatshops; he was the first Governor ever to make a tour of the sweatshop districts; he consulted labor leaders regularly on matters affecting labor's interests; and, as though to measure the change in his philosophy, put his signature to just such a bill as he had fought most bitterly while in the assembly, an eight-hour law for workers on government contracts. Although he identified himself closely with the authority of the state and the defense of property, he saw the justice and necessity of making authority benevolent and improving the condition of the people through social legislation. But any display of independent power by the masses, especially in the form of a strike, set off a violent reflex. He epitomized his philosophy during his Governorship when he remarked of a current dispute: "If there should be a disaster at the Croton Dam strike, I'd order out the militia in a minute. But I'd sign an employer's liability law, too." He still displayed, as Howard L. Hurwitz describes it, "a trigger-like willingness to use troops. . . .

His mind was a single track when it came to strikes, and that track always carried troops to the scene of the dispute."

Roosevelt followed events on the national scene with a similar impatience and showed the same penchant for sudden violence that appears again and again in this period of his life. At the time of the Haymarket affair he had written proudly from his ranch that his cowboys would like "a chance with rifles at one of the mobs. . . . I wish I had them with me and a fair show at ten times our number of rioters; my men shoot well and fear very little." The discontent of the nineties brought a new attack of hysteria. During the Pullman strike (when Mark Hanna was proclaiming before the outraged gentry of the Cleveland Union Club that "A man who won't meet his men half-way is a God-damn fool") Roosevelt wrote Brander Matthews: "I know the Populists and the laboring men well and their faults. . . . I like to see a mob handled by the regulars, or by good State-Guards, not over-scrupulous about bloodshed." He was among those who saw in the events of 1896 a threatened repetition of the French Revolution. "This is no mere fight over financial standards," he informed his sister in July.

It is a semi-socialistic agrarian movement, with free silver as a mere incident, supported mainly because it is hoped thereby to damage the well to do and thrifty. "Organized labor" is the chief support of Bryan in the big cities; and his utterances are as criminal as they are wildly silly. All the ugly forces that seethe beneath the social crust are behind him.

He had not forgiven John P. Altgeld for pardoning three of the Chicago anarchists or for protesting when Cleveland sent federal troops to Illinois to break the Pullman strike. He now refused to meet Altgeld personally, because, he said, he might yet have to face him "sword to sword upon the field of battle." While Hanna was snorting at his Union Club friends: "There won't be any revolution. You're just a lot of damn fools," Roosevelt was reported as saying:[7]

The sentiment now animating a large proportion of our people can only be suppressed as the Commune in Paris was suppressed, by taking

[7] Roosevelt heatedly denied having uttered these words, which were reported by Willis J. Abbot, an editor of the Democratic *New York Journal*.

ten or a dozen of their leaders out, standing . . . them against a wall, and shooting them dead. I believe it will come to that. These leaders are plotting a social revolution and the subversion of the American Republic.

The passing of the silver crisis, the diversion of the Spanish War, and the return of prosperity did not entirely dissipate Roosevelt's worried mood. In 1899 he was still writing Lodge from Albany that the workers and small tradesmen in his state were in a mood of "sullen discontent." Brooks Adams came to visit him during the summer, and the two talked of the danger to the nation of the trade union eight-hour movement and the possibility that the country would be "enslaved" by the organizers of the trusts. They were intrigued by the idea that Roosevelt might lead "some great outburst of the emotional classes which should at least temporarily crush the Economic Man."[8]

Roosevelt was none too happy over McKinley's victory in 1896. Anything, of course, to beat Bryan and Altgeld; but he looked on McKinley as a weakling who could not be relied on in a "serious crisis, whether it took the form of a soft-money craze, a gigantic labor riot, or danger of a foreign conflict." The triumph of 1896 represented, after all, the victory of the type of moneybags he had always condemned, and he wrote sadly to his sister after attending the Republican celebration dinner that he was "personally realizing all of Brooks Adams' gloomiest anticipations of our gold-ridden, capitalist-bestridden, usurer-mastered future."

Because he feared the great corporations as well as the organized workers and farmers, Roosevelt came to think of himself as representing a golden mean. After he had sponsored, as Governor, a tax on public-service franchises, which alarmed the corporate interests, he was accused by the incredible Boss Platt of being too "altruistic" on labor and the trusts. Roosevelt replied that he merely wanted to show that "we Republicans hold the just balance and set our faces as resolutely against the improper corporate influence on the one hand as against demagogy and mob rule on

[8] This was probably in reference to the distinction Adams had drawn two years earlier in *The Law of Civilization and Decay* between the imaginative, emotional, and artistic types of men and the economic man. Roosevelt wrote a significant review of this book for the *Forum*, January 1897.

the other." This was the conception that he brought to the Presidency. He stood above the contending classes, an impartial arbiter devoted to the national good, and a custodian of the stern virtues without which the United States could not play its destined role of mastery in the world theater.

III

"Wall Street has desperate need of men like you," Brooks Adams had taunted in 1896, as he urged Theodore Roosevelt to hire himself out to the commercial interests. The thought of being such an outright mercenary was revolting to the Rough Rider, and he was doubtless uneasy in the presence of Adams' cynicism. But the more independent and statesmanlike role of stabilizer of the status quo, of a conservative wiser than the conservatives, appealed to him. It became his obsession to "save" the masters of capital from their own stupid obstinacy, a theme that runs consistently through his public and private writings from the time of his accession to the Presidency. During his first term he was keenly aware, as Matthew Josephson remarks, that he was a "captive president" for whom it would be unwise to break the chains that bound him to the interests. "Go slow," Hanna advised him. "I shall go slow," the new President replied.[9]

The advisers to whom Roosevelt listened were almost exclusively representatives of industrial and finance capital—men like Hanna, Robert Bacon and George W. Perkins of the House of Morgan, Elihu Root, Senator Nelson W. Aldrich, A. J. Cassatt of the Pennsylvania Railroad, Philander C. Knox, and James Stillman of the Rockefeller interests. When his brother-in-law, Douglas Robinson, wrote from Wall Street to urge that he do nothing to destroy business confidence, Roosevelt answered:

I intend to be most conservative, but in the interests of the corporations themselves and above all in the interests of the country, I

[9] The relationship between these two became increasingly cordial. In 1909 Philander C. Knox, asked whether he had ever witnessed an argument between them, answered that he had—just once. Roosevelt had been maintaining that the Grangers, the agrarian reformers of the seventies, were maniacs, Hanna that they were useful citizens.

intend to pursue cautiously, but steadily, the course to which I have been publicly committed . . . and which I am certain is the right course.

Toward the close of his first term Roosevelt suffered attacks of anxiety for fear that some of his policies had offended the interests, and late in 1903 he did his best to assure them that his intentions were honorable.[10] Although the Democrats named a gilt-edged conservative candidate, Judge Alton B. Parker, Roosevelt held his own in business circles. Handsome donations poured into the treasure chest of the Republican National Committee from Morgan and Rockefeller corporations, from Harriman, Frick, Chauncey Depew, and George J. Gould. Roosevelt's opponent falsely accused him of having "blackmailed" the corporations and promising them immunity in return for their donations.[11] But Parker was overwhelmed at the polls. Roosevelt had convinced the people that he was a reformer, and businessmen that he was sound.

A qualification is necessary: some business elements did fear and hate Theodore Roosevelt. And yet, by displaying their opposition, they and the conservative newspaper editors unwittingly gave him the same kind of assistance that the Du Ponts later gave to Franklin D. Roosevelt: they provided the dramatic foil that enabled him to stay on the stage plausibly as a reformer. His attitudes toward many public questions were actually identical with those of the shrewder capitalists. This was particularly true where labor was concerned, and it was illustrated by Roosevelt's

[10] "The opposition to you among the capitalists is confined to a group of Wall Street and Chicago people," Lodge reassured him, June 2, 1903, "but even in Wall Street there is a large body of men who are with you, and I do not find here on State Street any manifest hostility on account of your merger [Northern Securities] case, rather the contrary."

Senator Orville Platt of Connecticut found late in the same year that the opposition to Roosevelt came "from both ends of the party—from the moneyed influences in Wall Street and the agitators in the labor movement —one as much as the other."

[11] According to Oswald Garrison Villard's report in *The Fighting Years,* Henry Clay Frick suffered from the delusion that Roosevelt had made positive commitments in return for the financial support he solicited. "He got down on his knees before us," Frick remembered angrily. "We bought the son of a bitch and then he did not stay bought!"

compromise of the formidable anthracite strike of 1902. The
frame of mind of old-fashioned capitalists was expressed during
that dispute by George F. Baer when he said that "the Christian
men whom God in his infinite wisdom has given the control of the
property interests of this country" were alone qualified to look
after the welfare of the workingman. The attitude of the more
statesmanlike business interests was represented by Morgan and
Hanna, both of whom pressed the mine operators to accept the
method of arbitration proposed by Roosevelt and Root.[12]
Throughout the controversy the President fumed at the obstinacy
of the mineowners. "From every consideration of public policy
and of good morals they should make some slight concession," he
wrote to Hanna. And: "The attitude of the operators will beyond a
doubt double the burden on us while standing between them and
socialistic action." "I was anxious," he recalled years afterward,
"to save the great coal operators and all of the class of big propertied men, of which they were members, from the dreadful punish-
ment which their own folly would have brought on them if I had
not acted. . . ."

Roosevelt worried much about the rise of radicalism during his
two administrations. The prominence of the muckraking literature
(which was "building up a revolutionary feeling"), the growing
popularity of the socialist movement ("far more ominous than any
populist or similar movements in times past"), the emergence of
militant local reformers like La Follette, the persistent influence of
Bryan—such things haunted him. "I do not like the social conditions at present," he complained to Taft in March, 1906:

The dull, purblind folly of the very rich men; their greed and
arrogance . . . and the corruption in business and politics, have
tended to produce a very unhealthy condition of excitement and
irritation in the popular mind, which shows itself in the great increase
in the socialistic propaganda.

His dislike of "the very rich men" caused Roosevelt to exagger-
ate their folly and forget how much support they had given him,

[12] "If it had not been for your going in the matter," Roosevelt said in
thanking Morgan, "I do not see how the strike could have been settled at
this time."

but his understanding of the popular excitement and irritation was keen, and his technique for draining it into the channels of moderate action was superb. (His boxing instructors had taught him not to charge into his opponents' punches but to roll with them.) In 1900 Bryan had puffed about the trusts, and Roosevelt responded in 1902 with an extremely spectacular antitrust prosecution—the Northern Securities case. Between 1904 and 1906 Bryan agitated for government ownership of railroads, and Roosevelt answered by supporting the Hepburn Bill, which made possible the beginnings of railroad rate-control by the Interstate Commerce Commission. During the fight over the bill he wrote to Lodge to deplore the activities of the railroad lobbyists: "I think they are very short-sighted not to understand that to beat it means to increase the danger of the movement for government ownership of railroads." Taking several leaves from Bryan's book, Roosevelt urged upon Congress workmen's compensation and child-labor laws, a railway hour act, income and inheritance taxes, and a law prohibiting corporations from contributing to political parties; he turned upon the federal courts and denounced the abuse of injunctions in labor disputes; he blasted dishonesty in business with some of the showiest language that had ever been used in the White House. Only a small part of his recommendations received serious Congressional attention, and in some instances—especially that of the Hepburn Bill—his own part in the making of legislation was far more noteworthy for readiness to compromise, than to fight against the conservative bosses of his party. But his strong language had value in itself, not only because it shaped the public image of him as a fighting radical, but because it did contribute real weight to the sentiment for reform. His baiting of "malefactors of great wealth" and the "criminal rich" also gave his admirers the satisfaction of emotional catharsis at a time when few other satisfactions were possible.

In retrospect, however, it is hard to understand how Roosevelt managed to keep his reputation as a strenuous reformer. Unlike Bryan, he had no passionate interest in the humane goals of reform; unlike La Follette, no mastery of its practical details. "In internal affairs," he confessed in his *Autobiography,* "I cannot say that I entered the presidency with any deliberately planned and far-reaching scheme of social betterment." Reform in his mind did not mean a thoroughgoing purgation; it was meant to heal only the most conspicuous sores on the body politic. And yet many people were willing and eager to accept his reform role at its face value. Perhaps the best proof that the progressive mind was easy to please is his reputation as a trust-buster. Let it serve as an illustration:

Roosevelt became President without any clearly defined ideas or strong principles on the question of big business. As early as August 7, 1899 he had written H. H. Kohlsaat that the popular unrest over trusts was "largely aimless and baseless," and admitted frankly that he did know what, if anything, should be done about them. But, as we have seen, he distrusted and despised the ignoble "bourgeois" spirit in politics. While bigness in business frightened the typical middle-class citizen for economic reasons, it frightened Roosevelt for political reasons. He was not a small entrepreneur, worrying about being squeezed out, nor an ordinary consumer concerned about rising prices, but a big politician facing a strong rival in the business of achieving power. He did not look forward to breaking up bigness by restoring competitive conditions. He did not have, in short, the devotion of the small man to small property that won the sympathy of such contemporaries as Brandeis, La Follette, and Wilson. Bigness in business filled him with foreboding because it presaged a day when the United States might be held in thrall by those materialistic interests he had always held in contempt, a "vulgar tyranny of mere wealth." Antitrust action seems to have been to him partly a means of satisfying the popular demand to see the government flail big business, but chiefly a threat to hold over business to compel it to accept regulation. And regulation, not destruction, was his solution for the trust problem. Psychologically he identified himself with the authority of the state, and jealously projected his own pressing desire for "mastery" into the trust problem. The trusts must never be allowed to grow stronger than the state; they must yield to its superior moral force.

From the beginning Roosevelt expressed his philosophy quite

candidly—and it is this that makes his reputation as a trust-buster such a remarkable thing. On December 2, 1902 he informed Congress:

Our aim is not to do away with corporations; on the contrary, these big aggregations are an inevitable development of modern industrialism, and the effort to destroy them would be futile unless accomplished in ways that would work the utmost mischief to the entire body politic. . . . We draw the line against misconduct, not against wealth.

He repeated this theme again and again. At the beginning of his second term he declared: "This is an age of combination, and any effort to prevent all combination will be not only useless, but in the end vicious, because of the contempt for law which the failure to enforce law inevitably produces."

In his *Autobiography* Roosevelt argued with brilliant historical insight for his thesis that regulation rather than dissolution was the answer:

One of the main troubles was the fact that the men who saw the evils and who tried to remedy them attempted to work in two wholly different ways, and the great majority of them in a way that offered little promise of real betterment. They tried (by the Sherman-law method) to bolster up an individualism already proved to be both futile and mischievous; *to remedy by more individualism the concentration that was the inevitable result of the already existing individualism.* They saw the evil done by the big combinations, and sought to remedy it by destroying them and restoring the country to the economic conditions of the middle of the nineteenth century. This was a hopeless effort, and those who went into it, although they regarded themselves as radical progressives, really represented a form of sincere rural toryism. . . .

On the other hand, a few men recognized that corporations and combinations had become indispensable in the business world, that it was folly to try to prohibit them, but that it was also folly to leave them without thoroughgoing control. . . . They realized that the government must now interfere to protect labor, to subordinate the big corporation to the public welfare, and to shackle cunning and fraud exactly as centuries before it had interfered to shackle the physical force which does wrong by violence. . . .

Roosevelt did, of course, engage in a few cleverly chosen prosecutions which gave substance to his talk about improving the moral code of the corporations. The prosecution of the Northern Securities Company in 1902, near the beginning of his first term, was his most spectacular effort.

The Northern Securities holding company, organized by James J. Hill, J. P. Morgan, and others, had established a gigantic railroad monopoly in the Northwest, embracing the Northern Pacific, the Great Northern, and the Chicago, Burlington, & Quincy railroads. The roads involved had been very much in the public eye because of an extremely bitter and well-publicized rivalry between Hill and E. H. Harriman. And yet the monopoly was anything but a vital concern in the life of the business community or the affairs of the House of Morgan. To prosecute it was a brilliant stroke of publicity that could hardly have been resisted even by a more conservative politician.[13]

Nevertheless, the announcement of the Northern Securities case caused a real shock in the ranks of big business and brought Morgan himself bustling down to Washington with Senators Depew and Hanna to find out if the President was planning to "attack my other interests." He was told that this would happen only if "they have done something that we regard as wrong."

Roosevelt was never keen to find wrongdoing among the trusts. "As a matter of fact," he admitted privately toward the close of his Presidential career, "I have let up in every case where I have had any possible excuse for so doing." A few outstanding cases were

[13] It is possible that McKinley might have undertaken such a prosecution had he lived. Hanna, who was as usual calm about the whole affair, refused to intercede: "I warned Hill that McKinley might have to act against his damn company last year. Mr. Roosevelt's done it. I'm sorry for Hill, but just what do you gentlemen think I can do?"

The prosecution, technically successful, did not restore competition. It is illuminating that Roosevelt, when he heard the news of the Supreme Court's decision in the Northern Securities case, proclaimed it "one of the great achievements of my administration. . . . The most powerful men in this country were held to accountability before the law." As Mr. Justice Holmes maliciously pointed out in his dissenting opinion, this was precisely what had not happened, for the Sherman Act logically required criminal prosecution of Messrs. Morgan, Harriman, Hill, and others involved in the company. Roosevelt never forgave Holmes.

tried during his second term—after he had weathered the trial of re-election with the help of large donations from business—but even such obvious subjects of antitrust action as Standard Oil and the American Tobacco Company were left untouched. There was a hundred times more noise than accomplishment. Historians have often remarked that Taft's administration brought ninety antitrust proceedings in four years, while Roosevelt brought only fifty-four in seven years. The most intense and rapid growth of trusts in American business history took place during Roosevelt's administrations.

The ambiguity that can be seen in his trust policies came naturally and honestly to Theodore Roosevelt. In his early days it had always been his instinct to fight, to shoot things out with someone or something—imaginary lovers of his fiancée, Western Indians, Mexicans, the British navy, Spanish soldiers, American workers, Populists. But before he became President he had learned that an ambitious politician must be self-controlled and calculating. His penchant for violence, therefore, had to be discharged on a purely verbal level, appeased by exploding in every direction at once. The straddle was built like functional furniture into his thinking. He was honestly against the abuses of big business, but he was also sincerely against indiscriminate trust-busting; he was in favor of reform, but disliked the militant reformers. He wanted clean government and honest business, but he shamed as "muckrakers" those who exposed corrupt government and dishonest business. (Of course, he was all in favor of the muckrakers' revelations— but only if they were "absolutely true.") "We are neither for the rich man nor the poor man as such," he resounded in one of his typical sentences, "but for the upright man, rich or poor." Such equivocations are the life of practical politics, but while they often sound weak and halting in the mouths of the ordinary politician, Roosevelt had a way of giving them a fine aggressive surge.

Roosevelt had a certain breadth and cultivation that are rare among politicians. He read widely and enthusiastically, if not intensely, remembered much, wrote sharply at times and with a vivid flair for the concrete. He had generous enthusiasms. He invited Booker T. Washington to the White House, elevated

Holmes to the Supreme Court, and gave Edwin Arlington Robinson a political sinecure. Thoughtful and cultivated men found him charming, and it is hard to believe that this was merely because, as John Morley said, he was second in interest only to Niagara Falls among American natural phenomena. Yet those who knew him, from shrewd political associates like Root to men like Henry Adams, and John Hay and Cecil Spring Rice, refused to take him altogether seriously as a person. And rightly so, for anyone who today has the patience to plow through his collected writings will find there, despite an occasional insight and some ingratiating flashes of self-revelation, a tissue of philistine conventionalities, the intellectual fiber of a muscular and combative Polonius. There was something about him that was repelled by thoughtful skepticism, detachment, by any uncommon delicacy; probably it was this that caused him to brand Henry James and Henry Adams as "charming men but exceedingly undesirable companions for any man not of strong nature," and to balk at "the tone of satirical cynicism which they admired." His literary opinions, which he fancied to have weight and importance and which actually had some influence, were not only intolerably biased by his political sentiments but, for all his proclaimed robustiousness, extremely traditional and genteel. Zola, for example, disgusted him with his "conscientious descriptions of the unspeakable"; Tolstoi he disliked because he preached against both marriage and war, and *The Kreutzer Sonata* he considered a "filthy and repulsive book"; Dickens, who did not like America, was no gentleman; Gorki, who came to the United States with a woman who was not his legal wife, was personally immoral, like so many Continentals, and in politics a "fool academic revolutionist."

The role in which Roosevelt fancied himself was that of the moralist, and the real need in American public life, he told Lincoln Steffens, was "the *fundamental fight for morality*." Not long before leaving Washington he predicted to Ray Stannard Baker that economic questions—the tariff, currency, banks—would become increasingly important, but remarked that he was not interested in them. "My problems are moral problems, and my teaching has been plain morality." This was accurate enough; Roosevelt's chief contribution to the Progressive movement had been his homilies, but nothing was farther from his mind than to translate his moral judgments into social realities, and for the best of reasons: the fundamentally conservative nationalist goals of his politics were at cross-purposes with the things he found it expedient to say, and as long as his activity was limited to the verbal sphere the inconsistency was less apparent.

His mind, in a word, did not usually cut very deep. But he represented something that a great many Americans wanted. "Theodore Roosevelt," said La Follette caustically, "is the ablest living interpreter of what I would call the superficial public sentiment of a given time, and he is spontaneous in his reactions to it." What made him great, commented Medill McCormick, was that he understood the "psychology of the mutt." While Bryan had been able to do this only on a sectional basis, Roosevelt spoke the views of the middle classes of all parts of the country, and commanded the enthusiastic affection of people who had never walked behind a plow or raised a callus. He had a special sense for the realities they wished to avoid; with his uncanny instinct for impalpable falsehoods he articulated their fears in a string of plausible superficialities. The period of his ascendancy was a prosperous one, in which popular discontent lacked the sharp edge that it had had when Bryan rose to prominence. Although the middle classes, which contributed so much to the strength of progressivism, were troubled about the concentration of power in political and economic life and the persistence of corruption in government, it is doubtful that many middle-class men would have been more willing than Roosevelt to face the full implications of an attempt to unravel the structure of business power, with the attendant risk of upsetting a going concern. The general feeling was, as Roosevelt wrote Sir George Trevelyan in 1905, that "somehow or other we shall have to work out methods of controlling the big corporations *without* paralyzing the energies of the business community."

This sentence is characteristic of the essentially negative impulses behind Roosevelt's political beliefs. It was always: We shall have to do this in order to prevent that. Did he favor control of railroad rates more because he was moved to correct inequities in the existing tolls or because he was afraid of public ownership? Did he force the mine operators to make a small concession to their employees because he bled for the men who worked the mines or because he feared "socialistic action"? Did he advocate workmen's compensation laws because he had a vivid sense of the plight of the crippled wage earner or because he was afraid that Bryan would get some votes? "There were all kinds of things of which I was afraid at first," he had said of his boyhood, ". . . but by acting as if I was not afraid I gradually ceased to be afraid." But did he lose his fears, or merely succeed in suppressing them? Did he become a man who was not afraid, or merely a man who could act as though he was not afraid? His biographer Henry Pringle has pointed out how often he actually underwent attacks of anxiety. In his anxieties, in fact, and in the very negative and defensive quality of his progressivism, may be found one of the sources of his political strength. The frantic growth and rapid industrial expansion that filled America in his lifetime had heightened social tensions and left a legacy of bewilderment, anger, and fright, which had been suddenly precipitated by the depression of the nineties. His psychological function was to relieve these anxieties with a burst of hectic action and to discharge these fears by scolding authoritatively the demons that aroused them. Hardened and trained by a long fight with his own insecurity, he was the master therapist of the middle classes.

IV

Of Taft, whom he chose as his successor, Roosevelt said revealingly to Gilson Gardner: "It is true he has never originated anything that would savor of progressiveness, but he has been close enough to this Administration to know what it stands for." Taft, however, could not mold public opinion, nor run with the hare and hunt with the hounds in the Roosevelt manner. When the ex-President returned in 1910 from his self-imposed exile to Africa, he found the Republican insurgents, who had never broken so far out of line, growing bold enough to challenge Taft for control of the party. "The Administration," he complained to Nicholas Longworth, July 11, 1910, "has certainly wholly failed in keeping the party in substantial unity, and what I mind most is that the revolt is not merely among the party leaders, but among the masses of the people."[14]

Roosevelt was too young to cease to care about his reputation or to abandon political ambitions. With his customary quickness he perceived that the Progressive impulse had not yet reached its high-water mark. Starting with his famous "New Nationalism" speech of August, 1910, he began to present himself as a "new" political personality. The "New Nationalism" was a transparent amalgam of the old Roosevelt doctrines with some of the more challenging Progressive ideas. Democratic ends, Roosevelt proclaimed, must now be sought through Hamiltonian means. A strong, centralized state, extended governmental interference in economic life, freedom of politics from concern for special interests—these were to be the main lines of development. Specifically Roosevelt endorsed the initiative, referendum, and recall, popular election of Senators, and direct primaries. He shocked conservatives by assailing the federal judiciary for obstructing the popular will, and advocated that decisions of state courts nullifying social legislation should be subject to popular recall. He supported compensation laws, limitation of the hours of labor, a graduated income tax, inheritance taxes, physical evaluation of railroad properties to enforce "honest" capitalization, and government supervision of capitalization of all types of corporations in interstate commerce.

Democracy, Roosevelt proclaimed, must be economic, not merely political. And labor? He echoed Lincoln: "Labor is the superior of capital and deserves much the higher consideration." "I wish to see labor organizations powerful," he added. But in the language of the old Roosevelt he made it clear that as they became powerful they must, like the big corporations, accept regulation by the state.

Among these proposals there were only a few things that

[14] La Follette remarked in his *Autobiography* that the Progressive movement in the Republican party made greater headway in Taft's first two years than in Roosevelt's two terms. "This," he concluded, "was largely due to the fact that Taft's course was more direct, Roosevelt's devious."

Roosevelt had not endorsed before, and nothing for which others had not worked for at least ten years, but an appearance of newness was provided by shearing off some of the familiar Roosevelt equivocations and intensifying his paternalistic nationalism. Elihu Root found the new Roosevelt suspect: "I have no doubt he thinks he believes what he says, but he doesn't. He has merely picked up certain ideas which were at hand as one might pick up a poker or chair with which to strike." In a moment of candor Roosevelt himself declared that he was still working along familiar strategic lines. "What I have advocated," he said in 1910, ". . . is not wild radicalism. It is the highest and wisest kind of conservatism."[15]

Roosevelt's practical aims were probably centered at first on the election of 1916. Professor George Mowry suggests that he anticipated Republican defeat in 1912 and would have been happy to see Taft bear the brunt of it, leaving himself to come back to the White House at the head of a rejuvenated and reunited party in 1916, when he would be only fifty-eight. If these were his plans, he altered them as the Progressive movement came to the boiling point.

Robert M. La Follette, by virtue of his accomplishments in Wisconsin and in the Senate, seemed the natural leader of the Progressives as they rallied for the 1912 convention. Roosevelt himself, who had written privately in 1908 of "the La Follette type of fool radicalism," praised him in 1910 for having made of his home state "an experimental laboratory of wise governmental action in aid of social and economic justice." La Follette seemed to have an excellent chance of capturing the nomination if he could get Roosevelt's backing. He subsequently charged that he had had a definite promise from Roosevelt. Although proof has never been offered, this much is certain: Roosevelt did at first give the Progressive leader informal encouragement, but withheld positive public endorsement and at length sapped the vitality of the La Follette movement by refusing to disavow his own candidacy. La

[15] On Roosevelt's Confession of Faith before the 1912 Progressive convention Frank Munsey made the charming comment: "While splendidly progressive it is, at the same time, amply conservative and sound."

Follette's friends grew indignant. "You would laugh if you were in this country now," wrote Brand Whitlock to a friend abroad, December 5, 1911, "and were to see how the standpatters are trying to bring [Roosevelt] out as a candidate for President again, in order to head off La Follette, who is a very dangerous antagonist to Taft." "The Colonel," Lincoln Steffens reported a few weeks later, "is mussing up the whole Progressive movement with his 'To be or not to be.' "

Roosevelt's seeming indecision helped to strangle the La Follette boom. By January, 1912, outstanding Progressives like the Pinchots and Medill McCormick had switched to Roosevelt. In February, Fighting Bob, ill, harassed, and worried, suffered a momentary breakdown. Soon afterward, in response to a carefully prearranged "solicitation" by seven Progressive Governors, the ex-President threw his hat in the ring and the La Follette boom collapsed entirely. One of the most interesting comments on the mentality of the Progressives is the fact that most of them turned to Roosevelt not only without resentment but enthusiastically, and when he bolted the Republican convention to form a third party, followed him with a feeling of fervor and dedication that had not been seen since 1896. As William Allen White later recalled, "Roosevelt bit me and I went mad."[16]

Having aroused the hopes of the Progressives and having sidetracked their most effective leader, Roosevelt went on to use their movement for the purposes of finance capital. One of several practical advantages that Roosevelt had over La Follette was his ability to command the support of men of great wealth. Most important among these was George W. Perkins, ex-partner in the House of Morgan, director of International Harvester, and organizer of trusts. Perkins belonged to that wing of business which was aroused by Taft's more vigorous antitrust policy, especially by the prosecution of so vital a Morgan concern as the United States Steel

[16] It is interesting that as late as October 27, 1911 Roosevelt could have written to Hiram Johnson: "I have no cause to think at the moment that there is any real or widely extended liking for or trust in me among the masses of the people." Events proved him wrong, but it may be that this projection of dislike and distrust upon the people represented the way he imagined they might be expected to feel about him.

Corporation.[17] He was among those who therefore preferred Roosevelt to Taft or La Follette; this preference was shared by Frank A. Munsey, the influential publisher, a large stockholder in United States Steel. Perkins and Munsey pressed Roosevelt to run, later supplied, according to the revelations of the Clapp Committee, over $500 thousand to his campaign, and spent even larger sums in indirect support. When Roosevelt failed to win the Republican nomination, they spurred him on to form a new party, Munsey with the grand promise: "My fortune, my magazines, my newspapers are with you." To the bitter disappointment of Progressives like Amos Pinchot, Perkins forced upon the Progressive platform a plank stating the Perkins-Roosevelt approach to the trust problem.[18]

The strong showing of the Progressives in the election—Roosevelt ran second to Wilson and almost 700,000 votes ahead of Taft—promised much for the future. But Roosevelt soon abandoned the movement. It would be impossible, he asserted, to hold the party together; there were "no loaves and fishes." Four years later when a forlorn group of Progressives again tendered him a nomination, he spurned it and tossed them a final insult by suggesting that they name his friend Henry Cabot Lodge, whose principles, if any, were thoroughly reactionary.

Roosevelt's attempt to promote Lodge was prompted by the fact that he had lost interest in the domestic aspects of the Progressive movement. War was now raging in Europe, and the colonel had little regard for the notions of foreign policy that prevailed among

[17] In an address on "The Sherman Law," delivered to the Economic Club of Philadelphia in 1915, Perkins scourged Taft bitterly for having betrayed the moderate plank on trusts prepared by Roosevelt for Taft's 1908 campaign, and expounded the Roosevelt-Perkins approach to the trust question.

[18] When Pinchot complained to Roosevelt about Perkins' influence in the party, Roosevelt assured him that the matter of the trust plank was "utterly unimportant" and attributed the Progressive party's defeat to its being "too radical." At last Pinchot aired in public the rift in the party over Perkins and blamed Roosevelt for the collapse of the movement. "When I spoke of the Progressive party," replied Roosevelt to Pinchot, "as having a lunatic fringe, I specifically had you in mind."

the more sentimental adherents of the third party. As he wrote to Lodge in the spring of 1917, the typical American Progressive was like his liberal brother in England—"an utterly hopeless nuisance because of his incredible silliness in foreign affairs."

Although in nominal retirement at the outbreak of the World War, Roosevelt was still in search of excitement. At first he seems to have been torn between the impulses of the hardened realist who could look upon the affairs of nations with detachment, and those of the strategist and man of action who would welcome an opportunity to engage the nation's power and see some fighting. His initial remarks on the war, although calm and impartial, were more friendly to Germany than prevailing opinion in the United States. Concerning the invasion of Belgium, which shocked so many Americans, he patiently explained that "When giants are engaged in a death wrestle, as they reel to and fro they are certain to trample on whomever gets in the way of either of the huge straining combatants." Disaster would have befallen Germany if she had not acted so resolutely in Belgium. The Germans had proved themselves "a stern, virile, and masterful people." The sole policy of the United States should be to protect her own interests and "remain entirely neutral."

As late as October 11, 1914, Roosevelt voiced a "thrill of admiration for the stern courage and lofty disinterestedness which this great crisis laid bare" in the souls of the German people, and hoped that the American public would show similar qualities should the need arise. To cripple Germany or reduce her to impotence, he warned, would be "a disaster to mankind."

Yet the preceding August Roosevelt had written to Stewart Edward White that if Germany should win, "it would be only a matter of a very few years before we should have to fight her," adding that he would consider it "quite on the cards to see Germany and Japan cynically forget the past and join together against the United States and any other power that stood in their way." By early 1915 this point of view had made its way into his public statements as he fulminated against Wilson for "supine inaction"—and for failing to help the Belgians! Thenceforth he devoted himself to baiting pacifists and scolding at Wilson's neu-

trality policies. The American people themselves, he once complained to Lodge, "are cold; they have been educated by this
infernal peace propaganda of the last ten years into an attitude of
sluggishness and timidity."

Long before the United States entered the war, Roosevelt was
thinking of participating. An army officer visiting him at Oyster
Bay in January, 1915, found him pacing the floor, protesting
American inaction, asserting his eagerness to fight. The boyish
demand for excitement—"you must always remember," Spring
Rice had written a decade earlier, "that the President is about
six"—was as strong in him as ever. He applied to the War
Department for permission to let him raise a division, and, antici-
pating rejection, told Ambassador Jusserand that he would lead
an American division to France if the French would pay for it.
Wilson's refusal to commission him brought on a new fit of rage.
Wilson was "purely a demagogue," "a doctrinaire," "an utterly
selfish and cold-blooded politician always."

But the last exploit was denied him. Ravaged by the strenuous
life, saddened by the loss of his son Quentin at the front, he grew
suddenly old and became ill. Lodge journeyed to his bedside and
the two schemed to spike Wilson's League of Nations. On January
6, 1919, Roosevelt died of a coronary embolism.

HOWARD K. BEALE

✪

Theodore Roosevelt and the
Rise of America to World Power

What . . . can one say of Theodore Roosevelt's role in international relations?

It is clear that his comprehension of the problems was extraordinary, and his ability in dealing with them was superior to that of most Presidents and Secretaries of State. He perceived the growing interdependence of the world and the intricate involvement of America in that more closely-knit world. He comprehended, for instance, the rivalries of Britain and Germany and of Germany and France and the threat that both constituted to the peace of the world. He early grasped the importance of the Pacific and the Far East. In regard to many details of his universe, he had unusual understanding. Thus his characterizations of the Kaiser were uncannily perceptive. His comprehension of the importance of helping a rival to save face when discomfited, and his ability to separate the nonessential from the important in international relations made him a skilled diplomatist. At his best, he could analyze problems and understand his opponents' motives with surprising perspicacity.

Many of his insights were prophetic. In reading his letters, one

Reprinted from Howard K. Beale, *Theodore Roosevelt and the Rise of America to World Power* (Baltimore: The Johns Hopkins Press, 1956), pp. 383–394. Reprinted by permission of the publisher.

155

is startled by the number of times he foresaw the future and its problems. Russian revolution he prognosticated and often talked about, as early as the nineties; and, when the third revolution in twelve years put the Bolsheviki into power, he wrote an article that showed extraordinary understanding of its background, in which he tried to see that in some sense what had happened might under Russian conditions be good for Russia.[1]

Then, too, Roosevelt saw world events and policies in terms of power. He was intrigued with power, with the problems of power, and with rivalries for power. In this, too, he was prophetic. In his day many of those that were urging imperialist and expansionist policies were thinking in terms of economic factors, and many opponents of imperialism were writing in terms of economic argument. A succeeding generation of historians and political scientists was to analyze the history of the foreign policy of Roosevelt's time with primary emphasis on economic motives and forces until the rise of the totalitarian dictatorships of Hitler and Stalin was to shock them into re-evaluations that brought recognition of the importance in human history of the urge to power. Charles Beard revised his economic interpretation to give the political man and the military man an important place beside the economic man. Indeed, in the end, he seems to have wondered whether the economic motivation that had dominated the making of history in the eighteenth and nineteenth centuries operated in the same manner in the mid-twentieth-century world. In Hans Morgenthau and others at the mid-century a preoccupation with power politics and a world struggle for political and military power has replaced Reinsch's and Hobson's and, for that matter, Lenin's economic doctrine of imperialism expounded in the day when Roosevelt was acting an imperial role. Yet even in that day Roosevelt, like Bismarck before him but unlike many of his American contemporaries, thought more in terms of power than of economics, though he realized that the two were interrelated. This concern of Roosevelt's with power relationships in international affairs was as

[1] "The Romanoff Scylla and the Bolshevist Charybdis," *Metropolitan*, XLIX (December 1918), 66–67.

noteworthy in his day as was his prevision of America's involvement in the world.

About the future of the British Empire, too, he showed prescience; he often talked about and deplored, though he did not want to face, the decline of British power. Many of the Roosevelt circle felt that England's power was doomed. "England is sad—to me very sad," Adams had written Lodge in 1900. "Like you I hope she may revive, but I admit my hope is faint. The current is flowing away from her."[2] "I do not apprehend any sudden or violent change," Adams continued, "but I fancy England will grow gradually more and more sluggish, until, at length, after our day, she will drop out of the strenuous competition of the new world which is forming." "What you tell me about England's decay," Roosevelt himself wrote Speck von Sternburg, "makes me feel rather sad, but it is in exact accord with my own observations and with what I hear from other sources."[3] "It certainly does seem to me that England is on the downgrade," he observed in 1901. "The English-speaking race shares with the Slav the future."[4] The structure of the British Empire, he lamented to another friend in the same year, is unwieldy. "She is so spread out that I think it will be very difficult to make a real and permanently workable imperial federation."[5] Yet for all his accurate prognostication of Britain's future he acted on his hopes about Britain rather than his sounder forebodings, and hence he miscalculated in his policies.

Roosevelt understood, as many people did not, the important effect of internal policies and domestic events upon the foreign policies of the various countries. Hence he was concerned about controlling China's internal affairs and thought the work of the missionaries there important because "it tends to avert revolutionary disturbances in China."[6] Hence, too, with the aid of Meyer,

[2] Brooks Adams to Henry Cabot Lodge, October 14, 1900, Lodge MSS.

[3] T.R. to Hermann Speck von Sternburg, October 11, 1901, T.R. MSS. See also T.R. to Cecil Spring Rice, May 29, 1897; to Anna Roosevelt Cowles, December 17, 1899, T.R. MSS.

[4] T.R. to George Ferdinand Becker, July 8, 1901, T.R. MSS. See also T.R. to C. Spring Rice, August 11, 1899, T.R. MSS.

[5] T.R. to G. F. Becker, July 8, 1901, T.R. MSS.

[6] T.R. to Lyman Abbott, September 7, 1908, T.R. MSS.

and Spring Rice, he watched events in Russia as revolution threatened. He came to understand that Russia's foreign policy depended on whether Witte was in power, or Kuropatkin and Bezobrazov and their palace clique gained control. And he learned always to qualify predictions about Russia's foreign policy with a question about internal disorder. His distrust of Germany's form of government and social structure contributed to his distrust of that country's foreign policy.

In spite of Roosevelt's vigorous talk, his reputation for brandishing the big stick, his determination to have a large navy so that he could support whatever policy he chose to pursue, and his undeserved reputation for making snap judgments, Roosevelt as President did not jump into international situations excitedly. He wished to be strong enough to take any action he might choose, but then, being strong, he chose his actions with caution. Contrary to the myth that has grown up about him, in international crises he was calm and careful in his decisions. He acted only after thought about all the consequences of action. Furthermore, he paid no heed to rumors and claims of the sort that were always exciting the Kaiser. "I am always being told," he wrote William, "of Japanese or German or English spies inspecting the most unlikely places—the Moro Castle at Havana, for instance, or some equally antiquated or indefensible fort; and now and then I learn of a high official in some West Indian island or South American republic who has been thrown into a fever by the (wholly imaginary) information that an agent of mine has been secretly inspecting his dominions." "I have no time to devote to thinking of fables of this kind," he protested; "I am far too much occupied with real affairs, both foreign and domestic. . . . No such tale . . . will ever cause me more than good-natured amusement."[7]

Furthermore, Roosevelt had one firm conviction that other nations and the government of his own country have often disregarded. He was unalterably opposed to bluffing, to making threats that he did not intend to back up. At times he took firm stands against other nations, but when he did he stood ready to make good with military force. One reason for his insistence upon a

[7] T.R. to William II, January 8, 1907, T.R. MSS.

large navy was that he wished to be in a position to support with action any threat he felt it important to make in pursuing America's role as a world power. Speak courteously but firmly, and then stand ready to support your words in action was his formula. Confidential records today reveal questions about plans for military or naval action in cases where the public did not know any was contemplated, because polite but firm words accomplished his purpose without his having to go to the public for support for the use of force. Roosevelt always believed that speaking softly sufficed because he carried a big stick, because it was known that *he* always stood ready to back words with deeds.

It was a short step from this determination not to take stands that could not be backed by force to a desire for sufficient power to be able to do as he pleased without restraint. Roosevelt admired the strong men of history—Frederick the Great, Napoleon, Bismarck, the elder von Moltke. At times he envied autocratic rulers their power. His strong conviction that he and his country acted from righteous motives made him oppose any international restraints upon his own power. His conviction that he could have handled his country's foreign policy more wisely had he not been restrained by selfish and weak-kneed elements in the population or in the Senate explains his often carrying out policies unbeknown to the public where he felt he could later win the public to support what he had done. His belief that he could handle foreign relations better by direct, secret personal relations with other rulers than through the normal channels of diplomatic negotiations prompted him to the bypassing of the State Department and to the personal diplomacy that characterized some of his most important foreign ventures. His aristocratic background, his established social status, his economic security gave him a freedom from social and political pressures that few Presidents and Secretaries of State have enjoyed, that in some respects resembled the freedom from restraint enjoyed for very different reasons by mid-twentieth-century totalitarian rulers at the head of one-party dictatorships.

In other hands his ability, his understanding of international problems, his interest in power, his desire to be strong enough to settle questions by might, his secret, highly personal handling of foreign affairs might have become dangerous to democracy and to the peace of the world. What was it that restrained Roosevelt and prevented his becoming dangerous? The democratic process with the chance to criticize government and to retire a leader from public office in the next election provides, of course, an important safeguard that is nonetheless somewhat offset by the President's power to put the country into war situations where the people would have to support the President however much they deplored his action. Roosevelt's own personal qualities, however, also prevented his use of power from becoming the threat the same power might have been in other hands. In part, Roosevelt was held back by a deep-seated concern about the well-being of his country, and in part by his cautious middle-of-the-road approach to all questions. Furthermore, to a considerable extent, it was the same American aristocratic background that gave him independence and freedom from ordinary social pressures that also restrained him. This background had given him a keen sense of the dignity of man and of the worth of the individual that was never acquired by the mid-century totalitarian rulers with the power he sometimes aspired to. His background, too, had given him a sense of social responsibility and above all an attitude of noblesse oblige that dominated him always. Too, he believed thoroughly in America and hence respected the American democratic tradition. And as part of that democratic tradition he respected public opinion. Though he was often frustrated by the inability or unwillingness of the public to see things as he did, still he conceived his role as a democratic head of state to be one of leading public opinion where he could, and yielding where he could not persuade until such time when able leadership like his would be able to persuade. Even in his secret handling of foreign affairs he sometimes refrained from actions he deemed wise, such as formally joining the Anglo-Japanese Alliance, when he felt he would not be able to carry public opinion with him when he made his action known. His belief that progress could be achieved by persuading people through democratic processes was in itself part of the Western world's nineteenth-century democratic tradition, and at the same time an effective restraint upon the abuse of power.

Indeed, he believed that popular support was as necessary as executive firmness and armed might. Roosevelt had no intention of being left unable to support strong words in foreign policy because the people would not back him. Better no strong words than strong words the people would not stand behind. A foreign policy that the voters would not approve in deeds was as bad as bluffing about something the executive lacked the intention or the power to carry out. Roosevelt never forgot that public opinion was important to successful foreign policy. Hence he devoted much time to creating public support for his policies. He was successful in stimulating in many of the people pride in the new imperial role he envisaged for America. He prepared the way for future comprehension of America's involvement in world affairs. But it was difficult to carry public opinion with him in support of the world role he felt America should play. Just before the end of his Presidency he listed Caribbean countries where he had interfered "for the immeasurable betterment of the people." "I would have interfered . . . [in several others]," he said, "simply in the interest of civilization, if I could have waked up our people so that they would back a reasonable and intelligent foreign policy which should put a stop to crying disorders at our very doors." "Our prime necessity," he declared, "is that public opinion should be properly educated."[8] "This people of ours," he wrote on another occasion, "simply does not understand how things are outside our own boundaries. Of course I do not desire to act unless I can get the bulk of our people to understand the situation and to back up the action; and to do that I have got to get the facts vividly before them. . . . The worst of it is that the educated northeasterners are not merely blind, but often malevolently blind, to what goes on."[9]

In his more mature years, Roosevelt became troubled over the relation of democracy to empire. How a democracy was to rule colonial peoples under democratic machinery was a problem that worried him as he gained experience. The colonials he felt were

[8] T.R. to William Bayard Hale, December 3, 1908, T.R. MSS.
[9] T.R. to Sir Harry H. Johnston, December 4, 1908, T.R. MSS.

not ready for democratic forms of government and so he believed
rule by a great power benefited them. But could the imperial power
itself maintain democracy at home and at the same time rule a
colonial empire? "The problem of the control of thickly peopled
tropical regions by self-governing northern democracies is very
intricate," he wrote in 1908. "A legislative body, most of the
members of which are elected by constituencies that in the nature
of things can know nothing whatever of the totally different conditions of India, or the Philippines, or Egypt, or Cuba, does not offer
the best material for making a success of such government."[10]
(James Bryce had seen this problem in the 1890's and had
sounded warnings to American imperialists.[11]) The weakness of
British policy in Egypt and India that he deplored in 1910 he
ascribed to this dilemma of democratic rule over empire. "I don't
believe for a moment," he conceded, "that . . . the English
attitude in Egypt is any worse than we would take, if at this time
we had [as England does under the Liberals] what the *Evening
Post* desires, a mixture of mugwumps, ultra peace advocates and
maudlin, hysterical sentimentalists, plus Bryanites to dominate our
foreign affairs. But it certainly makes the English look flabby."[12]
Because of this dilemma created by imperial rule through democratic parliaments, he came to have serious doubts about our
keeping the Philippines that he had once worked so hard to get and
keep. "The Philippines present . . . a very hard problem," he
had concluded as early as 1907, "because we must consider it in
connection with the country's needs and ideas also, and with what
it is reasonable to expect as a permanent policy of this country
with its alternating system of party control." "I am perfectly sure
that the best thing for the Philippines would be to have a succession of Tafts administer them for the next century," he told a
leading churchman, but he added, "I am not sure, either that under
changing administrations we would get a succession of Tafts, nor
yet that our people will patiently submit, as in my judgment they

[10] T.R. to Whitelaw Reid, September 3, 1908, T.R. MSS.
[11] James Bryce, "The Policy of Annexation for America," *Forum* XXIV
(December 1897), 388, 391–392.
[12] T.R. to Henry White, April 2 [1910], White MSS.

ought to, to doing an onerous duty for which they will get no thanks and no material reward; while from a military standpoint the Philippines form our heel of Achilles."[13]

In the end, for all his activity, his tremendous influence on foreign policy, his surprising insights and prophecies, Roosevelt failed in his most important objectives. He strove to create a stable world in which the great civilized nations would refrain from war upon one another. Yet in less than a decade after his much-heralded success at Portsmouth and his earnest efforts at Algeciras and The Hague, these "civilized" powers were at each other's throats in a gigantic struggle that was to destroy much of what he believed in and to prepare the way for a second world war that was to destroy much more. By balancing Russia against Japan in Manchuria and North China, without letting either one get strong enough to dominate, he believed he was creating a stable Far East open to the trade of all nations. Yet within three years of the Portsmouth Conference the two powers had combined to exclude all other imperial nations. He hoped he had created stability in China by preventing its partition and setting up large-power control over that nation. Yet during much of the next generation China was torn by internal strife, and forty years after he left the White House China was to fall under domination by Russia that was to exclude all the powers except Russia. By building American naval power he planned to provide a safe future for his country, since no nation would dare attack her. Yet thirty years after his death, with military might such as his wildest dreams could not have pictured, and with a navy more powerful than any other, his country had suffered losses in battle as great as ever before in its history and was living armed to the teeth in dread of destruction of her cities in an atomic war. He thought he had prepared the way for a century of the "English-speaking" man, and yet by the middle of that century Britain had lost much of her empire and was struggling desperately for survival. By joining forces with British imperialism, he imagined he was assuring the orderly government of colonial areas that domination of the "civilized" imperial powers would create. By the mid-century, nationalism among

[13] T.R. to Silas McBee, August 27, 1907, T.R. MSS.

colonial peoples had led to uprisings all over the world of a sort that military might and superior master races could not prevent or quell. America's tying herself to British imperialism had left her holding the bag and paying the price of liquidating, everywhere outside the Western Hemisphere, the imperialism Roosevelt had helped create. America was left fighting a costly rear-guard retreat in defense not only of British, but of Dutch and French empires in opposition to the aspirations for freedom that America would once have befriended. Instead of helping Britain maintain the balance of power in the *world* as Britain had more than once done on the Continent of Europe, the United States found itself the only remaining nation with power to stand up on one side of a balance that was precarious. Roosevelt's theory of saving democracy from autocracy by armed might had been strenuously pursued for forty years with the result that more and more of the free world had fallen under totalitarianism.

What had happened? Roosevelt and his friends had made several miscalculations. They had failed really to anticipate and take into account the rapid decline of Britain to whom they had tied America's fate, for while recognizing her decline and fore-seeing Russia's growing power, they had still believed Britain's pre-eminence would last out the twentieth century. They had seen that, without becoming "civilized," people could not produce compli-cated weapons of modern warfare, but they had overlooked the fact that, without becoming civilized in their terms, colonial peoples spurred by nationalism could do great damage to the imperial powers Roosevelt counted on to control them. In under-estimating the potentialities of China and failing to understand the aspirations of a New China, Roosevelt had inaugurated a Chinese policy disastrous for the future. That policy, continued by his successors, was ultimately to help lead China from initial friendli-ness toward America into communism, in the hope that the New China would obtain from communism the aid and sympathy America and the Western powers had refused it. Roosevelt and his friends had failed to comprehend modern war and the potentiali-ties of technology for destructiveness. They had not forecast the total nature of modern war. They had placed faith in a balance of power that could never be kept in balance. They had not divined that seeking safety through being more powerfully armed than rivals would only stimulate an armaments race in which no nation ever kept far enough ahead of its opponents to feel secure. They had refused to take seriously other methods than armed force in establishing international stability. In underestimating the destructiveness of modern war, they had overlooked the grim necessity of finding methods of organizing the world's will to peace so that there would be no war.

But could these factors have been foreseen? The answer is, of course, that many people did foretell them and did sound warning. There were Americans who felt that Roosevelt should have encouraged and befriended the forces of nationalism and freedom in China that instead he threatened to send an invading army to put down. Roosevelt himself saw dangers in China's developing modern techniques without accompanying changes in her values. "If the advantage to us is great of a China open to commerce," he warned, "the danger to us and to her is infinitely greater of a China enriched and strengthened by the material advantages we have to offer, but uncontrolled in the use of them by any clear understanding, much less any full acceptance, of the mental and moral forces which have generated and in large measure govern our political and social action." So far so good. What Roosevelt failed to see, in his contemptuous attitude toward the Chinese, was that neither America nor any other outside power could impose these moral and mental processes on China, but that she must come through her own development to new values in keeping with her own culture and history. There were those who saw that no stable situation in the Far East could come from a peace at Portsmouth drawn up for China by Russia and Japan. Such men felt that China should have been at the peace conference and that Roosevelt lost at Portsmouth a chance to protect China against both aggressors, and to win her friendship besides. In the field of colonialism, too, Bryce warned early that American institutions were "quite unsuited to the government of dependencies," where the population consisted of "elements utterly unequal and dissimilar."[14]

[14] Bryce, "The Policy of Annexation for America," pp. 391–392.

In 1907 Carnegie had protested against Roosevelt's easy justifi-
cation of wars that were "righteous." "Disputants," warned Carnegie, "are both seeking 'Righteousness,' both feel themselves
struggling for what is just." "Who is to decide?" he asked the
President. "No one; according to you they must then go to war to
decide not what is 'right' but who is *strong*."[15]

Roosevelt's old professor of anatomy at Harvard, too, foresaw
some of the effects of Rooseveltian policy. The year after the
Spanish War, William James protested: "We gave the fighting
instinct and the passion of mastery their outing . . . because we
thought that . . . we could resume our permanent ideals and
character when the fighting fit was done. We now see how we
reckoned without our host. We see . . . what an absolute sav-
age . . . the passion of military conquest always is, and how the
only safeguard against the crimes to which it will infallibly drag the
nation that gives way to it is to keep it chained forever. . . .
First, the war fever; and then the pride which always refuses to
back down when under fire. But these are passions that interfere
with the reasonable settlement of any affair; . . . Our duty and
our destiny call, and civilization must go on! Could there be a
more damning indictment of that whole bloated idol termed
'modern civilization' than this amounts to? Civilization is, then, the
big, hollow, resounding, corrupting, sophisticating, confusing tor-
rent of mere brutal momentum and irrationality that brings forth
fruits like this!"[16] Unlike William James, Roosevelt and his
friends assumed that economic power, the preservation of order,
and military might constituted the test of civilization.

Whatever mistakes Roosevelt made that led to ultimate catastrophe for the policies he pursued, they were not merely his
personal mistakes. They were the mistakes of a considerable
segment of the American people that gloried in his temporary
successes. One important element of his strength was that in so
many respects, among them the urge for power and the sense of

[15] Andrew Carnegie to T.R., April 10, 1907, T.R. MSS.
[16] William James to the *Boston Evening Transcript*, March 1, 1899, in
Ralph Barton Perry, *The Thought and Character of William James*, pp.
245–246.

superiority over other people, Roosevelt merely symbolized and gave voice to widespread American attitudes. Not only conservative Republicans, but Progressives were imperialists. Nor did Bryan and Wilson materially change the pattern of American expansionism when they succeeded Taft and Roosevelt. The men who had misgivings, of whom there were many, were not in the strategic positions of power.

So we return to the question with which we started. To what extent did Roosevelt and his fellow expansionists and fellow imperialists influence foreign policy? Concerned as they were, vigorous and active as they were in the key positions they occupied, were they able to direct foreign policy? Or was foreign policy determined by forces that would have sent America down the road of imperialism had these men never lived, or had their high positions in government been occupied by men as much against as they were for expansion and empire? Were they conscious creators of America's world power or were they merely driven on into expansion by a sort of political atavism.[17] Or were Roosevelt and his friends perchance the catalysts that aided the operation of forces they did not create? Or was America's role determined for her by other nations whose policies she could not control but whose actions determined her own? To what extent did the leaders choose at all? One can perhaps only say that, strategically located as they were in positions of power, and vigorous and able, they had as much influence on the course of events as men ever do and more than at many times or in many places men have succeeded in exerting.

Finally, to the extent that Roosevelt did choose, what was the effect of his choice between imperialism and its alternatives? One comes away from the study with admiration for Roosevelt's ability, his energy, and his devotion to his country's interests as he saw them, but with a sense of tragedy that his abilities were turned toward imperialism and an urge for power, which were to have

---

[17] Joseph A. Schumpeter leaned to this interpretation of early twentieth-century expansionism in a little volume he wrote in 1919. *Zur Sociologie der Imperialismen* (1919), translated into English in 1951 by Heinz Norden under the title *Imperialism and Social Class.*

consequences so serious for the future. Perhaps Roosevelt and his friends could not have led America along a different path. Insofar, however, as they did influence America's course, they influenced it in a direction that by the mid-century was to bring her face to face with grave dangers. Roosevelt probably had as much ability and handled foreign policy as well as any other statesman of his day. The trouble lay not in his abilities, but in his values and in the setting in which he worked, whether from choice or from necessity.

★

The Republican Roosevelt

So much of Theodore Roosevelt is comfortably familiar. There are the teeth, the famous intensity, the nervous grimace, impelling leadership, physical courage, moral fervor—sometimes frenzy. There is the falsetto exhorting the troops at the base of the San Juan ridge: "Gentlemen, the Almighty God and the Just Cause are with you. Gentlemen, CHARGE!" They did, of course, and they conquered. There are the busted trusts, the outdoor life, the nature fakirs, simplified spelling, rivers discovered, lions felled. There is the host of Armageddon dividing the Republican party with revivalist abandon. Like pages out of G. A. Henty—vivid, seemingly ingenuous. But Henty is now little reopened, and Roosevelt is more often remembered than reread.

This is regrettable. Roosevelt's recently published letters, like his long-available public papers, reveal a broadly roaming and occasionally penetrating intelligence, an incomparable energy, a vastly entertaining and remarkably knowledgeable Republican politician. Whether or not he was a great man is unimportant. It is enough that the contributions he made to American life, particularly public life, and the ways in which he made them were often magnificent.

Because in mid-century the spirit of Roosevelt's time has be-

Reprinted by permission of the publishers from John Morton Blum, *The Republican Roosevelt* (Cambridge, Mass.: Harvard University Press). Copyright, 1954, by the President and Fellows of Harvard College.

come foreign, the man appears often in caricature. He should be seen against the background of the confidence he shared and fed—the belief that hard work was in itself a good thing, that whatever this hard work did was right; the conviction that the world had since the beginning of time progressed, so that men lived in the best of all possible worlds. From Roosevelt the laborers in this vineyard drew inspiration, for he showed them new tasks for active hands. This, Stuart Sherman, that clement critic of the age of confidence, understood. Disapproving as he did of many of Roosevelt's policies, he nevertheless admired the vitality whose example more than that of any other man led from the brokerages a generation of watchers in the woods and at the polls.

With Roosevelt, it is true, this generation embarked again and again on crusades of relative insignificance or of dubious merit. But they embarked. Again and again Roosevelt himself achieved triumphs which, however brilliant at the moment, afforded only ephemeral gain. But he achieved. Much in his career seems in retrospect scarcely worth the strong emotions and heated righteousness with which his speeches and letters were filled. But even when his just causes were narrowly partisan, he felt strongly. Today's insouciant critics, unlike Sherman, censure as quixotic adolescence or dangerous diversion the intensity of act and feeling they no longer share. Even they, however, do not find it dull.

Nor need they find it empty. Misplaced it sometimes was, and more often unimportant. But something beside remains. The war with Spain, for one thing, Roosevelt's finest hour, for all its unhappy aspects was a momentous affair. It was for him a device by which the United States assumed, at last, its proper place as a responsible world power. If he swaggered too much, he also foresaw, welcomed, and later developed the nation's role in maintaining international stability and promoting international justice. Concomitantly he championed not only military and naval preparedness but also the physical development of the country and the moral development of its people which constituted the resources for national greatness. And this also he did with confidence and by example. Before the coming of two wars, he hastened to volunteer. This was not sheer bellicosity. Roosevelt looked upon military service as he looked upon public service—as the proper obligation of citizenship. The office did not have to seek the man.

If his just causes were sometimes not so just, his felt need so to define them was healthy. He had witnessed in his lifetime, as Americans only recently again have witnessed, the bankruptcy of public policy produced by callous disregard of morality. Honesty, he knew, was always an issue. Corrupt officials, like cruel forces of occupation, he found intolerable. Unlike most of the college breed of his generation, he did not choose to immunize himself. Mastering the tactics of the enemy, infiltrating their lines, in time occupying their strongholds, he ruled according to improved standards the domains they had held. As his motion was forceful, so his standards were high. In that combination Roosevelt had faith. By positive government he sought to promote national strength and to assure to each individual unfettered opportunity for realizing the dignity and the satisfactions of honest work. Whatever his shortcomings, his habit of action had enduring value. He made a virtue of dutiful vitality applied in an age of vigor and confidence. In a more troubled time the world learns painfully again the need for deciding firmly what is right and laboring assiduously to achieve it.

Roosevelt labored by his own choice as a politician. His decision to do so took courage, for his choice, when he made it, was disreputable. If he was, perhaps, called to politics by a craving for power, he needed nevertheless not only courage but also stamina to discipline that craving, to manage himself so that he could earn the chance to manage other men. This demanded what he called character, a splendid word which he never fully defined but never hesitated to use. Selecting a profession that satisfied his temperament, pursuing it with fortitude, he brought to it increasingly a perceptive practicability about the ways of gaining and utilizing high public office. Durable and sinewy were the roots of his career.

They had to be, for the roots of his convictions were also tough. From his patrician family, from his high-Victorian God, from Harvard, for which he had always a tender regard, from nature— raw on Western ranges or intellectualized in evolutionist tracts— from novels of romance and novels of realism, from history he read and history he wrote, he abstracted early in life principles of behavior which he honored to his death. He did not always abide by them. No politician could have. But he did attempt to abide, refusing either to abandon what he considered right or to let that consideration immobilize him. To his generation, as he would himself have said, he proved his truth by his endeavor.

He also demonstrated in a timeless way how Presidents succeed. The organization of his party, he knew, would determine his future; within the party, furthermore, the large decisions about the direction of public policy had to be made. A brilliant leader, he dominated his party, strengthening it as he worked. At the same time, if he did not dominate his constituents, he at least excited them and by pressure and persuasion won most of them to vote his way. So also with Congress. By negotiation, adjustment, discipline, and daring, he arranged that the laws he wanted most were passed. Because these operations took shape over long periods, only intimate examination of Roosevelt's professional performance reveals the joy and rigor in his relations, at once intuitive and controlled, with party, people, and Congress. Here was a rival for Mark Hanna, William Jennings Bryan, Nelson Aldrich; here a President who by tactics still significant resolved the persistent problems of his office; here a master among men who make things political work, make hustings howl with pleasure, conventions bow, and caucuses concede. Apart from anything Roosevelt attained, this virtuosity compels attention.

Roosevelt's proficiency in the processes of politics, administration, and legislation stamped him as a professional. Resting as it did on his unprotesting acceptance of established and relatively rigid political structures, this proficiency along with other qualities of mind and manner also suggested his affinity to latter-day conservatism. To be sure, Roosevelt was not a simple apologist for that familiar American conservative libation composed in equal parts of Herbert Spencer, Horatio Alger, and a protective tariff. Yet liberal historians—among many others Vernon Parrington, Henry Pringle, Arthur Schlesinger, Jr., and Daniel Aaaron—have quite justly cashiered him from their serried champions of embattled workingmen and farmers. He was never a Jeffersonian. This helps to place him. Furthermore, although there was not in

Roosevelt's life the stuff of a systematic philosophy of conservatism, in this country, in this century, perhaps, such a philosophy has not been systematic; certainly it has emanated from no one man, no Burke or Alexander Hamilton. And in Roosevelt's purposes and practices there appeared some attributes by and large common among those of his contemporaries whom liberals judged conservative.

These attributes can be enumerated. His preoccupation with the processes rather than the ends of government suggested that he considered democracy primarily a way of living. Valuing the institutions, forged in history, that mapped and stablized this way, he endeavored to preserve them. But perservation, he realized, depended upon change. "The only true conservative," he told a fellow Progressive, "is the man who resolutely sets his face toward the future." So he believed in change, but gradual change—change within established institutions, change obtained by adapting, managing, administering, change "on suspicion." This was not political science but engineering, development by cut and test. There were requisites and rules for this development. It had to be directed from a position of power by men who appreciated what was and what had been. They had to be informed and, much more difficult, to be moral. Their information they could best obtain from successful operators in the field, ordinarily in Roosevelt's day businessmen, lawyers, and financiers of parts and prescience. Their morality had primarily to come from character, ordinarily in Roosevelt's view a product of generations of good breeding or long seasons of hard work.

An institutionalist, a gradualist, a moralist, from the position he attained he ruled strongly and quite well. Learning the while, he developed large plans for the uses of power. These had one common, revealing objective: stability. The exercise of power at home, the concerts of power the world over were intended first of all to provide order. If this was essential, it was not enough, for Roosevelt more and more identified the dimensions of stability with the man who drew them.

Furthermore, power was as ever an inadequate judge of its own virtue and, out of power, Roosevelt a fractious judge of those who had it. Lacking, as he did, a systematic sense of governmental ends, particularly when out of office he allowed his ambition to corrupt his methods. He was in opposition always carping, sometimes conscienceless. Ultimately, morality and information failed to restrain him. For this as much as any other reason the liberals cashiered him.

Often lamentably wrong, now and then possibly dangerous, Roosevelt nevertheless commands attention now just as he did while he lived. He was, after all, man acting, and as such he made mistakes. But from him something about conservatism may be learned, rather more about the ways of American political life, and a great deal both engaging and pertinent about the vigorous and the resilient applied boldly to that life. Besides all this, there was for those who knew him, there may be again for those who read of him, and there is still endlessly for those who write of him "the fun of him." For this, when he is finally weighed, he is found not wanting.

•   •   •   •   •

"The word happiness," Lionel Trilling has proposed, "stands at the very center" of liberal thought.[1] It is a word which Theodore Roosevelt used rarely when speaking of himself and almost never when referring to other people. This was not an accident. Roosevelt concerned himself not with happiness but with hard work, duty, power, order. These conditions he valued not as prerequisites for some ultimate happiness but as ends in themselves. All interrelated, they blanketed myriad specifics. Hard work involved, among other things, an identity with task, whether the mining of coal or the writing of history; it was a part of duty and a preliminary of order. Duty demanded alike service to the nation, productive labor, and devoted attention to family. It demanded also physical and intellectual courage, honesty, and constancy. These qualities can produce frightening obstacles to personal happiness. There is a story that Roosevelt, more than two years after the death of his first wife, while contemplating his second marriage, for three days paced in a small guest room of a friend's

---

[1] Lionel Trilling, *The Liberal Imagination* (New York, 1950), p. xii.

home, pounding one fist into the other palm, expostulating the while to himself: "I have no constancy. I have no constancy." Not even in love was Roosevelt a liberal.

Roosevelt's politics, certainly, pertained not at all to happiness. There was none of Bentham, none of Mill in his public pronouncements or his private letters. Like those more reflective men, Roosevelt had a good deal of difficulty in defining his beliefs, but manifestly he believed in power and in order. With power he sought to impose order; only with order, he contended, could there be morality.

Because after his fortieth year Rooseevlt experienced no major change of thought, all this, inherent in his early thinking, contained the substance of his behavior as President. But during his Presidency he came better to understand himself, and with this new understanding he formalized, candidly and rather consistently, the principles that underlay his purpose. Distinct long before Herbert Croly wrote his *Promise of American Life,* these principles in 1912 provided Roosevelt with a rationalization, indeed with some motivation, for his devasting departure from the Republican party. Consequently they merit analysis not only in themselves but also as a measure of the conduct of the man.

Roosevelt began with power. Attaining it, he appreciated the chase and the reward. "There inheres in the Presidency," he observed, "more power than in any other office in any great republic or constitutional monarchy of modern times . . ." "I believe," he added, "in a strong executive; I believe in power . . ." This conclusion Roosevelt fortified with Hegelian conviction. The animal energy of that "bore as big as a buffalo" that so distressed Henry Adams provided the very force on which Roosevelt unerringly relied. Heroes, he knew, were not made by epigrams. His audiences of "townspeople . . . of rough-coated, hardheaded, gaunt, sinewy farmers . . . their wives and daughters and . . . children . . . ," he sensed, "for all the superficial differences between us, down at bottom" had "the same ideals . . ." "I am always sure of reaching them," he confided to John Hay, "in speeches which many of my Harvard friends would think not only homely, but commonplace." "The people who believed in me and

trusted me and followed me . . . ," Roosevelt asserted, felt that "I
was the man of all others whom they wished to see President."
Such confidence sustained heroic moods.

Every executive officer, in particular the President, Roosevelt
maintained, "was a steward of the people bound actively and
affirmatively to do all he could for the people . . ." He held
therefore that, unless specifically forbidden by the Constitution or
by law, the President had "to do anything that the needs of the
nation demanded . . ." "Under this interpretation of executive
power," he recalled, "I did and caused to be done many things
not previously done . . . I did not usurp power, but I did greatly
broaden the use of executive power." To this interpretation,
Roosevelt confessed, his temperament compelled him. So, of
course, did his profession; elected or appointed, the bureaucrat
would exalt his valleys. Realizing this, the second Charles Francis
Adams feared a regulatory bureaucracy as much as he despised the
competitive confusion it was intended to stabilize. Not so Roosevelt. He broadened power precisely for the purpose of establishing
order.

Throughout his life, Roosevelt displayed a morbid fear of social
violence which, he seemed to feel, lay ominously on the margin of
normal political life. He convinced himself that William Jennings
Bryan, Eugene V. Debs, the Socialist leader, and "Big Bill"
Haywood of the Industrial Workers of the World had inherited the
mission of Marat and Robespierre. This was not just campaign
hyperbole. In season and out, with wearing repetition he discovered the Jacobin in each dissenter of his time. To their evil he
apposed a twin, the evil of those "malefactors of great wealth"
who on lower Broadway held their court of Louis XVI. Un-
leashed, the energies of these extremes could in conflict wreck
society. They had therefore to be curtailed.

To modulate the threatening conflict Roosevelt in part relied
upon that indefinite composite which he called national character.
He meant by this not only personal morality but also the conglu-
tinations that history prepared, the accepted traditions of political
and social behavior by which people imposed order on themselves.
Yet these traditions, he recognized, depended heavily upon mate-

rial conditions which in the twentieth century were changing rapidly. The change Roosevelt welcomed; he foresaw more strength than danger in the new industrialism. But it demanded, he realized, concomitant political changes whose contours tradition could not draw.

If self-imposed order was in his time no longer to be anticipated, it had to be provided from above. This called for strong, disinterested government equipped to define, particularly for a powerful executive prepared to enforce, the revised rules under which the America of immense corporations, of enormous cities, of large associations of labor and farmers could in orderly manner resolve its conflicts. Definition and enforcement were needed at once, for within the lifetime of Roosevelt's older contemporaries social relations had changed "far more rapidly than in the preceding two centuries." The ensuing weaknesses in traditional political behavior strained the fabric of personal morality. In the United States of 1908, the President remarked in his perceptive last annual message to Congress, "the chief breakdown is in dealing with the new relations that arise from the mutualism, the interdependence of our time. Every new social relation begets a new type of wrong-doing—of sin, to use an old-fashioned word—and many years always elapse before society is able to turn this sin into crime which can be effectively punished at law."

Through mutualism itself Roosevelt hoped to stabilize social arrangements. His recommendations were designed first to create a political environment favorable to social and economic combinations which, he believed, the nation needed, and second, ordinarily through responsible administrative agencies, to prescribe the rules for the operation of those combinations. American industry afforded a salubrious example of "the far-reaching, beneficent work" which combination had already accomplished. In steel alone a Spencerian progression from the simple heterogeneous to the complex homogeneous suggested the almost limitless possibilities of power and productivity. Such a progression, Roosevelt believed, neither should nor could be arrested. But it had to be disciplined. Combinations in industry, susceptible as they were to the temptations of unbridled power, had to be made responsible through government to the whole people. They had, furthermore, to be balanced by other, also responsible combinations, voluntarily formed to promote the efficiency of less well organized parts of society. "This is an era," Roosevelt preached, "of federation and combination . . ."

"A simple and poor society," he later postulated, "can exist as a democracy on a basis of sheer individualism. But a rich and complex industrial society cannot so exist; for some individuals, and especially those artificial individuals called corporations, become so very big that the ordinary individual . . . cannot deal with them on terms of equality. It therefore becomes necessary for these ordinary individuals to combine in their turn, first in order to act in their collective capacity through that biggest of all combinations called the government, and second, to act, also in their own self-defense, through private combinations, such as farmers' associations and trade-unions."

Attempting as he did to apply this doctrine to agriculture, labor, and industry, Roosevelt envisioned an equilibrium of consolidated interests over which government would preside. To the farmer his purpose appealed least. Roosevelt was, after all, primarily an Eastern, urban man. He had never fully understood the dreadful anxieties that underlay the agrarian movements of the 1890's, or the deficiencies in national banking and credit arrangements that aggravated farm finance. He developed his program, furthermore, at a time when agricultural prosperity tended to obscure even for farmers the continuing weaknesses of their situation. Nevertheless, much of his advice was sound.

"Farmers must learn," Roosevelt proposed, "the vital need of co-operation with one another. Next to this comes co-operation with the government, and the government can best give its aid through associations of farmers rather than through the individual farmer. . . . It is greatly to be wished . . . that associations of farmers could be organized, primarily for business purposes, but also with social ends in view. . . . The people of our farming regions must be able to combine among themselves, as the most efficient means of protecting their industry from the highly organized interests which now surround them on every side. A vast field is open for work by co-operative associations of farmers in dealing with the relation of the farm to transportation and to the distribution and manufacture of raw materials. It is only through such combination that American farmers can develop to the full their economic and social power."

Through the Department of Agriculture, within the restrictive limits of its budget and authority, Roosevelt promoted farm cooperatives. To the recommendations of farm associations about changes in national transportation policy he gave a sympathetic hearing. "To ascertain what are the general, economic, social, educational, and sanitary conditions of the open country, and what, if anything, the farmers themselves can do to help themselves, and how the Government can help them," he appointed in 1908 the Country Life Commission. The report of this commission, although ignored by a Congress which refused even to appropriate funds for its printing, was a landmark in national thinking about the melioration of almost every aspect of rural life. To it, as to Roosevelt's own counsel, federal administrations later profitably returned.

Roosevelt intended that farm life should become increasingly institutionalized. While he urged this, he expected the farmers voluntarily to form their own organizations. Still the most individualistic-minded of Americans, they proceeded slowly. He could not command them, as he advised them, to exploit more fully the bicycle and the telephone; he could not force them to emulate the marketing cooperatives of Denmark. Consequently the immediate results of his advice were negligible. When he acted himself however, instead of simply urging them to act, he accomplished more. His employment of the strength of the government, especially of his office, imposed upon the country a conservation policy from which the farmers, however much they disliked it at the time, ultimately benefited.

Roosevelt sponsored conservation not so much to preserve a domain for agriculture as to preserve and enhance the strength of the whole nation. He was inspired not by farmers and ranchers but by intellectuals and interested commercial groups. Nevertheless, in effect his policy organized an essential element of prosperous rural existence. This it did directly through the irrigation act which compelled its beneficiaries to mutualism. Indirectly, Roosevelt's public power policy, resisting uncontrolled exploitation of water power sites, began to reserve control of power for the federal government. Through government agencies, interests of agriculture could be consolidated and advanced. By "planned and orderly development"—"essential to the best use of every natural resource"—these agencies could define and attain objectives which farmers' organizations, even if they had had the perspicacity to define, lacked the authority to attain. The varied purposes of his power policy, the need to restrain the haphazard and selfish methods of private direction, and the inadequacies of voluntary associations alike persuaded the President that for orderly development order had to be established from above.

Much more favorably than did the farmers, American labor responded to Roosevelt's doctrine of federation and combination. Agrarian spokesmen at the turn of the century, still antimonopolists in their orientation, proposed to solve the trust problem by disintegrating industrial combinations. The representatives of organized labor, on the contrary, intended to live with big business by bargaining with it. The general secretary of the United Garment Workers, the head of the United Mine Workers, and the president of the American Federation of Labor, among others, accepting the consolidation of industry as inevitable and salutary, sought to lead labor to comparable consolidations and to persuade government to protect the processes of combination and negotiation. Roosevelt spoke, therefore, to a receptive audience when he maintained that labor should reap "the benefits of organization," that wageworkers had "an entire right to organize" and "a legal right . . . to refuse to work in company with men who decline to join their organizations."

Repeatedly Roosevelt acted upon this principle. He drew upon the advice of the leaders of the railroad brotherhoods and the American Federation of Labor in fashioning his recommendations to Congress for legislation to govern the hours and working conditions of women and children, to extend the eight-hour day, to provide for comprehensive employers' liability, and to improve railroad safety precautions.[2] During the most celebrated strike of his term in office, his intercession defended the right of the anthracite miners to bargain collectively. Continually he endeavored to restrict the use of injunctions, the most formidable weapon against labor. The court's order prohibiting boycotting in the Buck's case he criticized severely; he ordered the Justice Department to assist an iron molders' local whose strike had been enjoined. There must, Roosevelt insisted, "be no . . . abuse of the injunctive power as is implied in forbidding laboring men to strive for their own betterment in peaceful and lawful ways; nor must the injunction be used merely to aid some big corporation . . . a preliminary injunction in a labor case, if granted without adequate proof . . . may often settle the dispute . . . and therefore if improperly granted may do irreparable wrong. . . . I earnestly commend . . . that some way may be devised which will limit the abuse of injunctions and protect those rights from which time to time it unwarrantably invades."

Encouraged to bargain, allowed to strike, the union was to consolidate the interests of labor. This had value for Roosevelt insofar as it promoted efficiency and order. But some unions, like the syndicalist Industrial Workers of the World, cultivated violence; some labor leaders, like the Socialist Debs, defending these unions, seemed to Roosevelt to court revolution. To handle such cases, he believed it "wrong altogether to prohibit the use of injunctions," for "there must be no hesitation in dealing with disorder."

The measure of order, difficult at best, Roosevelt would not leave to the judiciary. During and immediately after his tenure, the courts granted injunctions indiscriminately and nullified much of

[2] Roosevelt also agreed with Gompers and other craft union leaders who argued that mass immigration from the Orient and from southern and eastern Europe impaired labor's ability to organize. These immigrants—the labor unionizers held—willing to work for low wages, unfamiliar with American ways, were difficult if not impossible to organize. To protect American labor they therefore advocated the restriction of immigration, first of Asiatics, later also of Europeans. Roosevelt's attitudes toward immigration restriction were at most times close to those of labor leaders, not so much because they influenced him as because he shared their prejudices, as did so many Americans. Although he praised some unions for their work in Americanization, he generally failed to understand that the craft unions could not organize immigrant labor largely because they would not try.

the labor legislation he considered necessary and just. Underwriting as they did the status quo, they prevented the very changes upon which, he felt, a new social equilibrium depended. It was judicial interpretation of labor law that motivated Roosevelt finally to propose the recall of judicial decisions, a system which referred the interpretation of the needs of society to a momentary majority of the people. Conversely, Roosevelt was impatient with the legal impediments to silencing a Debs or a Haywood. Order for him was order. If a man incited violence, if he only endeavored to incite violence, indeed if he merely defended the prerogative of another man to incite violence, Roosevelt yearned at once to stamp him underfoot.

In dealing with radical newspapers and with the syndicalist Western Federation of Miners, Roosevelt, assuming the prerogatives of a steward of the people, decreed from his high office dicta of order with which many peaceable men could not conscientiously agree. By the same standard, while President he initiated a criminal libel suit—a suit presuming an offense against the United States—against a publisher who had criticized him, and he kept in prison without legal sanction a petty criminal who had violated not a law but his concept of the right. Such lawless uses of power, however meritorious or moral their intent, undermined the traditional principles of restraint upon which American order had been built. This created a danger that labor leaders recognized. They had too often been the victims of arbitrary power—ordinarily industrial rather than political—to trust completely any man who proposed himself to decide when their contests were safe and when they were not.

Labor had other reservations about Roosevelt. Just short of the full meaning of his preachments he stopped. On the issue of injunctions he retreated in 1908, when the Republican National Convention did. Bryan, Brandeis, and for a while Woodrow Wilson made no such forced marches. Furthermore, Roosevelt's doctrine of consolidation did not quite possess him. He would consolidate for order and also to establish the prescriptions for morality. But in the end he measured morality by the individual. "The chief factor in the success of each man," he asserted, "—

wageworker, farmer, and capitalist alike—must ever be the sum total of his own individual qualities and abilities. Second only to this comes the power of acting in combination or association with others." He judged on this basis that the "legal right" of wageworkers "to refuse to work in company with men who decline to join their organizations" might or might not, "according to circumstances," be a "moral right." There fell the union shop. Roosevelt reserved to himself definition of the moral right. He sustained the open shop in the Government Printing Office because he did not consider the circumstances a proper legal or moral basis for unionization. Where could he or his successor be expected next to draw the line?

The farmer could at once agree with Roosevelt about the primacy of individual qualities. The industrialist, protected by the legal fiction that a corporation—whatever its size—was an individual, could accept this dictum. Not so the labor leader. If the union did not contain every interested individual, its position relative to management suffered, and its victories benefited neutral noncontributors. This for labor leaders was a question not of morality but of money and of power. The President's ambivalence confused their issue.

In Roosevelt's program the farm community found discomforting unfamiliarity; about it union labor entertained anxious doubts. Businessmen were more enthusiastic, for from industry and transportation Roosevelt took his model. With accelerating tempo for two generations men of business had made consolidation their instrument not only of profits but also, more significantly, of order. Abandoning the insecurity and debilitation of competition, the enterprising in rails, steel, oil, copper, tobacco, sugar, salt—the list seems endless—had, after strife, in each industry organized stable structures. Their own achievement they admired. It was, they testified at symposiums on trusts, to Congressional committees, in essays, memoirs, and commencement addresses, the necessary and efficient way of business life, perhaps the only way of any life. With few exceptions they wished to have their institutions left alone. Here only did Roosevelt disagree. Because the consolidations were capable of doing much that was bad as well as much that was good, they had to be supervised. But they were not to be destroyed. "In curbing and regulating the combinations of capital which are . . . injurious . . .," he instructed Congress in his second annual message, "we must be careful not to stop the great enterprises which have legitimately reduced the cost of production, not to abandon the place which our country has won in the leadership of the international industrial world . . ."

Again and again during his Presidency Roosevelt made the distinction between size and behavior that characterized his speeches of 1912 on the regulation of industry. For the orderly system of control in which he believed, he first shaped his railroad policy. In developing that policy, he announced his preference for supervised pooling as an efficient regulatory device. Enlarging his thesis, he asserted late in 1911 that "nothing of importance is gained by breaking up a huge inter-State and international industrial organization *which has not offended otherwise than by its size.* . . . Those who would seek to restore the days of unlimited and uncontrolled competition . . . are attempting not only the impossible, but what, if possible, would be undesirable." "Business cannot be successfully conducted," he wrote in the same article, "in accordance with the practices and theories of sixty years ago unless we abolish steam, electricity, big cities, and, in short, not only all modern business and modern industrial conditions, but all the modern conditions of our civilization." This statement recognized associationalism as being as much a part of modern life as were the physical conditions that compelled it. Roosevelt also realized that, just as government could best supply a "planned and orderly development" of natural resources, so was oligopoly distinguished by its ability to provide experts to plan and to allocate from profits adequate resources to implement their plans—by its ability, therefore, to keep order without stultification.

But business had "to be controlled in the interest of the general public" and this could be accomplished in only one way: "by giving adequate power of control to the one sovereignty capable of exercising such power—the National Government." As an initial means for this control Roosevelt led Congress to establish the Bureau of Corporations. In his long struggle for the Hepburn Act he went considerably further. He next concluded and soon specifically proposed that "what is needed is the creation of a Federal administrative body with full power to do for ordinary inter-State industrial business carried on on a large scale what the Inter-State Commerce Commission now does for inter-State transportation business."

After leaving the Presidency, in the columns of *The Outlook* Roosevelt elaborated his plan. He would "regulate big corporations in thoroughgoing and effective fashion, so as to help legitimate business as an incident to thoroughly and completely safeguarding the interests of the people as a whole." The antitrust law, designed and interpreted "to restore business to the competitive conditions of the middle of the last century," could not "meet the whole situation." Size did indeed "make a corporation fraught with potential menace to the community," but the community could "exercise through its administrative . . . officers a strict supervision . . . to see that it does not go wrong," "to insure . . . business skill being exercised in the interest of the public . . ."

Criticizing the suit initiated by the Taft administration against the United States Steel Corporation, and deploring the vagueness of the Supreme Court's "rule of reason" in the Standard Oil and tobacco cases, Roosevelt explained how "continuous administrative action" might operate. The commission to regulate corporations was to have the power to regulate the issue of securities, thereby to prevent overcapitalization; to compel publicity of accounts, thereby to reveal the detailed techniques of business procedures; and to investigate any business activity. If investigation disclosed the existence of monopoly—of a consolidation that could control the prices and productivity of an industry—the commission was to have two alternatives. If unethical practices had produced monopoly—Roosevelt cited the oil and tobacco industries as examples of this—the monopoly should be dissolved under the Sherman Act. If, however, the monopoly resulted from natural growth—Roosevelt had in mind the United States Steel Corporation and the International Harvester Company—the commission was to control it by setting maximum prices for its products, just as the I.C.C. set maximum freight rates. This was not all.

Believing that administrative control should "indirectly or directly extend to . . . all questions connected with . . . [the] treatment of . . . employees," he proposed that the commission should have authority over hours, wages, and other conditions of labor.

Within each industry, then, consolidation was to establish order; acting in the public interest, the federal executive was to insure equity in this order. This fitted the grand scheme. It also offered to farm and labor groups, through the presumed disinterestedness of government, a countervailing force against the most advanced and, at that time, least controlled social group. By consolidation and administration Roosevelt would punish sin and achieve stability. To discipline consolidation, to make possible administration, his first requisite was power. The cycle was complete.

The question remains of how well this arrangement could be expected to function. Even a sampling of evidence suggests that it raised problems as large as those it presumed to solve. There was, for one, the problem of the natural growth of industrial combinations. Roosevelt considered it, in general terms, desirable. He believed, clearly, that an administrative agency could better judge what was natural growth than could the courts. Furthermore, as his relations with his Attorneys General and his directions to the chairman of the Interstate Commerce Commission indicate, he had considerable confidence in his own capacity to make administrative decisions pertinent to transportation and industry. How then explain the suit against the Northern Securities Company? The defendants in that case had by forming a holding company combined into a potentially efficient regional system the basic units of railway transportation in the Northwest. Railways had for decades been consolidating, naturally enough in the logic of railroad economics. The Northern Securities combination restored financial order among the rivals it merged and seemed capable of becoming a useful part of an orderly, integrated transportation network. Yet in 1902 Roosevelt proceeded against it. One suspects that he would have done so even if the I.C.C. at that time had had the authority to set maximum rates.

Two major considerations apparently motivated Roosevelt.

First, the farmers of the Northwest and their local political representatives wanted the holding company dissolved. It was good politics for Roosevelt to attack it. Second, as Roosevelt recalled in his autobiography, "the absolutely vital question" of "whether the government had power to control [corporations] . . . at all . . . had not yet been decided. . . . A decision of the Supreme Court [in the E. C. Knight case] had, with seeming definiteness, settled that the National Government had not the power." "This decision," Roosevelt continued, alluding to his prosecution of the Northern Securities Company, "I caused to be annulled . . ." He attacked to establish the government's power, for the while his power; he selected a corporation indisputably engaged in interstate commerce; he deliberately chose to charge a hill made vulnerable by popular opinion. Particularly when used by a man who has and loves power, such criteria may become terrifying.

This possibility Roosevelt intended partially to avoid by his reliance upon experts. Presumably the specialists who were to staff a regulatory commission would be restrained by the data they commanded. Unhappily this need not be the case. Emanating in large degree from the organizations to be controlled, the data explored by administrative commissions can often capture them. In such a pass, regulation may approach consent, and stability become stultification. Nor do experts, any more than other men, live by data alone. Besides common colds and ulcers, they develop loyalties and habits. In government, as in business or in education, administrators become to some extent the victims of their institutions. For many of them, lines of authority and procedure come to have an attraction of their own, an attraction that frequently induces a soporific insistence on inert routine, a fatal disinclination to innovation, sometimes to formalized action beyond the shuffling of bureaucratic dust.

Furthermore, even meaningful, objective data and personal energy and imagination do not necessarily make regulation by administration what Roosevelt thought it might be. He seemed to presume that politics would stop at the commission's water line. In a sense this is true. Railroads petitioning the I.C.C. may in that process be at once all Federalists, all Republicans. But in another

sense it is not true. The conflicting interests whose reconciliation
politics must effect continue to conflict before the tribunals of
administration. In a contest behind closed doors among spokesmen
of management, labor, and government, the adroit politician will
ordinarily prevail.

The possibility remains that the problems of competition, consolidation, and control can be resolved more equitably—though
perhaps with more waste—in the open environments provided by
the legislative or the adversary process. If it is hard to find good
Congressmen and judges, so it is hard to find good commissioners.
And whatever the deficiencies of parliaments and courts, they
concern themselves with concrete rules of conduct, written for all
to see, by which behavior can be measured. These rules pertain,
moreover, not only to citizens and corporations, but also to their
public servants.

The conclusion imperiously suggests itself that Roosevelt did
not want to be controlled, that he did not want to be inhibited by a
body of law, whether or not it was properly interpreted, nor
delayed by the impedance of legislatures. He proposed to govern.
Basically this was also the desire of the leaders of American
industry and finance. Relentless agents of consolidation, they
imposed and administered orders of their own. Many of them were
willing in the interest of industrial peace to go a long way in
condoning combinations formed by union labor. With the leaders
of these newer orders they were then prepared, man to man, to
bargain. Some of them foresaw that in the society they molded, big
government might have to provide balance. Most of them, however, as was the case with Morgan when Roosevelt moved against
the Northern Securities Company, thought that they could bargain,
man to man, with government. Here they miscalculated. Their rule
began to fade when Roosevelt began to make of government a
superior rather than a negotiating power.

Yet intellectually and emotionally he was always more one of
them than was he an agrarian reformer or a partner of little
business or of labor—a Bryan or a La Follette or a Brandeis.
Perhaps with a sense of this affinity to men of business, Roosevelt
called himself a conservative; and with reference to his differ-

ence—to his insistence that the governing was the government's—
he added that a true conservative was a progressive. This was the
position also of George W. Perkins, who for a time personified
articulate finance; of Frank Munsey, consolidator of journalism,
like Perkins a Bull Mooser; of Herbert Croly, who promised to
American life little that Rosevelt had not already offered; of
Brooks Adams, who would have arrested the disintegration of a
democracy he never understood by consolidation, conservation,
and administration—the very trinity of Roosevelt. To champion
consolidation as a means to order, to believe in administration and
to practice it well, this was the creed of a business elite in the early
century and of that conservative intelligentsia they helped to
inspire.

It rested upon a feeling about power that J. Pierpont Morgan,
prodded by a Congressional committee, disclosed, a feeling to
which Roosevelt thoroughly subscribed. Morgan saw nothing
wrong about the scope of his power, for he maintained that his
morality controlled it. He also arranged that the specialists in his
house helped exercise it. Roosevelt made a like claim and like
arrangements. Yet Morgan was neither virtuous nor successful in
his ventures with the New Haven railroad, and Roosevelt was just
as vulnerable to failures of the soul and errors of the flesh. In a
nation democratic by intent, Morgan's responsibility to a limited
number of investors made his power less acceptable than did
Roosevelt's responsibility to the whole electorate, but if their
power was relatively responsible, it was in both cases absolutely
corruptible.

To his great credit and doubtless greater pain, Roosevelt,
understanding this, surrendered his power. Explaining his decision
not to be a candidate in 1908, Roosevelt wrote: "I don't think that
any harm comes from the concentration of power in one man's
hands, provided the holder does not keep it for more than a
certain, definite time, and then returns to the people from whom he
sprang." This decision was a large achievement of restraint.
Roosevelt could certainly have had the Republican nomination
and would probably have won the election. The temptations to
continue were enormous. Nevertheless he declined. This strength

of character supported strongly the claims he made to the use of power; yet it was not enough.

Suppose only that Roosevelt was human and fallible—he need not have been paranoid or depraved, fallibility is here enough—and he claimed too much. Four years or eight years or twelve years, the number of terms is unimportant, may be in the history of this nation a brief and placid time or a tempestuous eternity. Roosevelt, it happened, ruled in a time of relative quiet. Even then he made mistakes. He made perhaps his worst mistakes, though he endeavored to be moral and informed, when his power was least restrained—mistakes possibly more of principle than of policy, but mistakes about which Americans since have often been ashamed: the episode in Panama for one, or the criminal libel suit against Pulitzer for his misinterpretation of that episode. During the last years of his life, after his power was gone, Roosevelt exhibited the characteristics that least became him, prejudices of mind and traits of personality that he had subdued while he felt the responsibilities of office. In office in time of turmoil he might not have conquered them. So too with any man. But Roosevelt especially may have benefited from the limits on Presidential power, which men who understood the problem in 1787 created. When he had to proceed with sensitivity for the constitutional balances to his power, the will of Congress and of the courts—or, indeed, for the institutional balances within his party—Roosevelt's performance was noteworthy. Then he demonstrated perception, knowledge, principle of a kind, energy tempered with restraint.

Consolidation, administration, stability—for these he used his power; but they turned on power itself, and power, while it must be, must not be all. . . . perhaps power particularly must not be all when it promises hard work, duty, order, morality—even welfare—but never mentions happiness. There was strength in Roosevelt's structure and potential for contentment, but in chancing very little, his order risked too much. The wonder is, intrepid though he was, that he never really knew this.

Bibliography

This can be no more than an impressionistic survey of a vast (and often repetitive) literature. There is no better introduction to the style, vitality, and range of Roosevelt's life than the distinguished edition by Elting E. Morison of *The Letters of Theodore Roosevelt* (8 vols., 1951–54). The most complete collection of T.R.'s published writings is Hermann Hagedorn, ed., *The Works of Theodore Roosevelt* (20 vols., National Edition, 1926). It includes, of course, Roosevelt's *Autobiography* (1913), a work of characteristic verve—and considerable myopia.

The major Roosevelt biographies are the near-contemporary, and eulogistic, William Roscoe Thayer, *Theodore Roosevelt, an Intimate Biography* (1919), and Joseph B. Bishop, *Theodore Roosevelt and His Times* (2 vols., 1920); the disparaging study by Henry F. Pringle, *Theodore Roosevelt: A Biography* (1931); and, among recent, more appreciative efforts, Edward Wagenknecht, *The Seven Worlds of Theodore Roosevelt* (1958), and William H. Harbaugh, *Power and Responsibility: The Life and Times of Theodore Roosevelt* (1961).

The first volume of Carleton Putnam's biography, *Theodore Roosevelt: The Formative Years* (1958), so far all that has appeared, is the most substantial treatment of T.R.'s early years. Two monographs focus on aspects of the pre-Presidential political career: Howard L. Hurwitz, *Theodore Roosevelt and Labor in New York State, 1880–1900* (1943), and G. Wallace Chessman, *Governor Theodore Roosevelt: The Albany Apprenticeship, 1898–1900* (1965). Edmund Wilson has a perceptive discussion of "The Pre-Presidential T.R." in *Eight Essays* (Anchor Books, 1954).

191

Interpretations of T.R.'s Presidency besides those included in this volume may be found in James Ford Rhodes, *The McKinley and Roosevelt Administrations* (1922), Matthew Josephson, *The President Makers* (1940), George E. Mowry, *The Era of Theodore Roosevelt* (1958), and Gabriel Kolko, *The Triumph of Conservatism* (1963).

The "Notes" to Harbaugh's biography are in effect a substantial critical bibliography of the most important printed works on Roosevelt.

Contributors

HAMILTON BASSO (1904–1964) was a novelist (*The View from Pompey's Head* [1954], *The Light Infantry Ball* [1959]) who also had a long career as an editor for *The New Republic, Time,* and *The New Yorker.*

HOWARD K. BEALE (1899–1959) was Professor of American History at the University of Wisconsin for many years. He wrote *The Critical Year: A Study of Andrew Johnson and Reconstruction* (1930), *Theodore Roosevelt and the Rise of America to World Power* (1956), and at the time of his death was at work on a major biography of Theodore Roosevelt.

JOHN M. BLUM, born in 1921, is Professor of History at Yale. He was associate editor of *The Letters of Theodore Roosevelt,* and has written *Joe Tumulty and the Wilson Era* (1951), *Woodrow Wilson and the Politics of Morality* (1956), *From the Morgenthau Diaries,* and *The Promise of America* (1965).

JOHN R. CHAMBERLAIN, born in 1903, has been a reporter, an editor of *Fortune* during the late 1930's, and in more recent years a staff writer for the *Wall Street Journal.* Besides *Farewell to Reform* (1932), he wrote *The American Stakes* (1940). A leading leftist intellectual in the early Depression years, he became after World War II a major spokesman of the American right.

LOUIS FILLER, born in 1912, is Professor of American Civilization at Antioch College. He has written *The Crusade Against Slavery* (1960) and *A Dictionary of American Social Reform* (1963).

RICHARD HOFSTADTER, born in 1916, is De Witt Clinton Professor of American History at Columbia University. He has been perhaps the most influential contemporary student of American political and intellectual history. His works include *Social Darwinism in American Thought* (1945), *The Age of Reform* (1955), and *Anti-Intellectualism in American Life* (1963). His work has won him two Pulitzer Prizes.

H. L. MENCKEN (1880–1956) was the great iconoclastic commentator on American mores during the 1920's and the 1930's. His pungent writings are collected in the Prejudices series and in such works as *Notes on Democracy* (1926). He also was a linguistic authority of the first rank, publishing *The American Language* (1919), which he continually revised and expanded.

STUART P. SHERMAN (1881–1927) was Professor of English at the University of Illinois and, for the last years of his life, literary editor of the New York *Herald-Tribune*. He was one of the most prominent middlebrow literary critics of his time and for this reason was a special object of Menckenian contempt.

DIXON WECTER (1906–1950) was Professor of American History at the University of California at Berkeley. His books include *The Saga of American Society* (1937), *When Johnny Comes Marching Home* (1944) and *The Age of the Great Depression* (1948).

WILLIAM ALLEN WHITE (1868–1944) was one of the great editor-commentators of early twentieth-century America. He published the *Emporia* (Kansas) *Gazette* from 1895 until his death, was a strong supporter and admirer of Theodore Roosevelt, and for decades was one of the major spokesman for liberal Republicanism. He wrote numerous novels, including *A Certain Rich Man* (1900), biographies of public figures such as Calvin Coolidge (*A Puritan in Babylon* [1938]), and his *Autobiography* (1946).

MORTON KELLER was born in Brooklyn, New York, in 1929, was graduated with highest honors in history from the University of Rochester, and holds advanced degrees from Harvard. He has taught at the University of North Carolina, the University of Pennsylvania, and Harvard University, and is now Professor of History at Brandeis. Professor Keller has been awarded Guggenheim and Social Science Research Council fellowships, and his book *The Life Insurance Enterprise, 1885–1910: A Study in the Limits of Corporate Power* won the Kulp Memorial Award. His other books include *In Defense of Yesterday: James M. Beck and the Politics of Conservatism, The New Deal: What Was It?* and the John Harvard Library edition of E. L. Godkin, *Problems of Modern Democracy.*

✪

AÏDA DIPACE DONALD, General Editor of the American Profiles series, holds degrees from Barnard and Columbia, where she taught American history, and a doctorate from the University of Rochester. Mrs. Donald has been awarded A.A.U.W. and Fulbright fellowships and has edited *John F. Kennedy and the New Frontier.* She is also co-editor of the *Charles Francis Adams Diary.*